"Outsiders still give Hamilton a bad rap. But hometown boy takes stock of the city's turnaround while it's still in progress. Informed, engaging, passionate—why can't we have more books like this about Canada's cities?"

Richard Harris, professor emeritus, School of Earth, Environment and Society, McMaster University

"*Shift Change* has the reach and the importance no doubt hoped for by its author. Combining wide-ranging comparative research with many rich interviews of key participants, the author outlines how Hamilton, Ontario, like many other de-industrialized cities and regions, is in the throes of an epic battle for its place in a post-industrial world. No longer a lunch bucket steel town, the combatants are not behemoth manufacturers versus powerful trade unions, but gentrifying developers and their Toronto-come-lately customers versus a determined, but far from united, array of affordable housing and anti-poverty activists and organizations, who draw upon the city's history of community solidarities and collective struggles to argue for a post-industrial pathway that retains Hamilton's egalitarian heart and soul. As *Shift Change* optimistically concludes, that remains a road that is there to be taken."

Robert Storey, emeritus faculty, School of Labour Studies, McMaster University

Shift Change

Shift Change

Scenes from a Post-industrial Revolution

Stephen Dale

Between the Lines
Toronto

Shift Change
© 2021 Stephen Dale

First published in 2021 by
Between the Lines
401 Richmond Street West, Studio 281
Toronto, Ontario, M5V 3A8, Canada
1-800-718-7201 · www.btlbooks.com

Library and Archives Canada Cataloguing in Publication

Title: Shift change : scenes from a post-industrial revolution / Stephen Dale.
Names: Dale, Stephen, 1958- author.
Description: Includes bibliographical references and index.
Identifiers: Canadiana (print) 20210241985 | Canadiana (ebook) 20210242086 | ISBN 9781771135535 (softcover) | ISBN 9781771135542 (EPUB) | ISBN 9781771135559 (PDF)
Subjects: LCSH: Urbanization—Ontario—Hamilton. | LCSH: Sustainable development—Ontario—Hamilton. | LCSH: Hamilton (Ont.)—Economic conditions. | LCSH: Hamilton (Ont.)—Social conditions.
Classification: LCC HT384.C32 H36 2021 | DDC 307.7609713/52—dc23

Cover design by Michael DeForge
Text design by DEEVE
Printed in Canada

We acknowledge for their financial support of our publishing activities: the Government of Canada; the Canada Council for the Arts; and the Government of Ontario through the Ontario Arts Council, the Ontario Book Publishers Tax Credit program, and Ontario Creates.

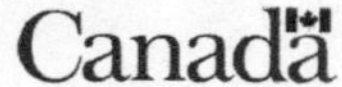
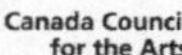

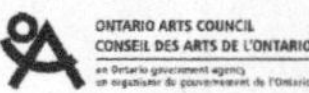

For Geoff and Elaine

Contents

Acknowledgements

'M GRATEFUL TO the multitude of people who contributed their time, ideas, and good will to this project. This book wouldn't have made it into print without you.

Shift Change relies heavily on first-person reflections and reminiscences. I'd therefore like to thank, first of all, the people who allowed me to interview them, whose passion animates these pages, and whose generosity and openness made a lasting impression on me.

There were many others who helped shape this book, particularly during the preliminary research, by sharing their knowledge of the social, political, and cultural landscape of current-day Hamilton. Noelle Allen, Ryan McGreal, Shawn Selway, Paul Weinberg, Rob Kendrick, and Jeff Martin were all involved in some formative early conversations and, in some cases, introduced me to key interviewees. Sarah Hipworth also contributed to those discussions and introductions, and later provided crucial feedback on a draft of the manuscript. Matthew Behrens and Jazz Cook carefully read the penultimate version before it went to print.

Untold hours of interviews became manageable thanks to the diligent transcription of Aha Blume.

Some of the research in this book first saw the light of day through a series of podcasts, produced with invaluable assistance from Lil Blume, Adrian Shuman, Jamie Tennant, and Victoria

Fenner. Two of those podcasts, posted on the Raise the Hammer website and elsewhere, received support from the Ontario Arts Council's Media Arts program. Another audio documentary on Hamilton's waterfront was commissioned by David Kattenburg for his excellent multimedia website, the Green Planet Monitor.

There aren't enough superlatives in the dictionary to describe the wonderful people at Between the Lines. In particular, I'd like to thank Jamie Swift for his enthusiasm and encouragement, as well as his insightful review of the manuscript; Amanda Crocker for her calm tenacity and wealth of useful suggestions; and eagle-eyed editor Tilman Lewis, whose skilful and sensitive work enormously improved the pages that follow.

I gratefully acknowledge the generous financial support of the Canada Council for the Arts, the Ontario Arts Council, and the City of Ottawa Arts Funding program.

As always, for the joy and the laughter, I'm thankful to Laura Macdonald and Ben and Matthew Macdonald-Dale, whether they're nearby or far away.

CHAPTER ONE
Tectonic Shift

AT ONE TIME, it seemed like it would last forever. The foundries standing like dinosaurs at the edge of Hamilton Bay—drawing water from and excreting poisonous effluents into that prized deep-water port—seemed to have been an inseparable part of the landscape since before anyone could remember. They were survivors from some primordial age, as solid and as permanent as the Niagara Escarpment and as much a force of nature as the seasons.

The foundries belched iron oxide into the atmosphere after sunset (as if no one would notice) and turned the night sky above Hamilton's industrial northeast a luminous red—an ominous likeness of the northern lights. The factories' rhythms became the rhythms of life for the humans who served them. A day was segmented into equal thirds that would begin and end—at seven in the morning, three in the afternoon, and eleven at night—with predictable, manic surges of traffic up and down the Sherman Cut and the Kenilworth Access, the two automotive arteries linking the suburban fringe with Hamilton's industrial heart. Lives were measured in hour-long units recorded on time cards and assigned value through regular, ritualistic contests (negotiations, strikes, lockouts) between the owners and the owned. This was the basis of life in Hamilton. The routine was grinding, predictable, and seemingly endless. Through most of the twentieth century, while the machine hummed hypnotically—spewing out smoke and steel and steady wages—there was no reason to think things wouldn't keep going like this for generations more.

In reality, however, the Steel Age came and went in not much more than a century. In 1910, the Steel Company of Canada (Stelco, as it would soon come to be known) was formed through the amalgamation of several smaller steel producers, chief among them the Hamilton Blast Furnace Company. That was a watershed moment in a process of industrialization that had gathered huge momentum by the 1890s. The next great landmark was the birth of the Dominion Steel Castings Company in 1912 (later renamed the Dominion Steel Foundry Company, then Dofasco).[1] These two steelmaking giants became the twin magnets drawing a range of second-tier manufacturers—National Steel Car, International Harvester, Frost Wire Fence, Otis Elevator, American Can, Firestone Tire, Westinghouse, and many others—into Hamilton's orbit, endowing the city with its undisputed status as the industrial capital of Canada and forging its cultural identity as the "lunch-bucket town."

But after a few prosperous decades, the machine suddenly lurched into reverse. In the face of a move towards globalized production and subsequent competition from low-wage countries, the smaller players (especially branch plants of multinational corporations) began closing down in the 1980s. Ominous headlines spoke of days when hundreds of jobs would vanish in an instant. The big players like Stelco and Dofasco cut legions of steelworkers adrift as foreign competition eroded their markets and new technology reduced the human component of steel production. Still, the symbolic end of an era didn't arrive until October 2013, when U.S. Steel—which had bought Stelco in 2007 but kept it mostly idle since then—acknowledged its intention to permanently cease making steel in Hamilton.[2]

To some extent, Stelco's archrival, Dofasco, has kept steelmaking alive in the city. Purchased by the world's largest steel conglomerate, ArcelorMittal, in 2006 and run as an autonomous division, it has remained competitive producing specialized steel products for the automotive and construction sectors, as well as more mundane items like tin cans. But this is just the exception that proves the rule, a distraction from the real story: that Hamilton's industrial age is effectively over. ArcelorMittal Dofasco's current workforce of around five thousand people is just a fraction of the fourteen thousand people employed by Stelco at its apex. Dofasco's numbers look even smaller when measured against the thousands more who worked in the other Hamilton plants that have disappeared since the 1980s.[3] Acres of abandoned industrial lands tell the same story of sudden, seismic change, as do the ghostly streetscapes standing in the shadows of the old factories. There are no more glowing skies after sunset and no traffic jams at shift change, although those hulking foundries still make an awe-inspiring impression on the waterfront.

This type of manufacturing apocalypse has become an almost archetypical feature of the contemporary North American narrative. The erosion or displacement of working-class culture—along with its rituals and values and the stability it represented—have been mythologized in Hollywood films like *Gran Torino* and television series like *The Wire*. The legacy of resentment, despair, and confusion that followed the crumbling of the blue-collar reality, meanwhile, remains a living, consequential force. Among other things, it was credited with delivering key American Rust Belt states like Michigan and Ohio to Donald Trump in the 2016 presidential election, giving him the path to victory he needed to move into the White House.

But in Hamilton there is a definite sense of looking forward rather than back, intimations that a new chapter has begun. So much has happened since all those factory gates were chained shut that Hamilton's long-standing identity as Canada's Steeltown is starting to feel like a historical footnote. Many tough years of decay followed by some determined strides towards recovery are bringing on a new set of questions about what kind of future is being constructed here, who's in charge of the process, and who will benefit (or lose) once this nascent post-industrial renaissance is fully formed. Discerning the potential long-term outcomes of current and ongoing attempts at transformation will be the central goal of this book. Something is happening here, but—as Bob Dylan sang—we don't know what it is.

Light at the end of the tunnel

From the mid-1980s through most of the nineties, Hamilton was being battered on all fronts. "The football team was losing, the industries were losing, and the businesses were moving out of town. The kids were starting to act up and look like little hoods. It was not a nice place," summarized Bill Powell, blue-collar bohemian, son of a steelworker, and founder of the Festival of Friends. In its heyday in the 1970s, this annual music, arts, and crafts festival was one of the few attractions that could entice outsiders (like smug Torontonians) to visit a city generally associated with belching smokestacks and rancid air.

When I talked to Bill a few months before his death in 2015, in the suburban bungalow that he shared with his wife, Lynne Powell, he had new reason for optimism about his beloved city's prospects. Around the turn of the new century, there were signs of a new spring. An influx of artists, drawn by cheap rents and the new possibilities that existed on a landscape they generally viewed as vacant, began to ignite a kind of cultural renaissance here. In particular, Bill credited the architects of Hamilton's Art Crawl and the spin-off Supercrawl—a kind of Mardi Gras tour of downtown studio spaces, expanded to include live music and related revelry on a closed-off street—with remaking the city's downtrodden downtown as the kind of place where people would once again want to live and work. Bill was hopeful that the new confidence that had come with this flagship event was "just the beginning. I think and I hope, and I knock on wood," he told me, "that things have reached a kind of crossroads and the city is pulling itself together again."

You'll notice a sense of uncertainty in that last sentence, and it's not unique to Bill Powell. Even as property values, incoming investment, and the unveiling of new development plans have accelerated, the question of what exactly is being constructed here remains uncertain; a definitive answer may not be apparent for another decade or so, perhaps two or three. Since the early 2000s—when an initial wave of artists, musicians, and other bohemian settlers cast their gaze on Hamilton, but before the interest of overleveraged Torontonians and assorted real estate barracudas was fully engaged—the city has been in flux, caught between conflicting visions of what the city could or should become.

The path of least resistance would be to allow Hamilton's fate to be shaped, unhindered, by the powerful forces of the real estate market. This is a well-worn road. Across North America and around the world, cities that were once diverse, with strong working-class and poor populations living alongside monied professionals—think Pittsburgh or Toronto—have been reshaped by the irresistible pull of the market as monoculture pastures of the well-to-do. The cycle is replayed in city after city: as incoming gentrifiers buy undervalued properties on a new urban frontier, whole neighbourhoods become absurdly expensive and lower-income people are banished to distant, decaying suburbs to live out of sight and out of mind. Aside from some historic pockets of social housing, this process leaves no place in the inner city for people who don't have buckets of money or an anomalously secure tenure downtown.

But there are people in Hamilton who are audacious enough to think that their one-time Steeltown could chart a different course and defy a market-driven narrative so commonplace and so powerful that it sometimes seems almost inevitable. It's still a long shot, they say—and the odds get worse with each day that business as usual continues—but a rare alignment of factors and some potential quirks of timing indicate that humble Hamilton might become one of the rare examples of a more equitable form of urban regeneration. These people point to its history as a union town and a historic battleground on social justice issues that, arguably, still has an influence on the way people think around here. That same history has begotten a range of nimble and innovative community organizations run by activists with a sophisticated understanding of policy and a penchant for deft practical fixes.

Those intrepid optimists also point out that Hamilton is small enough that solutions to social problems don't have to be implemented on an impossible scale. Then there is timing: Hamilton is dealing with its gentrification challenges at a time when the toxic effects of real estate gold rushes elsewhere have been well publicized, and some promising antidotes have been brought off the drawing board and put into practice. None of these factors guarantee success, of course, but they do provide a small opening within which it becomes possible to dream big, luminous, and rebellious dreams. That, today, is Hamilton—battlefield, laboratory, chessboard, where competing forces are in the midst of creating something whose final form is as yet unknown.

Looking for the right mix

One problem with trying to influence a city's future growth is that the city itself is a living, changing entity and therefore a moving target. The health of the city is never constant; conditions are rarely static. The importance of this fact kept coming up as I conducted interviews with numerous Hamiltonians who, cumulatively, form a kind of loose, informal alliance attempting to steer Hamilton's redevelopment in a direction that will benefit a range of citizens. My interviewees would float certain plans or scenarios based on the conditions at the time. Returning periodically over a handful of years, it became clear that a quickly moving chain of events was altering the underlying conditions, so that earlier predictions began to look less plausible and new outlooks and strategies were emerging to replace them.

I first tested the zeitgeist in my old home town in early 2015, just as an in-migration from more expensive real estate markets (namely, the Greater Toronto Area) and the resulting prospects of gentrification were routinely making headlines in the newspapers. Around this time, two popular conceptions of Hamilton's character—one fading, the other emerging—were competing for dominance. In one narrative, the city was a grim, post-apocalyptic repository of poverty and despair. In the other, it was an electrifying urban frontier where the entrepreneurship and enthusiasm of newcomers was flourishing, where endless new possibilities were emerging from the ruins of a landscape that had once embodied the drudgery of the manufacturing age.

The former image had been foremost in the public imagination at least since 2010, when the *Hamilton Spectator* published a series of in-depth articles under the banner "Code Red," using census data to rank lower Hamilton neighbourhoods by economic status, health and education outcomes, and so forth. Even since the early 1960s, the old city (conveniently separated from Hamilton's postwar suburbs by the Niagara Escarpment, or the Mountain, as it's known locally) had been losing its middle-class character. Industrial workers who'd grown tired of living in the shadows of the factories where they worked were decamping for the greener, cleaner suburbs on the Mountain. An ambitious "urban renewal" scheme in the early seventies, involving the construction of the Jackson Square shopping centre and adjoining office tower, and a new theatre and art gallery, failed to stem the migration of commerce to distant, car-friendly shopping malls.

Things spiralled even further downward during that rough patch in the eighties when the manufacturing base was being eroded and the new, gigantic Lime Ridge Mall, opened in 1981, fully undercut earlier efforts to revive the city core. In the face of all this, the main competitive advantages downtown Hamilton retained were its depressed rents and a critical mass of health and social services. Consequently, people who had been squeezed by the soaring cost of living in Toronto and the declining buying power of social assistance payments discovered that they had a better shot at survival in Hamilton: today, you'll hear stories of case workers in Toronto urging their clients to pick up and relocate seventy kilometres or so down the QEW (Queen Elizabeth Way). As a result, many Hamilton neighbourhoods below the Mountain soon became known for their formidable concentrations of people who were poor, socially disadvantaged, and often living with disabilities.

The statistical measures provided in the *Spectator*'s Code Red series provided chilling evidence in support of that portrait. The

Spec's number crunching revealed that eight neighbourhoods within three downtown wards had more than half of their children living in poverty. In Ward 2, which encompasses much of the central core, 40 per cent of inhabitants lived below the poverty line.[4] Since epidemiological data makes a strong case that "the wealthier you are, the healthier you are," as reporter Steve Buist wrote, it came as little surprise that a city with such high rates of poverty also produced tragic health stats.

The most obvious indicator of well-being is life expectancy. Here the numbers tell a remarkable story. Comparing an affluent west Mountain suburb with a neighbourhood in a northeastern slice of the downtown core,[5] the *Spectator* team arrived at a difference in lifespan of twenty-one years: life expectancy in the former was 86.3 years (five years above the Canadian national average) while it was only 65.5 in the latter. "Put another way," Buist elaborated, "the same North End neighbourhood would rank 165 in the world for life expectancy, tied with Nepal, just ahead of Pakistan and worse than India, Mongolia and Turkmenistan." The unflattering comparison with developing (or, as he put it, Third World) countries holds up across a range of indicators: "In parts of the lower-central portion of Hamilton, where poverty is deeply entrenched, some neighbourhoods live with Third World health outcomes and Third World lifespans—all the more shocking in a city with a major medical school and top teaching hospitals, in a country with universal, publicly funded health care."[6]

The incidence of cardiovascular emergencies is another measure of the divide between poor downtown and wealthier suburban citizens. The *Spectator* reported that while a neighbourhood in Flamborough, on the city's rural fringe, had a rate of one cardiovascular emergency per 1,000 people, the figure rose to 27 cardiovascular emergencies per 1,000 people in one east-end neighbourhood near Nash Road. There was also a large gap in the age at which cardiovascular emergencies occurred: in one suburban Stoney Creek neighbourhood, the average age was 79 years old; in that poorer neighbourhood near Nash Road, it was 57 years. That 22-year gulf suggests that lower-income people are likely to fall victim to cardio-vascular disease well before the wealthy.[7]

The pattern holds true for mental health emergencies, where one poor inner-city neighbourhood[8] experienced 88 psychiatric emergencies per 1,000 residents; 34 times higher than in a sample neighbourhood in Flamborough, where the rate was 2.6 per 1,000. All ten neighbourhoods with the highest rate of mental health emergencies were in the inner city.[9] As well, Code Red found that 8 per cent of babies born in Hamilton had low birth weight, which is one-third higher than the national average. Although twenty-four neighbourhoods had no low-birth-weight babies, there were seven neighbourhoods where the rate was over 20 per cent, which is higher than the rate of 15 per cent the World Health Organization pegs as the incidence of low birth weight in sub-Saharan Africa. Since low birth weight can be a prelude to later health problems, the implication is that a high percentage of babies born in downtown Hamilton may face a lifetime of struggle.[10]

Not long after the *Spectator*'s Code Red articles unleashed anguished soul searching among Hamiltonians, other appendages of the regional and national media also started to take an interest in Canada's tarnished steel capital. Inevitably, though, those stories offered more upbeat storylines focusing not on the concerns of long-time residents but on the dreams of a growing cadre of Torontonians who looked to Hamilton to provide an escape from smothering big-city mortgages. In these stories, Hamilton became a kind of studio backlot—adorned with quaint Victorian residential streetscapes, hulking warehouses, and romantically rusting facto-ries—on which the newcomers from down the road could act out their personal scripts about escaping the rat race and finding some space to live creatively. The locals mostly appeared as extras with brief walk-on parts, sometimes as impediments to the plans of new arrivals who had their own ideas about how people should conduct themselves in a real city.

Writing in late 2012 in the *Grid*, a now-defunct urban weekly published by the *Toronto Star*, Jason McBride reported that although disenchanted Torontonians had been making the trek to Hamilton since the turn of the millennium,

> in the past two years or so, Steeltown was being spoken about with the same romantic fervor that people once reserved for Montreal's Mile End. Suddenly, I knew a half-dozen people who had moved, or were thinking about moving, there. Those people were all relatively young. . . . They were also members of the so-called creative class and Hamilton, it seemed, was now offering fresh, alluring opportunities for that particular demographic.[11]

This would become a familiar theme: subsequent stories over the years reported on the relocation to Hamilton of fashion and film businesses (low-margin enterprises that require substantial space on limited budgets),[12] while an essay in the urbanist journal *Spacing* detailed the fascination that Hamilton held for a busload of city-watchers who had motored down the highway to witness the reinvention of the Steel City.[13]

Despite the rising buzz about Hamilton as a creative hive, however, even by 2017 *Toronto Life* seemed to be taken by surprise. The magazine opened its cover story on Hamilton-bound real estate refugees with that stale image of Toronto's industrial cousin as a place big-city sophisticates would normally shun. "When you approach the city from the QEW, it doesn't feature a skyline so much as a blockade of smokestacks—a veritable DO NOT ENTER sign made in steel and scrawled in soot," wrote Stuart Berman, himself a transplanted Torontonian drawn to Hamilton by "a sprawling . . . Edwardian home" with an irresistible price tag just shy of half a million. For most of his life, Berman continued, in his mind, "Hamilton was to Toronto what a backyard shed is to a house—a gritty appendage, perhaps, but not a place you want to hang out."

Although much of Berman's article advanced the revisionist notion that Hamilton isn't that bad after all, it's also coloured by an obvious condescension; the suggestion, for example, that what remains unchanged by the current round of gentrification in downtown Hamilton is somehow offensive and irksome to the true urbanite.

For all the activity reinvigorating the city, the Hammer [the city's nickname] is still a long way from L'Hammeur. Compared to Toronto's relentless modernity, large swaths of Hamilton remain frozen in time: its streets are dotted with derelict strip malls, concrete buildings, businesses that operate out of houses and video stores that have somehow managed to survive in the streaming age.[14]

Notably, that description hints at the presence of pre-influx residents without actually mentioning them. The features of the landscape so derided in this piece (stone-age video stores, home-based businesses) surely existed because they had a clientele: long-tenured, likely lower-income Hamiltonians. But they are important in this article only because they have reshaped the streetscape in a way that sophisticated newcomers will find unappealing. It's a clear dig at the culture that existed here before: incoming Torontonians are forewarned that the hidden price of discount real estate is having to tolerate the residual trappings of working-class life.

Will the real Hamilton please stand up?

Looking at these two distinct ways in which life in Hamilton has been reported on—through the investigative advocacy of the Code Red series, and then the lifestyle mag journalism unleashed after intra-urban migration became a discernable trend—it's possible to conclude that there are two self-contained solitudes here, with interests and mindsets that rarely intersect. One group is focused, to a major extent, on sheer survival. The other is pursuing the twenty-first-century urbanist dream—on the trail of restorable pre–World War II architecture, quirky bistros, and an amusing art and music scene, wrapped in a package that doesn't include astronomical mortgage payments and a crushing commute.

In reality, though, the fates of these two groups have become intertwined. Or at least, they are interdependent mostly in one direction, with the future of long-time residents in once-forgotten urban areas now determined to some extent by the activities of new-comers. This need not be a negative intersection. As reporter Emily Badger noted in the *Washington Post* in 2015, an injection of new money—for all the destruction it has created in gentrifying neigh-bourhoods across the globe—can also have a positive impact. It can help remedy situations where people with low incomes are confined to neglected neighbourhoods and lack access to basic amenities like supermarkets and drug stores, and even to civic services like garbage collection or transit, rationed by municipal governments that are often disinclined to assign funds to neighbourhoods that generate less tax revenue.[15]

This lack of services was clearly on display in Hamilton after the downturn. A Code Red story noted, for example, that a 3.4-kilometre stretch of Barton Street, once a thriving commercial strip, by the early 2010s had only 166 businesses in place of the 367 that had existed in the 1960s. There are now two pharmacies rather than the original eleven, along with a handful of convenience stores and thrift shops where once there were furniture shops, tailors, and pool halls.[16] In the wider North American context, Badger pointed out that although the opening of wine bars and pricey condos coaxed into being by new money won't improve life for lower-income people, other developments (like the arrival of gro-cery stores) can provide them with both services and employment opportunities. She wrote:

> The more useful question isn't whether "gentrification" is good or bad, but what it might look like to have new investment in a community that benefits existing and future residents alike. I know people who worry that this isn't possible—that new investment and old residents cannot coexist, that the former can only displace the latter. But I'm convinced there must be a way to do this.[17]

Bridging the two solitudes

This idea that the transformative effects of urban redevelopment can be harnessed to benefit people across a wide swath of society is very much alive in Hamilton. The aim is not just to provide lower-income people with access to employment and services, but to address the overall erosion of well-being that comes with being forced out of the mainstream and segregated from the rest of society.

"There's a lot of evidence to suggest that concentrated poverty is a bad thing," James Dunn, a McMaster University geographer with a background in epidemiology, told me. "Essentially, if you are poor and live in a neighbourhood of concentrated poverty, it creates an added disadvantage beyond being poor and living in a mixed-income kind of neighbourhood." Researchers who have studied this phenomenon in Scotland call it "deprivation amplification" and have measured its impacts on health outcomes, child development, school performance, and so on. The one compelling argument in favour of *not* mixing income levels, said Dunn, is that concentration will not dilute lower-income people's political voice the way deconcentration will. That is, keeping poor neighbourhoods uniformly poor generally leads to the election of representatives who clearly represent the poor—although it's debatable to what extent this advantage offsets the negative impacts on well-being.

In the United States, studies that have followed poor people who were given vouchers redeemable for housing outside disadvantaged neighbourhoods showed that some distinct improvements came with moving into a mixed milieu: "For adults and for girls it was very beneficial, although it was a little more ambiguous for boys." The most notable changes included "astonishing drops in obesity and diabetes," said Dunn. Researchers now claim they can attribute a portion of the differences between individuals' health and education outcomes to factors "that are explainable at the neighbourhood level."

This is the type of thinking that Dunn advocates putting into action in Hamilton, his home town. Having grown up in the city and staying on to attend McMaster University, he left in the early nineties and spent eleven years studying and working in Western Canada. Dunn then ventured back east in 2004 to take a job at St. Michael's Hospital in downtown Toronto, where he led a research project to assess the health impacts of redevelopment at Regent Park, a sixty-nine-acre public housing complex abutting the Cabbagetown district, a short walk from St. Mike's. Faced with enormous accumulated maintenance costs—the legacy of financial starvation by successive governments—Toronto's community housing agency had opted to invite private developers to redevelop Regent Park. They built high-density towers that included both market-value condos and subsidized housing where conspicuous low-rise clusters of public housing once stood.

In effect, said Dunn, the redevelopment became "a way to achieve a socially mixed community very quickly." While before, Regent Park "was visually distinct" and unmistakably separate from the surrounding neighbourhood, "what they've done in the redevelopment is to make it look like any other neighbourhood in the city. You can't tell the social housing buildings from the condo developments because the materials and the architectural design are all the same." Predictably, aspects of the redevelopment have over time been undermined: critics note the city has since reneged on its funding promises for crucial social development programs that were to complement Regent Park's material, structural changes, and negotiated increases in density have lowered the proportion of social housing in the redeveloped community from an anticipated 44 per cent to 25 per cent. This has caused lower-income tenants to sometimes struggle to compete for services, like recreation programs or daycare, alongside their market-value neighbours.[18] Still, Dunn said initial research indicated that residents' health and sense of well-being improved under the new conditions. Along with "statistically significant improvements in subclinical depression and anxiety," moving to new housing in the rebuilt mixed community produced "huge, eye-popping improvements—astonishing improvements—in people's perception of safety and feelings of security."

Several roads leading to mixed-income neighbourhoods

Dunn believes that Hamilton, facing a defining moment in its history, has many similar opportunities to encourage the creation of mixed-income communities that welcome and benefit a wide range of people. The first key to equitable growth, he said, is encouraging much higher density in underused spaces, such as the 25 per cent of Hamilton's downtown area (excluding streets) that's used as surface parking, as well as the once-thriving commercial thoroughfares lined with buildings that have either been boarded up or converted to impromptu living spaces. Transforming these badly underused spaces into sites for mid-rise or high-rise development would enable downtown Hamilton to generate significantly more tax revenue, which is key to funding needed infrastructure and social services.

Dunn is also keen on the city using its planning power to ensure new private developments help to meet public needs. For example, the city could impose inclusionary zoning regulations that allow cities to compel developers to set aside a certain percentage of new units at rents affordable by low-income residents. The concept has been enthusiastically embraced, said Dunn, in places like Montgomery County, part of the Washington, D.C., metropolitan area, where it allows lower-wage employees of local tech companies to live close to where they work.

Dunn also proposed a planning approach that would make Hamilton a southern Ontario hub for seniors. Simple adjustments like enhanced snow removal, more safety-conscious street design, and flexible transit services would encourage construction of senior-friendly housing that would allow aging citizens to live independently for longer; they could also defuse a demographic time bomb for the province. The number of people over eighty in the Greater Toronto Area is set to double (rising to two million) over twenty-five years, advised Dunn. With most of those people located in poorly serviced, car-dependent suburbs, the cost of caring for this growing group (either in remote suburban communities, or after circumstances have forced many to move prematurely into long-term care facilities) will be enormous. A new type of neigh-bourhood in a dense urban setting—welcoming to a range of res-idents but specifically designed to accommodate seniors—would bring multiple benefits. At an individual level, it would free many people from the torturous choice between staying in the suburbs in isolation and without adequate support, or moving into assisted living before it's actually necessary. At a public policy level, it prom-ises a more economical solution to circumstances that may soon coalesce as a significant social challenge.

Several kilometres to the east of Dunn's office in the leafy, serene surroundings of McMaster University's Westdale campus lies the caffeine-powered, bare-brick charm of the Mulberry Coffeehouse, smack in the centre of "once rundown James Street North, which is percolating with a vibrant arts scene, inventive farm-to-table restau-rants, edgy start-ups and cool shops," as a recent travel piece in the *New York Times* puts it.[19] It's here that I caught up with Don Jaffray, an understated, soft-spoken man who had worked for Hamilton's Social Planning and Research Council (SPRC) for roughly thirty years, serving as its executive director for much of that time. Like Dunn, Jaffray had been doing a lot of thinking about how to encour-age socially mixed communities in Hamilton. Also like Dunn, he was born and raised here. But instead of leaving the city to find his calling in life, Jaffray was drawn to social work after following several family members into a quintessentially Hamiltonian career path, toiling in the service of Big Steel.

"I used to work in a punch-press shop where we pounded out steel bars," he explained. "It was actually a pretty interesting job and I made a lot of money. When I left the Steel Company and went to work for community services, I started working for a soup kitchen operation downtown as the welfare advocate, making sure that people had access to the benefits they were entitled to. It was an interesting challenge, but it didn't pay spit. I came from a family of people who were involved in manufacturing and steelworking, and they all laughed, like, 'What's the matter with you? You seem like a smart kid. Why in the world would you walk away from a good job to do that for spit?' I didn't have a good answer for that. I guess

I was following what interests me, and what interests me is what's going on with people around me. I like to live in a good place where people look out for each other, so I went to work on that."

Amid the clattering of dishes and the steam-powered hiss of a gleaming cappuccino machine (the closest thing to industrial noise pollution you'll find around here these days), Jaffray explained that trying to ensure that Hamilton becomes—or remains, depending on your perspective—that "good place where people look out for each other" is an essential goal of the SPRC's work. In particular, he pointed to a project known as the Neighbourhood Action Strategy (which was underway at the time of our 2015 interview but has since concluded), initiated by the City of Hamilton and involving the social planning council as an executing partner. An exercise in community animation, its goal was to unleash the energy of local communities so that residents would have some say in how their neighbourhoods evolved.

"Just like in the old days," said Jaffray, "they hired a team of community developers to go into communities and try to get people to pay attention to each other, to watch each other and help each other, to try to have an influence on what's going on in the neighbourhood. They ask people, 'What is it about your neighbourhood that you like? What would you like to improve?' In communities with a lot of low-income people, you want to give people a little more support, to let them know how they can get information, to take special efforts to hear their concerns, and to commit more resources to improving their neighbourhoods."

Partly, the Neighbourhood Action Strategy was designed to address some of the unspoken issues raised by the *Spectator*'s Code Red series. Many people living in downtown Hamilton's more modest neighbourhoods didn't like the newspaper's portrayal of their communities as pools of despair. The action strategy began from the contrary assumption that there were plenty of positive qualities and social resources in those communities that would be essential to improving material conditions. The project also anticipated that the heating up of the real estate market would put social pressure on Hamilton neighbourhoods. The idea was that, by shoring up social cohesion in those places, community animators could help old-guard Hamiltonians harness what they needed to stand up to the inevitable tide of new migration, economic pressure, and social change.

Both Dunn and Jaffray spoke with me in the spring of 2015, as the real estate boom was starting to make itself felt. At the time, Dunn remarked on some classic early signs of gentrification that were beginning to appear in Hamilton: "I am hearing now of a building on John Street [a block from ground zero of Hamilton's arts- and culture-driven redevelopment on James North] where people are being offered a two-thousand-dollar bonus plus last month's rent if you move out within sixty days." This is one of several means (some of them more coercive and less honest) that are commonly used to circumvent the provincial rent controls that allow established tenants to stay put with only nominal annual rent increases.

Although those signs of gentrification were appearing in scattered pockets of the city, there was no consensus, back in 2015, on how quickly or broadly they would spread. University of Toronto geographer Alan Walks, who has monitored the gentrification of cities across Canada, told me around the same time that researchers "haven't detected gentrification in Hamilton yet. It's not a problem in Hamilton." Nor did he foresee it becoming a problem in the near future. Although some newcomers were migrating to neighbourhoods close to transit links to Toronto, "those are small entry points," he said, "and there's still a lot of city left in Hamilton."

For Walks, the prospect that Hamilton's gentrification would remain contained suggested an entirely different development strategy. Real estate prices had become inflated in nearby Toronto, he said, largely because of the new dominance of the financial sector, which had replaced the manufacturers that had typically moved their operations to lower-wage countries in the preceding decades. Walks proposed, in defiance of conventional wisdom, that the financially driven status quo in Canada and the U.S. need not stay in place forever. Since wages in Canada and competing countries like Mexico have come closer into line, and since there's no real reason why financial services should remain the backbone of the Canadian economy, it may soon make sense to "shift back to producing things in Canada that are used in Canada, things like washers and dryers and kitchen ranges. Hamilton would be the perfect place to make those. It's a good place to focus new production facilities because it has so much industrial land." (That argument resonates even more in the shadow of COVID-19, as countries worry about their dependency on distant producers for essential products.)

In turn, reviving Canadian manufacturing, Walks suggested, would safeguard lower-income communities: since gentrifiers don't like to live near factories, bringing industry back to Hamilton would reduce the competition for homes in neighbourhoods close to industry. (Dunn, meanwhile—despite conceding that a manufacturing revival would help working-class Hamiltonians by creating jobs—said it would do little to increase the tax revenue needed to fund social services, as industry is taxed according to a different formula than residential areas.)

An unanticipated real estate frenzy

For his part, Jaffray was uncertain about the pace at which gentrification would likely proceed in the coming years. Still, he was mightily convinced of the question's importance. If redevelopment unfolds slowly and gradually, said Jaffray, "then we have enough tools and investment and partners that there's still a way to make things work for more people." On the other hand, "if the transformation is too quick, driven by a handful of people with a ton of resources, then there won't be a fair opportunity to help shape the transformation."

Likewise, Dunn agreed that timing was critical to the success of any plans to ensure Hamilton's future inclusivity. "The window to act is when land values are still relatively low," he said. "I would suggest that the city should be doing land banking now," so that, as the owner of the land, it has extra leverage to insist that requirements such as inclusionary zoning are part of developers' plans.

Of course, the pace of gentrification in Hamilton is no longer the subject of conjecture. Confounding the most common predictions, the real estate market in Hamilton exploded in the period immediately following these discussions. Canadian Real Estate Association figures show that, between August 2014 and August 2015, Hamilton had the largest growth in real estate prices of any municipality in Canada: 16.6 per cent; higher than the country's two most robust markets (Vancouver, at 12.2 per cent, and Toronto, at 10.3 per cent.)[20] Cumulatively, housing prices in central Hamilton rose by 126 per cent between 2006 and 2016,[21] while prices in newly discovered neighbourhoods made enormous jumps. In Hamilton East, for example, the average home price jumped from $244,000 to $317,000 in 2016 alone.[22] By 2021, Hamilton had the third-least affordable housing in North America, according to Oxford Economics North America, whose index cross-references a city's housing costs against the incomes of its inhabitants.[23]

This kind of rapid price inflation has proven disastrous for the most vulnerable of Hamilton's low-income residents. "When my wife and I moved here ten or eleven years ago, the realtors would say, 'Don't buy here because you'll never get your money back out of it,'" recalls Jeff Neven, Hamilton East homeowner and executive director of the non-profit housing agency Indwell, which recently opened a gleaming high-rise building on the neighbourhood thoroughfare of Main Street. On the street where Neven and his family live, "most of the homes were owner occupied, primarily by elderly women. About half had renters: on my street you used to be able to rent a half-decent apartment without bedbugs for four hundred bucks a month. In the last eighteen months, on my block sixty per cent of the houses have sold and those rental apartments are just gone. A similar unit on our street would now be eleven hundred or twelve hundred dollars, if it's available."

Neven says the disappearance of those affordable rental units has led directly to tragedy. "In the last year and a half we've had three fires with three or more people dying in each. And then you read that fifteen people had been living there and it makes sense. Before you could rent an apartment for around four hundred dollars, then just a room in a rooming house, and then just a bed in a room in a house—and that might be a furnace room that has no windows. People are living in harsher and harsher circumstances." Neven believes that people perishing in fires is a consequence of Hamiltonians on fixed incomes being forced out of decent accommodation and into overcrowded and unsafe lodgings as housing prices rise across the city.

There have been parallel processes of displacement unfolding across the city, for example, in high-rise apartment towers. Investigative reporter Joey Coleman, who publishes a website called the Public Record, has followed moves by deep-pocketed real estate investment trusts to buy up a large number of Hamilton apartments and move them upmarket. Toronto-based Greenwin, for example, bought two buildings downtown and applied to convert 70 three-bedroom units, suitable for families, into one-bedroom units that might appeal to childless professionals moving from Toronto. Coleman reported that the average 2017 cost of renting a smaller single unit ($1,075 monthly) had risen to roughly the same as the old price for a family-sized three-bedroom unit, which was $1,090 in 2013. With financial resources that enable them to be patient, the company has offered cash incentives to residents to entice them to move, and was, in 2017, keeping 51 of the 70 three-bedroom units vacant while it waited to convert them to the more profitable one-bedroom apartments.[24]

In their 2018 report "Out of Control," the Social Planning and Research Council of Hamilton, the Hamilton Roundtable for Poverty Reduction, and the Hamilton Community Legal Clinic confirmed that efforts by landlords to squeeze greater profits out of properties once geared to low-income tenants have had a real impact on affordability across the city. In 2017, rents in Hamilton rose by an average of 5 per cent, compared with 1.5 per cent in Quebec City, a city of similar size and growth. The report also showed a 95 per cent jump, between 2010 and 2016, in the number of landlords applying to the Landlord and Tenant Board for evictions.[25] As prices rose and decent accommodation was being replaced by crowded and unsafe housing, the *Hamilton Spectator* reported the appearance of groups of homeless people living in tents near trails on the Niagara Escarpment and near major intersections downtown.[26]

When I spoke with Don Jaffray in 2015, before the full extent of Hamilton's real estate boom was evident, he was acutely aware of how difficult it would be to encourage the creation of communities with a mix of people from different incomes and social backgrounds, one where the fruits of incoming development and an expanded tax base would benefit people from across the social spectrum. The challenge would be to avoid the sequence of events that followed gentrification in Toronto, where monolithically low-income neighbourhoods became momentarily diverse before becoming uniformly affluent.

"The area around here," he said, referring to the newly hipsterized section of James Street North where our conversation took place, "has gone from being a place that's had a very high concentration of very low income people to one that's had an upward arc. At some point, it will probably be somebody's ideal of a mixed community. The problem is, it doesn't stop there. It carries on. The question is, when things do reach that ideal of being a mixed neighbourhood, what can we do to stabilize it, to hold it there?"

Since Jaffray articulated that dilemma, a rush of events has transformed Hamilton in a way that suggests the dream of an economically diverse and inclusive city may already have moved out of reach. Beyond the sharp rise in property values and rents, and the resulting incentive for landlords to force out low-income tenants, is the accelerated accumulation of large chunks of property by speculators who, encouraged by Hamilton's new popularity, are awaiting new waves of upper-middle-class migration and subsequent redevelopment that will allow them to cash in. This makes much of the old city off limits to agencies that might want to develop affordable housing in Hamilton. There are also some discouraging features on the political landscape—the 2018 election of a fervently business-centric provincial government and a persistent urban-suburban split on city council that disadvantages the downtown—that bode poorly for any future urban development plans that are shaped not solely by the marketplace's unrelenting demands, but rather by the desire to create mixed, inclusive communities.

Still, many people in Hamilton are willing to bet that the horse has not left the barn, that much can still be done to encourage an urban renaissance that breaks with the standard narrative of social polarization that has accompanied economic upturns in countless other cities. In a changing city, there are many competing visions of what kind of tomorrow should emerge. These competing visions have certainly already led to conflict and have the potential to feed further animosity and social exclusion. But as we will see, there's enough inventive thinking and constructive dialogue happening in Hamilton to suggest that the outcome, here in the shadows of those hulking foundries that monumentalize a lost era, might somehow be different.

CHAPTER TWO

Boom, Bust, and a Double-Sided Bohemian Renaissance

OLD HAMILTON CANADA Photos is a volunteer-run Facebook group that posts historical images of Hamilton for close to eight thousand members, some current residents, others Hammerheads-in-exile. Under the watch of former east-ender Doug Southon and his band of administrators, the popular page with a prosaic name performs a kind of magic. It resurrects the spirit of a place that passed into oblivion decades ago, transporting readers beyond the mists of time to an era when Hamilton was a viable city teeming with activity, excitement, and life.

For those who know Hamilton from its post-apocalyptic phase, after the industrial meltdown of the 1980s, that characterization seems unlikely. But the pictures support the myth—offering proof that this industrial-era Shangri-La actually existed. We see shots of the majestic Eaton's department store on James North, where elevator operators wore white gloves, pearls, and unflinching expressions as the cages they commanded descended at stomach-churning speeds. Along with other larger retailers—Robinson's, the Right

House, Home Outfitters furniture, Eames menswear, Woolworths, and Kresge's—Eaton's anchored a downtown core that was also populated by dozens of specialty stores. Among people whose childhoods unfolded within this milieu, the names of those places— Mills China Shop, Waddington's musical instruments, Anne Foster records, and dozens more—quickly evoke a sense of melancholic nostalgia.

Scrolling through Old Hamilton Canada Photos is like stumbling across an old Frank Capra film on TCM. Its mementos capture an urban reality more stylish, more personable, arguably more optimistic than the one that would replace it. Before the fortress-fronted Jackson Square swallowed acres of the downtown core, blaring neon signs lit up the night on King Street with the exuberance of a down-market Las Vegas. The second- and third-largest movie theatres in Canada—the Palace and the Capitol, both with frescoed ceilings and marble staircases—welcomed hundreds of patrons. Large crowds filled wide sidewalks during the day, and trolley buses—sometimes idled by downtown traffic jams, as bizarre as the notion now seems—were often standing room only. My own interior snapshots of this place date back from the mid-1960s through the early seventies, but Hamilton had been a bustling place with a distinctive personality for generations before then.

It wasn't until the late eighties that Hamilton's full-scale decline—with distinguished buildings replaced by parking lots and legendary local businesses supplanted by dollar stores, head shops, and peep shows—was clearly on display. Still, the disintegration of the Frank Capra version of Hamilton had started long before that, even by the early sixties.

In 1963, city controller Brian Morison implored fellow councillors to get behind a massive downtown redevelopment project, declaring, "I'm voting for this proposal because I want the downtown to live. I've been on council for twelve years and I've seen our downtown core dying."[1] Bulldozing and then rebuilding the centre core was also advocated by "downtown businessmen who were deeply concerned that much of their business was being gradually eroded by suburban plazas and shopping centres,"[2] writes Martha

Hewitt in *Their Town: The Mafia, the Media and the Party Machine*, a 1979 collection edited by Hewitt and Bill Freeman.

The political realities of the time favoured the bulldoze-and-rebuild approach. The National Housing Act of 1954 committed significant federal funds for urban renewal projects, and Hamilton had already successfully accessed federal cash for projects such as a redevelopment scheme at Van Wagner's beach and the replacement of numerous houses and factories in the North End by a hundred-unit high-rise public housing complex, accompanied by a park and a school. This way of working had an administrative advantage. The feds' financial might allowed for the assembly of large packages of land (with the federal government picking up 50 per cent of expropriation costs, the province 30 per cent, and the city 20 per cent) that could then be transferred to private developers. And so, city council embraced its Jetsons-style future: in 1964 it approved a revolutionary Civic Square proposal submitted by Toronto architect Murray Jones and then set about levelling a massive forty-four-acre swath of the downtown core on which a new type of city would emerge.

"The possibility of massive redevelopment downtown, transforming the city core into monoliths of steel and glass, sparked the imagination," writes Hewitt. Besides commercial space, the rebuilt area was to include "a theatre auditorium, planetarium, education centre, library, farmers' market, art gallery, and trade and convention centre." (All of those facilities, except for the planetarium, eventually wound up being built, although the ratio of commercial to public buildings shifted in favour of the former, and there were years when vast tracts of land sat vacant.) The underlying idea was that surrounding businesses would be buoyed by the increase in traffic as the new amenities attracted people back to the central core. The city also anticipated a rise in tax revenue with flourishing high-end shops occupying the new commercial space.

In the pursuit of this glistening dream, city politicians essentially abandoned the more marginal merchants who had served the working-class and largely ethnic communities that had stayed in downtown Hamilton. Although expropriated merchants were offered first right of refusal on new space in what would become

Jackson Square, the exorbitant rents made this impossible, forcing smaller enterprises to seek more affordable quarters elsewhere. "In the end," according to Hewitt, "somewhere between one-quarter and one-half of the merchants failed to relocate and were forced out of business." Meanwhile, some higher-tier businesspeople found a profitable way of gaming the system. A trio of well-connected speculators who had scooped up small retailers' land for as little as twenty-five dollars around the time of the redevelopment announcement offered to resell the properties to the city for a cool $2 million. (The city eventually brought them down to $1,186,500).[3]

Although some private interests profited handsomely, the public good that was promised from downtown redevelopment never materialized. After the first consortium contracted to build the Civic Square (First Wentworth, spearheaded by the local Pigott family) went broke, in 1970 a Montreal firm named Yale Properties stepped in and rescued the project. Although it did get built, the project did not catalyze an urban renaissance. Demand for new office space remained low as it had for the earlier, heavily subsidized high-rise projects Terminal Towers and Century 21. As a result, the rust-coloured Stelco Tower sprouting from the street-level Jackson Square shopping mall remained only partly occupied. Hewitt and Freeman argue that politicians essentially misread Hamilton's economic development potential: the city was fundamentally industrial, not commercial, and office-dwelling enterprises like insurance or financial services companies had little reason at that time to locate in a blue-collar town.

While Hamilton did gain an impressive art gallery and a top-notch performance space in the central core, the anticipated retail growth was underwhelming. Ergo, there was no spike in property taxes and no boost for surrounding businesses. In fact, concludes Hewitt, "by almost every yardstick [urban renewal] has been a disaster. . . . Rather than attracting people to the downtown, the redevelopment program drove them to the shopping plazas even faster."[4]

Added to the impacts of a failed reconstruction were the later crippling injuries to steel and other manufacturing industries in the

1980s; together, they accelerated the pace of decline and set the stage for a new age of misery. Any expatriate Hamiltonian who, like me, made the occasional trip back home in the nineties would be struck by the deterioration. By the mid-nineties, not only had most of the old businesses on King Street packed up; what seemed like half of the storefronts in the new Jackson Square were also papered over. Regal old buildings continued to be abandoned and demolished. The streets that were once awash in neon and mischief were now, at most times of day, mostly silent.

Finding the future in the past

In the midst of all this, a few optimists valiantly plotted Hamilton's comeback. In 1998, a time of peak bleakness, the Labourers' International Union of North America (LiUNA) made the unlikely (others said foolhardy) decision to buy the old CN railway station and adjoining lands on James Street, deep in Hamilton's North End. The train station had once been a focal point of this proud but faded working-class neighbourhood, which had by then evolved into a downscale pastiche of persistent mom-and-pop retailers, small Victorian and pre-Victorian residences, empty lots, abandoned industrial lands, public housing, and low-rent sixties-vintage apartment towers. It was also nearby the Royal Hamilton Yacht Club and a wonderfully rehabilitated stretch of public waterfront called Bayfront Park, opened in 1993, which enhanced its gentrification potential. The CN station had been derelict for at least a decade before the union purchased it.

Joseph Mancinelli, LiUNA's Hamilton-based international vice-president and regional manager for Central and Eastern Canada, recalls a city councillor named Frank D'Amico approaching him with news the property was on the market and the suggestion that LiUNA put in a bid. When Mancinelli and his colleagues first visited the station, "it was February and minus twenty-eight degrees and there were no windows left in the place because the kids in the neighbourhood had broken them all. Thousands of pigeons everywhere. Ice on the floor. We kind of looked at each other and said, 'Do we really want to do this?—because this building is in really bad repair.'"

What decided the question in the affirmative was the structural engineer's report "that basically said the building was as sound as the day it was built, because it had been built like a tank and just built so well." At first the union wanted to open a nursing home on the premises, but provincial authorities wouldn't allow a health-related facility to be constructed on brownfield property where environmental amelioration was required. So LiUNA set its sights on a convention centre. With a contract to host a construction industry convention in May 2000, the new owners had to pull out all the stops to open on time. Besides the building trades shindig, an impressive queue was forming for weddings, long before the building actually opened. "Brides would come down and have to step over construction materials," says Mancinelli. "It was a bit of a nightmare."

LiUNA's approach to renovating the CN station ran precisely opposite to the sentiment that had guided Hamilton's earlier redevelopment efforts. In a city that seemed bizarrely eager to tear down its most impressive heritage buildings in the hope of replacing them with something shiny and futuristic, LiUNA was committed to celebrating the past. "We didn't destroy anything," says Mancinelli of the train station renovation. "We restored the bronze, the terrazzo floors, any of the wood we could salvage from the offices we used to enhance the bar areas. And rooms that didn't have much original stuff left were replicated in materials from the era."

Betting that suburban merry-makers would be willing to ignore an increasingly desperate downtown core en route to a restored CN station brought an element of risk for LiUNA. But there was a substantial upside if things panned out. By investing its pension funds in the project, the union aimed both to generate some healthy returns and to create employment for its own membership. (LiUNA no longer represents just labourers but all of the skilled trades involved in construction.)

The strategy dates back to 1981, when interest rates in excess of 20 per cent had sparked massive unemployment in the construction sector. That year, LiUNA bought a chunk of land on Lake Ontario, abutting Hamilton's southern suburban fringe, with its own contribution augmented by $2 million in federal funding through a program designed to help the industry escape its near-death experience. By offering a combination of work and training programs at the lakefront site, says executive board member Riccardo Persi, the union met the terms for extending workers' unemployment insurance benefits, "which allowed many families to get back on their feet."

That experiment also left a material legacy in the form of LiUNA Gardens, another banquet centre, which became the model for future union forays into land development. LiUNA's pension fund "is now one of the largest investors in rental properties along the QEW," says Mancinelli, referring to a swath of glass-fronted, Triple A–rated corporate office buildings that line the highway between Hamilton and Toronto. LiUNA also has a non-profit arm that runs affordable housing projects, including six hundred units downtown and a series of "beautiful, nicely maintained" townhouses on the Mountain.

As well, the stately old office building on Hughson Street—LiUNA's headquarters for eastern North America and the site of my conversation with Mancinelli and Persi—is another example of LiUNA's pension funds and member expertise at work. I have a particular interest in this building because it rests on the same parcel of land where my father used to work in the 1960s, in the service of Canadian Canners' accounting department. When I mention this to Mancinelli, he confirms that we are indeed in what was once the office of the president of Canadian Canners (the corporate entity that produced Aylmer brand canned foods, later bought by Del Monte of California). "Basically, it's the shell of an 1830s building but an entirely new building inside," says Mancinelli. Meanwhile, the neighbouring grey-painted, more utilitarian office block where my dad surrendered his weekdays was flattened years ago and is, like so much of downtown Hamilton, a parking lot.

LiUNA owns this entire block, however, and has plans to eventually build residential towers (with a mix of retail and office space occupying lower floors) on the rest of the site. This is one of several initiatives that makes the LiUNA pension fund a major player in the redevelopment of downtown Hamilton. Mancinelli walks over to an easel in the corner of his office and runs through a list of projects sketched out in a series of architects' drawings. On James North, just below King William, is a now-constructed twenty-storey student residence, made feasible by the expansion of McMaster University into the downtown core. The tower is built in steps—rising to higher altitudes by degrees, so that the tallest part of the building is set back significantly from the road. At street level is the facade of the historic William Thomas Building, which had been taken down in pieces that were then numbered, stored, and later reassembled like a 3-D jigsaw puzzle on the original site. LiUNA is taking a similar approach on King Street, across from Gore Park, where its two residential towers (likely a condo and a rental building) will be fronted by the old Kresge building, whose welcoming working-class face was also dismantled, numbered, and warehoused for later reassembly.

LiUNA is certainly not the only developer to launch transformative projects in Hamilton's core, but its early commitment sets it apart as an essential, catalytic force in the city's redevelopment. With a few strategic land purchases, a shrewd reading of emerging trends, and, apparently, a bit of luck, LiUNA arguably set the stage for the current frenzy of gentrification. Its purchase of the CN station—along with the earlier acquisition of the Lister Block, a gorgeous mid-rise office block at James and King William with a pedestrian arcade at ground level—made those projects the "bookends," in Mancinelli's words, that delineated Hamilton's first frontier for gentrification along a soon-to-be-hipsterized section of James Street North. "The naysayers thought we were crazy," he says. "But we were convinced that if we did something inspiring at two ends of James Street, it would encourage others to move in between those two points. Sometimes people need to see something inspiring in order to take their own leap of faith."

A spark that helped set the real estate market on fire

Doubling down on its wager that other investors would be drawn to the area, LiUNA scooped up properties adjoining its own projects. For example, it resold land it had bought across the street from the CN station to the transit agency Metrolinx, which needed property for a train station for its new commuter service between Toronto and the North End of Hamilton. The Lister Block, picked up by LiUNA at a discount when a Toronto developer pulled the plug on its speculative leap into Hamilton, also came packaged with ancillary properties; among them, the William Thomas property on which the student residence would rise, the Kresge property, and a space on King William sold to another developer with dreams of building high-end lofts.

From the beginning, the union displayed a steely confidence that people would be attracted back to Hamilton's traditional business district. But did it foresee the extent of the stampede that would eventually follow, with exponential price rises, fierce bidding wars, and newspaper stories proclaiming that Hamilton had become Toronto's Brooklyn?

"No, we weren't that smart," responds Mancinelli. "We thought that gentrification would take place, and when it began we weren't surprised. But what did surprise us was the number of artists that came in and how quickly that happened. Just a few short years after the train station was redone, a long time before the Art Crawl, a number of buildings along James Street turned into galleries. That happened fast. And the number of Hamilton homes bought by Torontonians was really staggering. We didn't anticipate that. In 1998, you could buy any home here for under two hundred thousand dollars. Now if you find a house in downtown Hamilton, you'd better grab it fast because in a week it will be gone."

To what extent LiUNA's bookend investments on opposite ends of James North encouraged an influx of artists is open to debate. Surely, the fact that someone saw Hamilton's forsaken architectural treasures as worth gambling on would have sent a positive signal to other would-be pioneers. But it is also true that artists had congregated close to James North long before there was any suggestion of the area becoming trendy: for example, Hamilton Artists Co-op (now Hamilton Artists Inc.) had been an institution on the street since the early 1970s. From the beginning, the primary attraction luring artists to the city's crumbling core was the amazingly low property values, and that continued to be the main draw for the next wave of artists and arts-related entrepreneurs in the nineties and beyond. Not having to struggle to make the rent or the mortgage made almost anything possible. Here you could dream big, live according to your values, and make art or music without having to serve the master of commercial success. You didn't have to spend your days worrying about the state of your bank account or whether you'd be evicted next month. The low price of real estate left you free to create.

Cheap rent spawns an underground arts scene

Kevin MacKay, a driving force behind a nouveau-Hamilton institution known as the Sky Dragon Centre, housed in a multi-storey Victorian gem on a now chic section of King William, says the economics of downtown life was only one of the revelations that penetrated his consciousness after he moved into the city core in the early nineties. Enrolled at McMaster University in 1989, "like a lot of students, [he] just stayed around McMaster." He says, "There was almost an invisible barrier between Westdale and downtown Hamilton, which was seen as a very dodgy, very scary kind of place where you didn't want to go. Sadly, I just took this as accepted wisdom and almost never explored other parts of Hamilton."

By his third year at university, however, he was painting a lot and had heard rumours of cheap studio space in the city centre. With another student, MacKay rented an upper-storey expanse near the corner of James North and Rebecca Street, above what for years had been a health food store, with a sink in the studio and washrooms outside. "Just to give you a sense of what prices were like, we paid a hundred dollars a month for that, and it was a big space," he says. With this move came the realization that downtown—although many of its residents faced harsh deprivation in their lives—was not the crime-ridden wasteland he had been warned about: "They talk about the donut phenomenon—where there's a hole in the middle of post-industrial towns—and Hamilton was a living, breathing example of that. But once you got down there, you could see a lot of cool stuff going on below board. There were a lot of empty spaces that were just being appropriated and used."

In the midst of this impromptu creative playground, "you obviously don't just want to paint," continues MacKay. "You also want to do events. So I started looking for a bigger space." That facilitated a relocation to a "big, big room" a couple streets over on King Street, with high ceilings, a view of Gore Park (the city's epicentre), and an inspiring artistic past. The premises had been inhabited, at different times, by photographer José Crespo and painter Bill Powell, symbolically linking the space to that mid-twentieth-century era "when Hamilton was a vibrant, happening cultural centre. It was almost like young artists of my generation were creeping in amongst the ruins of that," says MacKay. The price tag, to return to more crass concerns, was still only $200 a month.

It was here, on that third-floor space on King Street—combined with the fourth floor, which MacKay and his associates occupied when another group of artists moved out—that the first iteration of the Sky Dragon Centre took shape. (The name, says MacKay, was a recognition of the new premises' multiple roles as "a meditation, martial arts, and arts space, which makes no sense apart from the fact that those are the sorts of things I was into.") Sky Dragon was one of a handful of informal meeting places in Hamilton where the 1990s counterculture began to coalesce. "Lots of performances and parties and film screenings and community events happened there," recalls MacKay, who adds that they uniformly occurred outside the gaze of regulatory agencies and occasionally attracted the (mostly amused) attention of the local enforcers of public order. Since these events were attended largely by young white people with suburban backgrounds, their transgressions were dealt with much more leniently by the police than they would have been, so experience suggests, if the partygoers had been from racialized backgrounds.

"It was still very underground in a lot of ways," recalls MacKay. "At every event we had, we'd be selling alcohol. We tried to be as responsible as possible: these weren't total bacchanalian free-for-alls, but they were highly illegal. When the space started to get more popular, we'd have the police showing up, and those were always fun moments. A lot of times they'd walk up and they'd have this kind of quizzical look on their faces. Everyone would be chilling, some people would be painting, and there would be enough pot smoke to kind of choke the officers on the way up the stairs—it was that kind of scene. I think they really didn't want to break it up; a few times they'd kind of walk around and say, 'Okay, well, just don't do it again.' Eventually, you would get somebody who was a bit of a dick. There was one beat cop who, at least twice, made us shut down parties that were really rocking. But we did have four to five hundred people shoved into a space that was probably not supposed to have fifty."

MacKay describes these chaotic gatherings as the genesis of the new, arts-centred Hamilton that would attract increasing media attention (as well as the scrutiny of real estate speculators) as the new century continued to unfold. The spark that led the Hamilton scene to catch fire was "all the artists and local people who saw the incredible opportunity that was possible because of the cheap rents, who would put on events."

Dave Kuruc offers a nearly identical appraisal. Kuruc and his wife, Teresa Devries, ran Mixed Media, an art supply store on James North, between 2005 and 2018. Raised in the East End, Kuruc was a teenager in the early 1990s when Sky Dragon was scraping together rent money by illegally selling booze at parties. The scene was a formative influence on Kuruc and surely a factor in his decision years later to open a business in the geographic heart of the scene.

"This was my hangout, right?" says Kuruc. "The downtown you see today sort of grew out of that subculture that you saw in the nineties—a really underground thing of gallery showings and indie bands, all the stuff that exists here now, only it didn't exist on the ground floors. What people see today on James Street and in the clubs, it existed in the eighties and nineties, but you had to climb three or four storeys to get to a gallery or go into a basement through an alley."

Contemplating a more stable foundation

Despite the romance of the underground era, many people knew at the time that it couldn't last. In the case of Sky Dragon, "we realized that we were renting a building that was slowly falling apart and that the owners didn't really care about," says MacKay. "The roof was leaking like a sieve and we saw all the energy we were pouring into it just dissipating. We thought we wanted something more stable." MacKay adds that the core group at Sky Dragon were all aware that, alongside "this really beautiful artistic community" were conditions of poverty and neglect that were creating hardship and despair for many of their neighbours, and they were convinced they could do something to help. "Basically, we wanted to fix up some of this decaying infrastructure downtown and use it for community purposes. We believed that having a creative and open space had the power to build community."

And so, MacKay and his friend Dan Smith, a finance student at McMaster on his way to earning an M.B.A., enlisted a group of Mac professors as the nucleus of a new community development co-operative. They took inspiration from the Spanish co-op Mondragon, founded in 1956 by graduates of a technical college in Basque, a massive worker-owned organization that's grown to oversee 160 businesses, a university, and a hospital. Sky Dragon's plans were obviously more modest but similar in intent: its initial aim was to refurbish crumbling buildings and to serve as an incubator that would nurture community enterprises. Ultimately, Sky Dragon wound up renovating only one old building (that elegant Victorian structure on King William Street), but the group stayed true to its aim of providing community programming, despite the surrender of the rest of the street to trendy restaurants and boutiques. My introduction to Sky Dragon was as a participant in a joint book launch in 2014[5] (featuring lots of spirited discussion, just like you'd expect in Hamilton)—a typical kind of activity for this place.

In the beginning, Sky Dragon operated a café called Bread and Roses and was home base for a magazine entitled *May Day* (both names providing a clue to the political sympathies that dominated around here). The magazine is now defunct and the café space has gone through a couple of different incarnations. Throughout its life, the co-op has offered space to activist groups, New Age practitioners, musicians, artists, and assorted other visionaries, iconoclasts, and eccentrics. MacKay says there were also plans to develop affordable housing when it bought its building in 2005, although the challenges of merely keeping up with the bills soon pushed housing off the agenda, at least for the time being.

The fact that Sky Dragon has been able to remain a kind of community hub, in the face of the consolidated commercialism that now dominates the neighbourhood, suggests a conscious awareness of (and a desire to avoid) the fates of earlier low-rent little Bohemias that had been swept away by sudden tidal waves of real estate dollars, victims of their own success and their perilously attractive mythologies. One such cautionary tale had played out in the 1980s a mere hour's bus ride away from downtown Hamilton, on a strip of Toronto's Queen Street West between McCall Street and Spadina Avenue, where visual artists, musicians, and assorted exiles from the suburbs had been gathering since the sixties. By the mid-eighties, as curator and art historian Rosemary Donegan wrote in a 1986 *Fuse* magazine article, as the area's resident artists and musicians began to "grumble about escalating rents, tourists, teeny-boppers and uptowners taking over their local hang-outs," it was becoming clear that Queen West, as an incubator of creative thought, was barrelling towards extinction.

Success stories and death spirals

Donegan delineated a series of (often overlapping) stages between the area's initial discovery by cultural producers and its final, indisputable takeover by big money. "What attracted the artists, musicians and their cohorts to the area in the mid-60s," she wrote, "was that it was cheap and central. It had photography labs, typesetters, copy shops, generous studio space in loft buildings and an accessible transit system," as well as proximity to the Ontario College of Art and, of course, "a few inexpensive bars," some of which had been operating since the nineteenth century. A second wave of artists arrived in the 1970s, some of them responsible for establishing a range of artist-run spaces such as Trinity Square Video, A Space, YYZ, and Chromozone, among others, which solidified the identity of the Queen West area as an artists' community. Then with the arrival of commercial galleries in the eighties, "suddenly Queen Street was a major centre of the art market, not just in Toronto, but nationally." This contributed to the growing media attention paid to the Queen West scene, meaning that—in the context of eighties Toronto's real estate boom—death by investment became assured.

"As the 'scene' becomes progressively recognized outside its real or imagined borders," noted Donegan, "the pressure mounts to turn a higher profit, and it becomes an inevitable place for investment by outside interests which have no historical or cultural commitment to the area. These investors will naturally demand the highest possible rate of return, whether from retail or real estate investment." And so, retail chains push out the local bookstore; the artist who's fixed up her cheap space gets bounced by a well-heeled renovator or a condo developer. While Donegan documented this process based upon what was occurring in the mid-1980s, since then Queen West has been much more thoroughly transformed, with massive high-rise infill development towering behind the rows of storefronts, and with that storefront space, in turn, now being mostly controlled by large corporations.

Of course, this cycle of artists moving into a downtrodden area, glamourizing it, and being turfed when the neighbourhood is discovered by outsiders hardly began with Queen Street. In fact, Donegan cited the celebrated German cultural critic Walter Benjamin's complaint that in a formerly bohemian sector of Berlin in 1932, the artists had been nudged out by "stock market speculators" and others who coveted the area's ambience as a relief from the dreariness of their daily lives. Toronto itself had sprouted earlier bohemian enclaves that rose to prominence in some secluded corner and then, for a variety of reasons, dissolved. The Gerrard Village near Bay and Gerrard, for example—anchored by institutions like Mary Johns restaurant, which was once patronized by "everybody from the Group of Seven, Stephen Leacock, Ernest Hemingway to doctors from the nearby hospitals"—had been the slightly shady nexus of the city's bohemian subculture from the 1920s until the sixties. Its demise came not at the hands of private real estate interests but rather a land-hungry public institution: this long-time playground for artists and artisans was eventually levelled to make way for an expansion of the Toronto General Hospital.[6]

In the case of Queen West, artists became especially vulnerable when the broken-down industrial spaces they had turned into live/work spaces suddenly became more marketable. "Owners of buildings . . . are watching market activities carefully, awaiting the right time and environment in which to launch sale or redevelopment of their property," stated the Toronto Arts Council's 1986 report "No Vacancy." "In an effort to keep their options open they are frequently choosing to sign only very short leases [with artists], or no leases at all, leaving tenants with no security of tenure and making tenants' investment of significant capital for renovations imprudent."[7]

At the same time, "the City was cracking down on illegal live/work spaces in warehouse buildings citing health and safety concerns," according to a historical summary posted by Artscape, an organization that was born during the artists' housing crisis of the 1980s and which, in the decades since then, has built a considerable amount of accommodation and workspace for artists.[8] Despite the legacy of Artscape, things looked bleak for this community of artists in the late eighties: caught in the pincers of the city's rulebook on the one side, and the financial incentives for owners to sell or redevelop on the other, most of the cultural producers who had given the Queen West area its new cachet had no option but to pull up stakes and move.

Some old Hamiltonians get behind the New Guard

In Hamilton, the situation that evolved since the turn of the 2000s was, in many instances, distinctly different from its antecedent on Queen West in the 1980s. Sometimes—rather than being at the mercy of their landlords—Hamilton artists found themselves in a more productive relationships with building owners that allowed them to achieve greater security of tenure by buying their buildings. Such was the case with Sky Dragon. In 2005, Kevin MacKay and Dan Smith struck a rent-to-own type of deal with Margaret Ashfield, the King William Street building's former owner.

"She was a wonderful person, and the building had been in her family for maybe fifty years," says MacKay. Having housed an art gallery, the Allan Petteplace Bookseller and Framing Gallery, "it was almost perfect for us because it was an artistic building which had been used so well, but it was really falling apart. There was a huge whole in the roof. Lots of water damage. It was probably on the way to becoming a vacant building that would be knocked down in three or four years, which is really the Hamilton way: you know, buildings go to hell and then they get knocked down."

Sky Dragon's principals proposed a creative—if somewhat con-voluted—alternative. They negotiated a one-year lease with Ashfield with "a pre-agreed purchase price at the end of that term, which was around two hundred thousand dollars." After taking possession, the group started renovating the building. The idea was to restore the structure to respectability so that a bank would give it a decent appraisal and provide a mortgage. A friend who worked in the co-op movement in Toronto suggested they could finance the renovations by selling community bonds—a strategy that did indeed provide a tenuous financial footing allowing Sky Dragon to proceed. "The bonds were a thousand dollars each," says MacKay. "Obviously, most of our friends could not afford these but we did know some people who were professors and professionals. Surprisingly, it worked." The renovations were completed (partly by hiring workers, and partly through Kevin and Dan exchanging their own labour for shares in the co-op once the funds had run out). When the renovations were finished, the building was appraised at $300,000 and the teachers' credit union extended a $200,000 mortgage.

There are some similar stories around these parts of upstart enterprises lacking in capital launching themselves with sweat equity and a ridiculously favourable real estate deal, courtesy of some benevolent onlooker. Take Sonic Unyon, which today is the closest thing in the new Hamilton to a vertically integrated conglomerate. The company's three founding partners (Mark Milne, Sandy McIntosh, and Tim Potocic) launched the firm as a record company and music distributor in 1993. Although McIntosh left the firm to become an architect, and the distribution arm was sold in 2008, Sonic Unyon has gone on to great heights as an artist management, record production, and event organization/promotion company. Its three-storey studio/office building on Wilson Street, a few steps from James North, has become a defining landmark in the neighbourhood. A more important indicator of Sonic Unyon's central role in the James North arts scene, however, is the company's involvement in organizing Supercrawl, the signature event in downtown Hamilton, which in 2015 attracted 150,000 people to a neighbourhood that, a couple decades before, had been mostly forgotten by the outside world.

All of this began modestly—and sometimes comically—when three friends who played in a band for beer on the weekends decided that the business side of music might provide an alternative to finding a conventional day job. In the late 1990s, Tim Potocic, a Hamiltonian who had "lived all over Hamilton, with grandparents in the East End and grandparents in the North End," had been studying business at Western University in London and making his way back to Hamilton each week for band practices with his friends. A self-taught drummer, his participation in the indie band Tristan Psionic was an outgrowth of a childhood that revolved around music. "I grew up playing in Croatian orchestras. There was always music in my house. My dad played weddings, in addition to his job as an engineer at Dofasco," says Potocic, who today is one-half of the ownership of Sonic Unyon and the unpaid director of Supercrawl.

Potocic learned that his two bandmates had started to dabble in record production and distribution, "and [he] said to Mark and Sandy, 'I'm not doing anything, and I want to use my education, so are you serious? Is this a real company?' And they were like, 'Well, not really.'" Nonetheless, Potocic continues, "we decided to incorporate it as a partnership." Each partner contributed $2,000, never expecting to get it back. At first the distribution company was located in Sandy's parents' basement in suburban Burlington, "in a room that was about ten by fifteen [feet]—the furnace room. Within a couple of months, we had taken over their entire basement with stock and with me sleeping on the couch and us working out of this room. It seemed pretty obvious we'd have to move, and Sandy's parents were cajoling us, basically saying, 'I think you guys are growing fast enough the you can afford rent . . . but *somewhere else.*'"

That precipitated a move above ground, to an upper-floor space in the Radigan Brothers cleaning supply building on Ferguson Avenue in downtown Hamilton. It was, says Potocic, leaning back in a swivel chair in his current second-floor Wilson Street office, "a thousand-square-foot, really cool, loft-style space. We stayed there maybe a year or a year and a half and that time went really quickly. We put a bunch of records out, although we weren't earning any money." (There would be no paycheques for quite a while after that. Potocic says that it wasn't until 1997, after four years or so of hard slogging, that the three partners paid themselves $1,000 each—"but we were building a business, right?")

The Sonic partners wanted to accommodate the continued growth by taking over the other rental space in the Ferguson Avenue building, but the Radigans liked to rent to multiple tenants, not just one, and refused their offer. Then came another luminous downtown Hamilton moment, Sonic Unyon's variation on the experience that Sky Dragon had with Margaret Ashfield, the landowner willing to offer exceptional terms to someone who appreciated what her building stood for and the role it had played in downtown Hamilton life. In Sonic Unyon's case, the white knight was Ron Weston Sr., who had run a local retail institution known as Sam Manson sports.

"Ron felt bad because he had this property where there was a thriving business for forty years, but he had sold [the business] to people who bankrupted it and now the building was gathering dust," says Potocic. "He felt guilty because he was a big Hamilton booster—an ex-Tiger-Cat and a guy who loves the city."

Potocic's aunt, while working at Hill Park high school on the Mountain, used to buy sports equipment for the phys-ed department from Sam Manson's and had gotten to know the Westons. She introduced them to her nephew, who, along with Milne, McIntosh, and outside investor Mark Furukawa (who operates the Dr. Disc record store next door), was eyeing the Wilson Street property as Sonic Unyon's new home and a hub for arts-related enterprises. Ron Weston Sr., wanting to salvage some of the building's legacy as a component of a formerly thriving downtown, offered to sell it to the four upstarts "for a song." The investors scraped together the money, bought the building in 1996, and in 1997 (before the partners started paying themselves) Sonic Unyon moved in.

Hey, let's put on a show!

Once they'd relocated, the local music moguls became aware of the sense of community that had solidified around James North. Supercrawl—the weekend-long art and music festival that, each September, now draws massive crowds to the North End—grew out of collaborations that had been underway for several years. A few galleries on the street were co-ordinating their efforts by staying open one Friday night each month, so patrons could wander between exhibitions, get a feel for the neighbourhood, and develop a sense of connection with the local art scene. Sonic Unyon joined in by organizing musical performances to coincide with the gallery events. (These monthly Art Crawls still take place). Then, in the late aughts, Sonic Unyon summoned a couple dozen community members to talk about spinning off an annual street party from the lower-key gallery event. "People were saying, maybe we should just pick a day and do it on the same day every month," Potocic remembers.

That idea bore fruit with the staging of the first Supercrawl in October 2009. "A bunch of people in the community rallied round—it was all volunteers—and we pulled it off. It wasn't a nice night, there was pouring rain, but we estimated that about three thousand people came out. At the time, we were like, 'Holy crap— this is a gigantic success.'"

Potocic believes that the boost in foot traffic that first Supercrawl night persuaded many businesses to "raise the level of what they were doing" so people would come back to their stores outside of the festivities. The crowds at Supercrawl produced mutual benefits for both businesses and the artists who participated in the event: with the festival helping to make James North a destination for people interested in restaurants, bars, galleries, and shops; and the street's growing cachet, in turn, helping Supercrawl boost its attendance from 3,000 to some 150,000 people, and its budget from $30,000 to a high-water mark of over a million.

Starting from scratch or rediscovering a rich history?

The spectacle of this section of downtown Hamilton awash with thousands of music fans and gallery-goers, sipping lattes as they inspect the goods in the street vendors' booths, is a far cry from its prior image. Namely, the down-in-the-mouth version of James Street North, struggling to deal with the cumulative impacts of misguided urban renewal schemes, flight to the suburbs, official neglect, and public disinterest. Listening to Tim Potocic describe the pre-renaissance James Street, he seems to come close to imply- ing that this neighbourhood was just a wasteland—a blank canvas waiting for someone to come along with a few tubes of paint, some turntables, and a marketing plan.

"It was pretty grim in downtown Hamilton," he says, his thoughts drifting back to the 1990s. "There wasn't a lot going on. We were doing shows at the X-Club once a month, and there was Mark [Furukawa's Dr. Disc] and a few record shops. But it was pretty quiet; there wasn't a lot of vibrant business going on. There were the old Portuguese businesses, some trinket shops, a few relevant businesses that had weathered the storm, and quite a few empty stores. That was about it. You really could walk down the street and run into nobody that you knew. There were no cool coffee shops . . . you had to go into the mall for a coffee."

But not everybody saw it that way. For Dave Kuruc, who spent over a decade in business on James North before he and his wife moved their Mixed Media shop to Westdale, the neighbourhood's primary attraction was a sense of history that neither urban renewal, nor changing fashions, nor economic misfortune could ever completely erase. "People said the neighbourhood was down and out when we opened up, but that's not true," says Kuruc, over the mechanical clang of his shop's over-the-transom bell. "The fish markets and the bakeries were still here. The main Portuguese church and the social hall are still right there. The thing that was noticeable was that the population base was much older, so the kids and grandkids only came down for special events and didn't actually live here. And you were starting to see older people move away for lack of services. But ten or twenty years from now, I'm sure the Portuguese will still feel this is the centre of their community, even if their businesses are no longer here."

And it's not just the Portuguese who can lay claim to James North. Although the Portuguese were the most recent arrivals in this area, they represent just one wave of immigrants who found in this street a safe haven within a large and unfamiliar land. At different times, the neighbourhood received Scots, Italians, Hungarians, Yugoslavians . . . each group arriving at Hamilton's port on Lake Ontario, or at the CN train station where wedding parties and conventioneers now gather, and then making their way slightly north to this stretch of inexpensive apartments above storefront family businesses. A kind of urban archaeologist, Kuruc points out that the range of ethnic churches here reveal, like sedimentary layers of rock, the various waves of immigration. (There's even a large Anglican church down the street, indicating that this place was once primarily English.)

Kuruc's reverent tone suggests that he views this place as a kind of sacred ground. On the streets around here, people sometimes lived out their entire lives, rarely straying beyond their comforting confines. Immigrants adjusted to the demands of a new country. Neighbours and families helped each other out. The particulars of this larger story came to life for Kuruc in fragments, after he bought his building and began ripping out walls and burrowing beneath the floors during renovations. Bundles of newspapers used as insulation hinted at the social context that former inhabitants lived in. In the store that housed Mixed Media (a pharmacy for many years before that), there were *Toronto Stars* and *Hamilton Spectators* of post–World War II vintage; next door, the long-time place of business for a Hungarian tailor, the walls were stuffed with Hungarian-language newspapers. "That gives you a bit of a sense of how diverse the neighbourhood was," says Kuruc. "Canada is diverse now, but in the fifties and sixties, Hamilton was incredibly diverse."

And then, he continues, "opening up the floorboards to fix the floors, we found random bits of people's lives: old packaging, post-cards, bills. One woman, her name was Thelma, would have lived on the top floor for a long time, because we were finding things from different eras. She would have raised her family there. You get a sense from the stuff that she purchased that her life was centred around James Street and downtown, based on the addresses [on the bills]." This portrait of Thelma's neighbourhood as a complete and self-contained ecosystem is supported by stories Kuruc has heard from a friend's grandmother, who as a child "lived just above one of the storefronts here" and later worked at Firth Brothers clothing manufacturers a few blocks away. "She said that, when she was grow-ing up, James Street was her front yard, her backyard, and her play-ground. She had three churches she could go to; she didn't belong to any of them, but she could always sit there. There was always the yard of some church or a civic space where she and her friends could play. Listening to stories like this, it's different than hearing the politicians who said that this neighbourhood was blighted."

Of course, later events dealt some cruel blows to the James North area. An obvious example is the urban renewal schemes that undermined business downtown and demolished nearby York

Street (another immigrant thoroughfare deemed unsavoury by local politicians) in the sixties and seventies. "You know," muses Kuruc, himself the child of immigrants, former farmers in Croatia, who settled in Hamilton's east-end Parkdale neighbourhood in the 1970s, "this was a Liberal town and urban renewal was undertaken by Liberal governments. It's ironic that the biggest Liberal supporters were immigrants, but the party was enacting policies to destroy their neighbourhoods."

Alongside the work of the wrecking ball downtown was a process of suburbanization that undermined the downtown's viability by providing new housing options within reach of a wide range of families. As a result, three-bedroom apartments above downtown stores, which no longer attracted families with kids, "were chopped up into single-occupancy places, bachelor apartments, so as to fit in as many people as possible," says Kuruc. "That's what you'd get instead of these large open spaces, and the vibrancy was lost. Buildings would be bought by out-of-town landlords, people who'd show up because real estate was affordable, not because they wanted to take care of them. Things started going into decline, and then the only people who lived here were the people who had no choice. A lot of businesses started to go bust, and this all contributed to the impression people had that James North was a place to avoid. For a lot of people, anywhere north of York Street was too far north; they would turn back at that point. There was a weird kind of bubble around the neighbourhood."

Across the street and a few blocks south, Morty Morgenstern expresses similar consternation at the ways outsiders have misunderstood the neighbourhood. Morty runs Morgenstern's, the retail clothing store opened by his mother in 1968. His family's story and the story of the neighbourhood surrounding James North are tightly intertwined.

Morty spent a lot of time in the store as a kid. When he went to college in Toronto, Morty would take the bus back to Hamilton on weekends, loaded up with stock that he'd picked up from Toronto garment dealers. He briefly moved to Vancouver after he got married, but when his father got sick, Morty faced the stark choice of either returning to Hamilton or seeing his father close the store. He chose to return home. That was in the 1980s, when Hamilton was going through tough times, but he never gave up on the neighbourhood that had given his family a shot at a prosperous and secure life.

"That's my mother," Morty says, pointing to a photograph above the cash register. "That's really not a very good picture of my mother—she was much older by then. I'm the taller guy, the goofy-looking guy, and the other goofy-looking guy is my brother [Mark] who owns [the restaurant] Charred, across the street. My brother and I both worked for my parents in the store, and where the restaurant is now is where the store first started."

The family put down roots on James North after a long and tumultuous period of dislocation. Morty's mother was a Holocaust survivor and his father had been a forced labourer during Nazi rule in Europe. They emigrated to Israel after the war but moved on to Canada in 1963, settling in Montreal. At first, while the couple learned English and got used to their adopted homeland, Morgenstern recalls that "[his] dad worked in the garment industry as a shipper at a factory, and [his] mother worked at a factory making drapes." Moving to Hamilton in 1968, Morty's mother opened the clothing store while his father joined with a relative who had also moved from Hungary, a mechanic, as co-proprietor of a BP service station on Barton Street. Soon after, his father left the BP station and joined his mother at the store.

From here, the family assumed an ongoing role within that self-contained neighbourhood ecosystem Kuruc described. Morgenstern's was one stop on a circuit of essential provisioners that made it possible for immigrant families to get everything they needed without leaving the North End. "On market days," recalls Morgenstern, "the ladies would come in and buy things, walk down James to the [farmers'] market and then pick up their purchases, which they had left here, on their way back home."

The store carried products geared almost entirely to the needs of the Italian and Portuguese immigrant communities: work clothes for the men, who were primarily employed in construction; work smocks for women working in garment factories; suits and dresses for church on Sunday. What set Morgenstern's apart from many other clothing stores on the street, undoubtedly contributing to its longevity, was the early decision to hire "sales ladies who spoke Portuguese and Italian," says Morty. "Most of the stores on the street were Jewish and the shopkeepers didn't speak the language of the customers. At one time we had two Portuguese, two Italians, and one Yugoslavian, so it covered all the bases. People like to speak their own language—especially when they arrive and they feel rather shy and uncomfortable."

The ethnic bonds that made Morgenstern's customers feel more at home were also important to the family itself as mater and pater familias established the business. The Morgensterns rented their first store from a fellow Hungarian, an older man whom Morty's father assisted by collecting rent cheques from tenants while the owner wintered in Florida. One day, says Morty—launching into his own variation of the unconventional handshake-and-good-faith real estate deal story told by more recent émigrés to the neighbour-hood—the owner asked the senior Morgenstern if he wanted to buy the building.

"So," Morty continues, "he said to the old man, 'I'd love to buy the building but I don't have any money.' And the old man said to my dad, 'I didn't ask you for money. I said, Do you want to buy my building?' My father said yes. The old man said, 'Okay. You give me whatever down payment you can. If you can't, that's fine too. And I'll give you a mortgage on the property.'"

Today, Morgenstern owns four buildings on James Street North, having sold a fifth in the 1980s when interest rates were exorbitant. The recent upswing in the street's cachet has been of obvious mate-rial benefit to Morty Morgenstern, but he chooses to focus on the quasi-parental pride he feels towards his renters, people who have helped redefine the area as an artistic hub. "I admire them. I respect them," he says of the current crop of renters. "I have tenants work-ing in fields that have nothing to do with the arts—because that's how they support themselves—but art is what they love to do." He stresses that the rising fortunes of the neighbourhood were driven by the people who live and work here, not by city hall. But approving of this district's change of character should not be mistaken for an endorsement of the view that the neighbourhood was a write-off before the artsy crowd moved in. Which brings us back to Morgenstern's dismay at the way the street used to be seen, especially during that period when the economy began to tank.

"See, my view is different from a lot of other people," he says. "A lot of people used to say that in the eighties and nineties James Street was an unsafe place. Like I said, we've been here forty-eight years. I've had shoplifting and a few incidents like break-ins and so forth. And there have occasionally been some violent crimes on the street. But I also recall reading about violent crimes at Lime Ridge Mall, and violent crimes in Dundas, a nice little quiet community. The difference between downtown and those places is that they put a lot of social programs down here, so the people you would see are not necessarily the most attractive-looking people. I call it perception over reality."

Morgenstern recalls a high-level police official (who, as it turned out, used to live in one of the Morgenstern family's apartments) telling a gathering of agitated local businesspeople that crime statistics did not support the idea of James North as a hotbed of malfeasance. But because almost everyone moving into the neighbourhood at that time was poor, people with more secure lives were quick to assume the worst. "It's perception," Morgenstern reiterates. "The area just looked seedy."

Mark Furukawa, the proprietor of the Dr. Disc record store (and one-time investor in the Sonic Unyon building, who has since been bought out by the remaining partners) sees things in a similar light. To be clear, he credits the influx of artists and hipsters, over the past decade or two, with moving the neighbourhood off life-support and towards viability. "Fifteen years ago," he remembers, "a bank wouldn't lend you money to buy a building down here, because there would be no way for them to get their money back should you default on the loan. I'd say the recent scenario is preferable for almost anyone living downtown. Knowing that there is development interest and fewer people are afraid to come downtown, I think, is overall a positive thing."

But yes, it's unfair to extrapolate from this that James North had been reduced, during the lean years, to some sort of crime-infested wasteland, that there was nothing interesting or worthy here before the artists arrived. When Furukawa prepared to move to Smog Town from London, Ontario, in 1991 (after completing "a seven-year B.A.," thanks to London's various cultural distractions), his friends' reaction was "Hamilton? Why would you want to move to Hamilton?" Furukawa soon discovered that their skepticism was unwarranted.

Like Morgenstern, he experienced some shoplifting and petty crime in subsequent years, but he's convinced that outsiders vastly overstated the dangers of life in downtown Hamilton. And the city had abundant charm. The presence of seven record stores within a few blocks of King and James was an indication that the punk/alternative music scene which had thrived here in the seventies and eighties (producing bands like Teenage Head and the Forgotten Rebels) was still alive and drawing nourishment from the local soil. Most importantly, he says, there was an open, welcoming, and unpretentious quality to Hamiltonians that was especially refreshing if, as Furukawa did, you grew up in an uptight, monochromatic community like Barrie, Ontario.

But has commercial success eroded some of those qualities that attracted outsiders to the neighbourhood in the first place? Dave Kuruc answers in the affirmative. The banks certainly won't hesitate to provide mortgages for North End properties these days, but if you're an artist, success should be measured by something less tangible than financial security and having a foot on the property ladder.

Although Kuruc is happy his business is more stable now, "there was something more interesting about the way [the street] was, with people hanging out and the old shops still there," he says. It's clear that things are moving further away from that mix: "I think James Street will continue to be successful, it just won't be as interesting. There will be condos going up and maybe the chain stores will come in at a certain point. This will keep going, and the neighbourhood will be a destination. But what everyone loses sight of in a process like this is the fact that the little points in between things are the most interesting."

In a gentrifying neighbourhood, the enemy of diversity, experimentation, and individuality is rising rents. When the circling sharks smell heightened profit potential, quirky old-timers and marginal newcomers soon find themselves in circumstances where they can't compete. In Hamilton's case, says Kuruc, this dismal prospect has been mitigated by the reality that many newer landholders are locally based owner-operators who bought low (meaning that they are not at the mercy of either crushing mortgage payments or rent-raising landlords) and retain a commitment to preserving the street's uniqueness.

"Some of the smaller galleries are able to do what they do," Kuruc explains, "because they bought the building for a price that people would drop their mouths at, and they rent the apartment upstairs to subsidize the gallery, right? So where you have these owner-operators, you'll still have these spaces existing where you can see something interesting."

There are other situations where galleries lacking hefty financial encumbrances commit to keep the rents low for artists who rent space on their upper floors, out of a sense of professional camaraderie. Either way, the few low-rent oases that do remain provide a nurturing habitat for the endangered species—artists, musicians, and so on—whose survival depends on a carefully calibrated mixture of plentiful espresso and cheap space.

But these circumstances have become the exceptions. In general, Kuruc believes that cash has trumped creativity on James North. He sees proof of this in what he believes is a wave of consciously orchestrated, manufactured boosterism, which to him has the ring of a commercial campaign. Many upstart businesses "are flying the Hamilton flag," he says, "but they are doing it without any substance or history or caring. It's all about, 'If we fly that flag, we are definitely going to make money.'" What downtown Hamilton needs is not slogans or cheerleading, he's convinced, but "people who do things that make the city better. We need to deal with affordable housing and space for artists and things like that."

Simultaneously, the sense of experimentation and non-conformity of earlier years has become formalized to the point where the street is now neither experimental nor non-conformist. "Some of the earlier Art Crawls just sort of popped up," he says, "and people were saying, 'What's going on here? What's happening?' You would see weird installations. You'd see a storefront that would make no sense in the world of the Portuguese men who would come by and shake their heads at it. What was so interesting about the early days was that you could take a chance, and have some Portuguese men come by and scratch their heads and be amused. Now, everything is, 'Oh, I'm going to open up a Japanese artisanal restaurant on the street' and its going to be run by two non-Japanese guys, right? And nobody is shaking their heads at that. They are, like, 'Yeah. Of course. I'm going to eat there.'"

Multiple perspectives on a single landscape

The influx of newcomers who have transformed North End Hamilton over a number of years is not a single force but a multitude. The wave is made up of distinct segments with separate interests and competing visions of what their adoptive community should become. Among its ranks are people who are drawn to the city for an opportunity to pursue a personal artistic quest (local politics may be largely extraneous for this group); entrepreneurs who see opportunities in transforming an undervalued landscape into a thriving site for business; evangelical urbanists committed to an ideal of the city as a functional, beautiful machine, modelled on the great North American downtowns laid to waste by postwar suburbanization; social justice activists who believe the city should be an inclusive place accommodating people of all income levels, classes, and backgrounds; real estate refugees seeking more reasonable housing prices; curious college kids; and many others. Their own individual trajectories and the nature of their interactions with their counterparts will change over time. Sometimes, these disparate groups will coalesce as something resembling a movement. Other times, there will be a sense that several locomotives are steaming towards each other from different directions, with an immense clatter and hiss that foretells some awful collision.

One such collision took place, in fact, one night several years back at the Sky Dragon Centre. Real estate prices had started climbing in the area surrounding the James North artists' district, leading to the displacement of low-income tenants and the mobilization of a movement against gentrification.

"This group of anti-gentrification activists had gone around to all the galleries downtown and put Fat Cat stickers on their windows—real subtle, right?" says Kevin MacKay. "That enraged the artists. So there was this real tension in the community and a lot of anger and yelling. Stupidly, we said, 'Let's hold a big community meeting at Sky Dragon and let's invite everybody. If you're an anti-gentrification anarchist, come on out. If you are a person trying to open up a gallery, come on out. If you're a lawyer who bought a building downtown because it's kind of hip and groovy now, come on out.' At first, we thought, 'Oh shit, nobody's going to show up,' but strangely, everybody showed up. All those camps were there, and the tension in the room was insane."

The organizers had anticipated that this attempt to find common ground among the warring parties would require some finesse, so MacKay (who had taken on a day gig at Mohawk College) employed some "teacher thinking" to devise a format that divided the large gathering into randomized groups, with members of each faction assigned to a discussion group by picking playing cards. Some of MacKay's colleagues from Mohawk agreed to act as facilitators. "It was incredible because these groups were all mixed, with gentrifiers and anti-gentrifiers within the groups. There was great discussion, some really good ideas, but a lot of tension. I remember thinking, 'Oh my god, we're going to get through this before it all blows up,' and then at the very end I did the stupid thing of saying, 'So now we'll open up the floor for general comments.' Right away three people stood up and just started yelling their heads off. The whole thing just blew apart."

MacKay says he and his Sky Dragon associates had planned to strike a committee, drawing from the competing stakeholders who came to the meeting, to promote ideas for dealing with the negative effects of gentrification and mapping out some way towards a more inclusive form of downtown development. But they recoiled when it became clear how high emotions were running and chose instead to focus on dealing with Sky Dragon's mounting financial challenges, so as to keep the centre alive and be able to fight another day. Having originally thought they could stir some optimism among the participants, instead they wound up on the receiving end of fierce hostility.

"By trying to bring everyone together," says MacKay, "you either come out being the safe space or else everyone turns their guns on you. For us, it was more the latter. The anarchists thought, 'You're just gentrifying scumbags.' And the artists were like, 'You hang out with those anarchist anti-gentrifiers.' To this day, there are people who won't talk to me because of that night."

Those "anarchist anti-gentrifiers" MacKay refers to are a group that used to meet at the Sky Dragon but left on bad terms and opened their own space, the Tower, first located on Cannon Street and later (after attacks by alleged neo-Nazis, police raids, and the landlord's discomfort led to their eviction in 2018[9]) further north and to the east on Barton. The name of the space, one of the group's websites explains, is a reference to "the Tower tarot card [which] represents crisis, upheaval and liberation—the ruling order, built on false foundations, is toppled by the strike of lightning, taking with it the power, values and influence of a small elite."[10] Adjacent to this description (which continues at length), is a drawing of a slightly askew tower with cracked bricks that's spewing flames and smoke— if we are to take that image as political allegory, it makes a pretty clear statement about the old system being corrupt and deserving of being burned down.

So you can anticipate that this group of contrarians would see what's been happening on the streets of Hamilton in entirely different ways than the commentators we've encountered so far. Essentially, they view Hamilton's culture-driven renaissance as a cover for a business-orchestrated con aimed at upwardly revaluing Hamilton's bargain real estate and dumping the poor people who've lived here, through the years of hard times, onto the street. They are not interested in celebrating the flourishing local arts scene or discussing the virtues of restoring pre-suburban forms of community in the city core. They are not even willing to discuss how social housing or improved transit can make the city more livable and egalitarian—this, they propose, would merely legitimize an illegitimate system that should be eliminated.

In fact, communiqués from Hamilton's anti-gentrification radicals (who do not explicitly identify themselves as being associated with the Tower, but are assumed to be so by their enemies and targets) make it explicit that any engagement with "urbanist" debates around how to improve the city's quality of life is counterproductive. "We are not interested in a conversation about what development in Hamilton should look like—development is not a conversation, it is an attack," reads a pamphlet distributed in 2015.[11] "Fuck your transit . . . Drop out of art." So what's the solution? The same pamphlet prescribes as follows:

> A purely negative orientation . . . helps bring fault lines to the surface and force the contradictions that urbanists and leftists plaster over. . . . In the short term, a purely negative approach might look like graffiti and propaganda targetting transit, anti-poverty, and environmental groups that seek to present development as a social good. . . . So far, the most effective tactics in Hamilton have been ones that drive open fissures and force belligerent, defensive responses from gallery owners and social entrepreneurs convinced that their self-interest is good for everyone.

These types of tactics have indeed been unleashed in Hamilton—consistently over several years and with an increasing intensity and sense of menace. It began with that plastering of gallery windows and doors with Fat Cat and Fuck your Boutique—Defend Hamilton stickers. Then, in the summer of 2016, a Try Hamilton bus tour that brought potential investors from Toronto was met by masked protesters bent on confrontation. An anonymous account on an anarchist website recounts: "We decorated the buses and as many participants as we could with silly string and fist-fulls of greasy condoms. Two human-sized pigeons circled, shitting rancid milk on the real estate goofs from squirt guns."[12] This was followed by the so-called Locke Street riot. In March 2018, as the *Toronto Star* reported, "a masked mob of about 30 people in black clothing marched down Locke Street throwing rocks at cars and businesses, breaking windows and lighting fireworks. They caused about $100,000 damage."[13]

The Tower always denies having organized acts of vandalism and/or assault such as these. But given that this is precisely what local anarchists have called for—and that the Tower has expressed solidarity with these anonymous actors after the fact[14]—it's not surprising that, when locks are gummed up with glue or some chic restaurant has its windows smashed, onlookers invariably cast their accusatory gazes towards the Tower.

Somewhere in between those two signature explosions of anti-gentrification theatrics—that is, just after the disruption of the Try Hamilton tour and well before the vandalism spree on Locke Street—a group of people involved with the Tower sat down with researcher Sarah Hipworth and me to discuss their views of what was going on beyond their storefront window. The terms of our discussion were that participants from the Tower would be identified by first names, and that these could (but might not) be aliases. Apart from the scorching, un-air-conditioned heat of that mid-summer day, the Tower's then-intact Cannon Street space was comfortable, with big, overstuffed old couches and a heavy set of drapes in the plate glass window of this formerly commercial ground-floor expanse. Joining the humans was a delightful, friendly but sleepy old dog, whose name never made it into my notes but whom I remember fondly.

I also remember being struck by the fact that the people gathered to answer questions that afternoon spoke in a way entirely unlike the communiqués on the Tower's Facebook page or the anti-gentrification pamphlets that appear under the guise of various fictional/virtual entities with names like the Hamilton Institute. The latter lean heavily towards simple declarations, angry invective, and frequent use of curse words, particularly the exclamatory "fuck" or some variation thereof. There was none of that during our in-person conversation. Instead, there was a detailed discussion on arcane topics such as the mechanics by which speculators depress land prices so they can extract more profit when they drive them back up, a couple references to key books on gentrification (the conversation did take place, after all, in a space our interviewees referred to as a library), and a general tone of calm and cordiality.

But let's be clear: their disinterest in discussing possible solutions with other groups, alongside a disinclination to denounce property damage as a tactic, places this group far outside of the orbit of the multitude of Hamilton progressives grappling with the city's crisis of inequality. While the latter have tried to engage with the system to bring about change—preparing briefs for council, pushing progressive policy options to politicians and through the media, supporting volunteer and social service initiatives to try to soften the blows of poverty—the people who congregate at the Tower shun all of that. More mainstream critics of the status quo therefore write off the movement that revolves around the Tower as ineffectual: as a group of people who enjoy listening to their own rhetoric without contributing tangibly to the community. The crusading ex–city councillor (later the NDP member of Parliament for Hamilton Centre) Matthew Green referred to the Tower collective, in a later conversation with me, as "a book club."

Still, this group's underlying analysis of how market forces have impacted the poor in Hamilton doesn't, in itself, seem that far removed from that of the city's "progressive urbanists," as they are scornfully referred to in those raging pamphlets.[15] The descriptions of displacement and day-to-day suffering that I heard at the Tower that scorching afternoon will surely ring true to those mainstream progressives on the other side of the methodological divide, and even to the casual onlooker wandering through one of the inner city's neighbourhoods in transition.

"I work with the homeless people downtown who are involved in treatment for addictions," says a soft-spoken woman who identifies herself as Sarah. It's been her observation that many of those people's challenges in recovering from addiction became more grave when they were turfed from their accommodation downtown.

"When they're being transitioned into affordable housing, it's further and further east, even though the communities they've been a part of—oftentimes longer than I've even been alive—are all downtown. The social services are also still downtown," she says. That means that it's necessary to budget for transport to access services or to see someone familiar downtown, and for people on social assistance, it's not easy to do that and also pay rent. Thus, a new downward spiral begins: the extra transit expense likely means not being able to afford a place to live, and being homeless makes it nearly impossible to conquer an addiction.

More tales from the streets: "There's been such an increase in the amount of misery people experience," says Peter. "In the last few years, as rents have gone up, the shelter waiting lists have gone through the roof. And there has been a big increase in violent crime, as people are getting forced into the black market to make up this difference" (between what landlords charge and what's affordable). But while people engaged in conventional political processes propose measures to increase the stock of affordable housing or to raise social assistance payments, Peter's not looking towards institutional solutions to make things better. Instead, he sees his role as helping to cultivate a spirit of rebellion and resistance.

"I try to encourage people to point their hostility in the right direction," he says. "A lot of frustration is turned against other people in the same situation. I am friends with some families who recently immigrated here from Syria in the last six months, and they're living in terrible housing conditions and don't have a lot of ability to complain to make those conditions better. At the same time, [their landlord] is having this influx of tenants coming to them and trying to get housing. A lot of them are white folks being displaced from downtown. And [the landlord] doesn't have enough units or is renting them for too much money.

"An excuse that they have been giving people is that they don't have any apartments because the government is making them rent them to Syrians. So people who are benefiting from this misery are trying to pit people against each other on the basis of race and citizenship status. I try to reach out and talk to people and provide some information, like, 'Hold on a second, don't get fooled, here are the people who are benefiting from this, here are the people who are profiting off your suffering.' It doesn't necessarily point towards an immediate solution, and personally, I am not interested in trying to produce policy. I am interested in helping people get together so we can fight our enemies."

Besides landlords, the commentators assembled at the Tower also have some unflattering words for the police. A key theme in the anarchist critique is that gentrification requires a scaling up of surveillance culture and a criminalization of activities like panhandling, which are extensions of being homeless. "A couple of weeks ago," recalls Tammy, "I was walking down King Street and there was a new art gallery opening—they are opening all the time. People were talking outside the new art gallery and there was construction work going on. A couple of storefronts down I saw two Hamilton police from the action squad, harassing and ticketing a homeless woman on the street, trying to move her away, hassling her. Just seeing those things side by side gives a good indication of what's currently going on in Hamilton."

Blaming creative types for dislocation

And then there are the artists, musicians, arts-related entrepreneurs—the "creative" types—whom the people gathered in that sweltering Cannon Street parlour characterize as the "foot soldiers of gentrification," responsible for creating the early sense of buzz that attracted all that money to Hamilton, triggering the city's tsunami of evictions and displacement.

Although artists now play a lesser role in Hamilton's journey upmarket (and in many cases are themselves being displaced as prices rise), "at a certain point," says Peter, "they are important because they act as a lobby group—a pro-investment and pro-policing force—and that creates the political conditions that allow bigger companies to come in and raze entire blocks and build fancy offices and apartments and condos where there used to be nothing. So [the artists] are producing new value in [the art district of James North] and that transforms the values in surrounding areas. That process reaches far further than the couple of blocks of displacement that the art galleries are directly responsible for."

By pursuing their own creative dreams, unconcerned that they are preparing the terrain for the arrival of Toronto-based financial interests that "are pushing for mass evictions of entire blocks of buildings," Peter contends, artists have been "played for dupes, essentially. I feel a lot of folks in the arts scene who set out to do something local, something good for their community, have ended up on the wrong side of this without ever necessarily deciding to. And they've ended up on the wrong side against their own interests."

Besides its "lobbying" function, Peter charges that the arts community has aided real estate interests' purge of low-income residents by providing public relations cover—that is, by manufacturing a new civic image that both masks the negative aspects of redevelopment and provides an advertising vehicle for real estate sales. A significant chunk of the work that sells in James Street galleries, he points out, is Hamilton-themed, offering a romantic view of the city's past as a blue-collar, "gritty" steel town.

"They've produced a brand for the city," he says, "that was based on a previous identity that was under attack at the same moment [that the redevelopers started moving in]. Like, I don't think you can turn anything into a mascot without killing it first. And I think [the artists] weren't the ones who killed or who broke the back of working-class strength in this city. But they were definitely the ones who stuffed and mounted it."

Although this commentary sounds more measured than the pamphlets that screech about "arts industry fucks," there's no disguising the deep mutual disrespect between the two camps. Those painters, musicians, and arts-related entrepreneurs whom Peter at the Tower sees as pawns of developers—too self-absorbed to see how they are being manipulated—in turn have their own unflattering critique of the role and approach of the rowdy horde associated with the Tower. Many will point to their rejection of anything that could improve an underserviced, impoverished city (rapid transit, bike lanes, art shows) as proof that they are driven by an unbending ideology that's out of touch with the real needs of poor Hamiltonians. The people who reject the Tower's approach insist that the innovations promoted by progressive urbanists should be seen for their obvious material benefit in the here and now, rather than as invariably tools for manipulation by developers. Sometimes an umbrella is just an umbrella. Sometimes the installation of bike lanes or improvements to transit are just things to help people get around better, not an implement of some devious plot.

"Some people think Supercrawl is part of gentrification," remarks Kevin MacKay, who himself was influenced by political anarchism of a different sort. "But you go out on Art Crawl and you see kids sitting out there with their paintings on the sidewalk—to me that's awesome. That's what bugs me about the anti-gentrification folks: they try to paint it all with the same brush. And it's so obviously not that simple, right?" MacKay says he agrees with Tower-aligned people's objections to phenomena such as "this 'clean up the streets, more policing, get rid of problem tenants' kind of thing—this very narrow, middle-class, entrepreneurial discourse" that's grown with the rising value of downtown real estate. But the way to combat those things is to engage with existing institutions, he says, not to withdraw. "They're just not effective," he says. "They don't address how it is that you create structural change."

Other targets of anti-gentrification rage complain that they've always been on the side of people with very little money, that they've helped improve the lives of long-standing residents downtown. The militants at the Tower may see small businesses—in the same way that they see Supercrawl—as collaborators with the enemy, but Dave Kuruc protests that his role on the street is miles away from that of "the fat cat with the top hat and the diamond-studded cane." After his storefront was plastered with Fuck your Boutique stickers, "your shoulders kind of slump a bit," he says. "We're like, 'Are you kidding? Really?' We're in our little store, just trying to contribute to what we consider our little slice of paradise in Hamilton, and they think of us as fat cats. We try to laugh it off, but we know there are people out there who seriously believe in this stuff, you know?"

Kuruc's Mixed Media store sold things like paintbrushes, posters, and postcards for a few bucks each. Just down the street, Mark Furukawa at Dr. Disc remarks that—despite the fact that he's pleased about James North's economic revival—his business also does not cater to the carriage trade. Many of the businesses that have been here for a while, he insists, brighten the lives of people without much money who otherwise would pass their days in a city doesn't give them places to go or things to do.

"We find a lot of music buyers or artists are close to the poverty line or below the poverty line, but if you can buy a coffee, you can buy records here," Furukawa says. "We have always catered to a lower-income clientele. When we opened, a record that would sell for six ninety-nine was three dollars here. We've got records downstairs that are three for a dollar. We're not the gallery space where you walk in and the paintings are two thousand dollars. If someone's got an old turntable at home, for five dollars they can get a week's worth of entertainment from us."

There's a common refrain around the neighbourhood that this area stands a greater chance of retaining its bargain-basement quality—of resisting the logic of the market and its determined push towards gentrification—because artists themselves got in on the ground floor and bought many of the buildings on James North when they were still ridiculously cheap. "There are a lot of people who are owner-operators, and I think that's how we control development," offers Kuruc. "So we continue to rent to cultural spaces. We have a gallery next door that could not afford anywhere else on the street, but we own the building and we are going to keep it affordable for them. We're not going to renovate the space and charge them twice the rent."

Ways of imagining an equitable mixed-income community

Providing some security of tenure for low-wage artists, of course, does not address the influence of the James North cultural district in making surrounding areas more attractive for real estate development, thereby contributing to a cascading, often crushing problem for lower-income people outside the artistic community. It's this reality of ordinary people being pressured, enticed, or tricked into vacating their lower-rent lodgings that moves the activists at the Tower and elsewhere to hurl invective (and possibly other substances) towards the artists and small business owners they portray as the welcoming party for an incoming wave of plunderers. Meanwhile, just about everybody who tracks the state of the city—the social planning council, the Roundtable for Poverty Reduction, the churches, academics, and downtown councillors—have called for action to resolve the crisis in low-income housing associated with Hamilton's interconnected cultural and financial resurgence.

Even the very people who helped remake James North as Hamilton's epicentre of hipness profess to be acutely aware of the problem and are quick to advance their own solutions. Joseph Mancinelli from LiUNA, the organization that arguably started this entire process with its restoration of the CN railway station, says the key to boosting affordability in Hamilton is to add significant rental accommodation into the development mix—in other words, to build more housing of various types. LiUNA, he says, is taking this approach with its high-rise student residence beside the Lister Block and its redevelopment of the Kresge property, which will contain both rental and condo towers.

"Projects like this that have condos and rental," he argues, "are a smart approach to solving that issue because what you'll have here is rental units that people can actually afford to live in, which is really important. And condos like these won't be like Toronto condos that are really high-end and expensive. They are still fairly affordable, although not for everybody. Obviously, some people can't afford to buy, so they can rent."

How far this goes towards addressing the affordable housing shortage hinges on how you define the word *affordable*. For Torontonians accustomed to a market where the average price for a detached home is over a million dollars[16] and where a studio apartment is considered a bargain at $1,200 a month, Hamilton may indeed seem affordable. But if you were crowded out of the Toronto market years ago, if you made the trip down the QEW because Steeltown's crumbling housing stock offered a way to keep a roof over your head on the budget that comes with social assistance or a disability cheque, then the outlook in Hamilton will remain bleak, regardless of any expansion of the rental market. Since Hamilton's boom began, in fact, there have been multiple skirmishes over apartment tower owners in the North and East Ends who have been trying to evict poor residents en masse and replace them with more affluent renters.

Mancinelli's response is that this scenario underscores the need to build more social housing, preferably within mixed-income developments like Toronto's reimagined Regent Park. Had it been uttered by a typical developer, it would be easy to dismiss this remark as mere buck-passing (dropping the issue into the laps of governments that have, for decades, shown an obvious disinterest in expanding social housing). But LiUNA's track record as the builder/operator of over six hundred units of social housing around Hamilton suggests sincerity.

Building new subsidized units is a far better prospect, says Mancinelli, than wishing for the continuation of the old status quo—where poor people often live in poorly maintained, unsafe, or unhealthy housing. He contrasts the kind of subsidized housing run by his organization with long-standing conditions downtown, where many lower-income Hamiltonians have found themselves at the mercy of absentee landlords who take the biggest chunk of their tenants' income while making only the most minimal investments in maintaining the property.

"Children and families should be living in nice places regardless of income," he says. "I don't understand why they don't. Just because you don't have a good income, you find yourself living in squalor—that is unacceptable. That's why we have nice affordable housing. Some of our members live there, and some units are accessible for people with disabilities—ten per cent of our projects have wheelchair access. So let's do more of that. What we've seen in the last fifteen years is a reduction in the amount of affordable housing units that are being built. That's a mistake."

Mancinelli's preference for new social housing to be woven into mixed-income developments is also in step with the visions of evangelistic urbanists like Dave Kuruc. Diversity, says Kuruc, is key to a vital, interesting urban space. It's the way that people used to live when places like downtown Hamilton were thriving. A city needs "lots of different spaces, lots of different levels for people to live in to create community," he says. "You don't want everything all of one kind; you don't want a wall of condos. That doesn't create the diversity you need for places to succeed. You want a city where it's possible to be a part of things, whether you're a struggling artist, whether you're a family, whether you're somebody who just arrived here from another country. We don't maintain those type of neighbourhoods in Hamilton very well."

Even the most vehement advocates of redevelopment in the downtown recognize the need to accommodate people who have been bumped from their spot on the civic landscape. Supercrawl's Tim Potocic is unyielding in his view that much higher densities are necessary for the business experiment in the neighbourhood around James North to continue. "Having foot traffic is the key, it's the absolute key to downtown survival," he insists. "If you don't have people there every day, walking out of their apartments or their condos and shopping in the local businesses, it's challenging." Asked what he'd like to see take shape downtown in the coming years, he offers this list: "Twenty to thirty thousand more people living downtown. We've got great transit, bike lanes, walkable streets—people walking the streets at all hours. There's a general vibrancy. That would be my ideal world. And that would come with some towers, for sure."

But Potocic protests that he's not the kind of guy who's unconcerned with the displacement of low-income residents. To ensure that low-income people are not exiled from this promised land (or at least, to ensure that *more* people are not cast out), he says the city will have to exercise its powers to impose inclusionary zoning. Under the former Liberal provincial government of Kathleen Wynne, municipal governments were given the power to compel developers to set aside a percentage of their new units for people on low incomes. Potocic believes the city must use that tool.

"You force developers who are developing new properties to deal with the issue," he says. "There's probably not a lot of developers currently in Hamilton who can handle it, to be completely honest. So we have to look to developers who have the ability to do mixed-income developments. Hamiltonians should be able to accept that someone buying a four-hundred-thousand-dollar condo could be living beside someone on social assistance. It's working in other cities in Canada and the U.S. It could work here."

During my wanderings through the arts district around James North, the promise of inclusionary zoning was held up by many as a kind of panacea that could reverse the process of displacement accompanying rising property values. It became clear that's one reason many people in the arts community embraced the idea so enthusiastically: it's a solution that other parties (government and large developers) would be responsible for, which wouldn't require those small investors who play a role in downtown revitalization to do anything differently (or to feel responsible for gentrification's negative impacts).

Kevin MacKay believes the unwillingness of new players in the local real estate market to accept their role in creating the social problems arising from the boom makes it incumbent upon governments to step in and impose conditions on future developments. "A lot of these folks moving into Hamilton are doing really cool stuff, opening up these little studios and transforming spaces," he says. "They do have money, according to Hamilton standards, but they are not necessarily rich people. They probably have very progressive values. But they are not going to let that get in the way of them starting up their little businesses and moving somebody out, if they have to. When you're talking about values, the rubber really hits the road when your economic interests are at stake. I find a lot of social democrats are very flexible in their values when they're in a situation where, 'Well, we've got to flip this property; it's part of our ten-year plan; it's part of being able to buy the cottage; it's part of the kids going to college.' I mean, that's the reality of class in

Hamilton. The machine will keep moving unless there's legislation to force developers to do certain things . . . If the city said, 'Listen, if you're going to build housing downtown, fifteen per cent must be affordable,' it's not like they wouldn't develop—they still would. But we'd get those affordable units."

Regrettably, though, post-2016 the concept of inclusionary zoning hasn't panned out. The provincial legislation only provided for the voluntary use of affordability quotas by municipalities, and Hamilton's politicians have been unwilling to use that power to impose significant obligations on large-scale developers. In the few cases where inclusionary zoning requirements have been written into new development plans, the percentage of units designated as affordable has been ridiculously low, and the definition of affordability has been set high enough that it only helps the middle class, not people who are poor.

Still, inclusionary zoning is just one item in a medicine cabinet stocked with potential remedies for the social inequalities exacerbated by gentrification. There are abundant ideas on how to encourage the formation of mixed-income communities that are as nurturing for the poor as they are for the monied. But the problem is not ideas. The problem is finding the will to put those ideas to work. Sadly, the recent history of urban redevelopment in cities around the world reveals more failures, in this respect, than successes. That accounts for the nihilism of some of Hamilton's anti-gentrification activists, and it foretells a tough struggle ahead.

CHAPTER THREE

The "Creative Class" Creates a Global Urban Clash

T HE NAME *STEELTOWN*, though still uttered with affection, is clearly a misnomer when applied to current-day Hamilton. Through all those years of industrial decline and downtown decay, some important (but largely unremarked upon) structural changes were transforming the essential nature of the place. Significant parts of Hamilton's workforce have migrated to the new frontiers of high-tech industry, medicine, academic research, and services. This new workforce is more female and not as unionized as it used to be, although Hamilton arguably remains a strong labour town—just not a *blue-collar* labour town.

There are also more people who live in Hamilton but don't work here. These commuters can be considered citizens of the new mega-region that emerged as the space between Hamilton and its pretentious cousin, Toronto, got filled in. This is what the *Toronto Star* now habitually refers to as the GTHA (Greater Toronto and Hamilton Area), which sometime in the last decade replaced its three-letter predecessor, the GTA. More evidence that the fates of people on both sides of the once-formidable Hamilton-Toronto divide are closely intertwined is found in the way news stories produced by *Hamilton Spectator* reporters are frequently reproduced in the *Star* (the *Star* now owns the *Spec*) and vice versa.

And with all this, a radically different chapter of history begins. Hamilton and Toronto had been on distinctly different trajectories since the mid-1800s. Although Hamilton once aspired to become a financial and commercial Mecca for central Canada, this dream evaporated when the city was bypassed by the Grand Trunk Railway, which linked Toronto and Montreal with centres such as Stratford and Sarnia to the west. Connected to the outside world by the competing Great Western Railway, which ran along a less advantageous route, Hamilton had to be content with developing as an industrial, rather than financial, centre.[1]

Although this entrenched division of duties was the wellspring from which an enduring cultural chasm, a ferocious football rivalry, and countless sneering jokes had arisen for most of the twentieth century, these distinctions started to fade in an age of massive, consolidated regional economies, like the one that now covers much of southern Ontario. As Hamilton is increasingly drawn into the orbit of the monster metropolis whose epicentre is seventy kilometres down the QEW, the city becomes less distinct, less in control of its own destiny, and subject to the same seemingly irresistible economic and social forces that shape life in Toronto.[2]

Parallel to this process of regionalization was the discovery by overmortgaged Torontonians of a stock of Victorian housing just down the highway, ready to accommodate the New Urbanist's particular tastes for a fraction of the cost elsewhere. In the age of the regional behemoth, there emerged an impeccable logic beckoning Torontonians to decamp and head to Hamilton. McMaster's James Dunn noted (when we spoke in 2015, before the drawbridge of soaring prices had shut out many potential émigrés to Hamilton) that the appeal is initially economic but that also translates as the possibility, especially for families, of living a vastly healthier lifestyle.

"There will be droves of people," he correctly predicted, "who say, 'Oh, wait a second, I can buy a gutted and fully renovated three-storey Victorian home in Toronto, or I could get the exact same house for one-third of the cost in Hamilton.'" That financial difference will in turn prompt many people to ponder, "Why don't we go down to one income, or have one-person commute, and save on all the housing costs?"—an option that promises a huge reduction in stress for people who live in nuclear families. The idea became even more viable with the 2015 opening of a GO commuter rail station in downtown Hamilton that offers rush-hour connections to Toronto's commercial district.

A cultural shift takes place when gentrifying out-of-towners move into a former industrial town, but that story is hardly unique to Hamilton. Versions of it have played out in a multitude of one-time manufacturing powerhouses across North America. In Pittsburgh, Baltimore, and Buffalo, to name but a few examples, hulking brick warehouses and manufacturing plants, often resting on prized real estate overlooking an impressive body of water, are gutted and remade as luxury condominium complexes. Modest diners and cut-rate retailers on nearby commercial streets are squeezed out as property values rise and a new kind of clientele make their preferences known. The fifty-cent cup of java is replaced by the artisanal vanilla soy latte. You can't get a grilled cheese that isn't made with sourdough bread and embellished with organic beetroot chutney.

At least, that's the caricatured version of the process. A stereotype has emerged of the new urban pioneer who rides into town on a wave of real estate speculation, amid clouds of swirling plaster dust, that's as unsympathetic as the words *gentrifier* and *gentrification* have become. These negative associations have arisen in belated recognition that the arrival of people with money in old city cores almost inevitably displaces long-time lower-income residents. Dunn described this process as a weakening of the whole ecosystem that supports low-income people: besides the loss of lower-cost housing, the non-profits and discount stores that serve the poor are unable to compete with incoming enterprises for commercial space. Thus, people without a lot of money face multiple pressures (lack of housing, lack of services, declining access to affordable shops) to move to neighbourhoods that aren't designed for living on a limited budget.

In Hamilton, says Dunn, "you will see people displaced to these more far-flung areas that have poorer services and 'transit deserts' and those sorts of things. It's going to cause isolation and disconnection and an inability to get to jobs and services. It's very problematic because these communities with a lot of apartment towers were built under the assumption that everyone would have a car."

A repeat of the Toronto fiasco

This is precisely the process that's remade the map just down the road in Toronto, where an influx of wealth into the city core, underway since the late 1970s, has transformed the postwar suburbs of picket fences and sizable backyards into something distinctly less idyllic. The "isolation and disconnection" that Dunn spoke of have become hallmarks of large swaths of Toronto's older suburbs (in particular, Scarborough and Etobicoke) where "poverty has become more prevalent and concentrated," as city-watcher John Lorinc writes in the *Walrus*. Toronto's experience is consistent with the North American trend:[3] a study of sixty-six metropolitan areas by the University of Virginia's Weldon Cooper Center for Public Service found many of those places (with notable exceptions such as Seattle, Boston, and Minneapolis) conform to a "new donut" model where a prosperous urban core is ringed by poorer, aging suburbs, beyond which is another layer of newer, more prosperous "exurbs."[4]

In Toronto's case, conditions in the older suburbs offer a startling contrast to those in the revitalized old city, where soaring property values have brought many urbanites windfalls that enable them to upgrade their homes with granite countertops and stainless-steel ranges and prowl the streets in BMWs or Jaguars. The social divide is inescapable. As Lorinc notes: "With some of the country's highest real estate prices . . . affordable rentals remain scarce, while tens of thousands of families who earn as little as $20,000 a year languish on waiting lists for often-substandard subsidized housing."

While they wait, many lower-income Torontonians—a large proportion of them immigrants who, since their professional credentials go unrecognized in Canada, work in low-wage service jobs—live in the vast array of high-rise towers that line suburban Toronto's thoroughfares. Lorinc elaborates:

> Increasing numbers of immigrant families have taken refuge in the city's 1960s-era slab apartment towers; Toronto contains more suburban high-rises than any other North American city. A 2006 United Way study, *Poverty by Postal Code 2: Vertical Poverty*, found that 40 percent of the tenants living in these spartan buildings were poor (based on StatsCan income categories), up from 25 percent in 1986, and the number is no doubt higher today. Many of these complexes are languishing in a state of chronic disrepair, often with malfunctioning elevators, security problems, and unreliable heating.[5]

Beyond poor housing conditions, lower-income suburbanites get shortchanged in the provision of government services. A report from York University's City Institute entitled *Switching Tracks* maps numerous so-called transit deserts—that is, places where bus service is less frequent and less reliable—in low-income areas of the inner suburbs. A *Toronto Star* newspaper report elaborates on the institute's findings, citing instances where children have waited for hours for a bus to school in freezing winter conditions and workers have lost their jobs because the bus service doesn't run late enough for them to get home from work. This fits a pattern of "transit inequity" wherein "the people most dependent on transit, who pay a higher portion of their income to ride it, also get the worst service." The *Star* story also refers to a Martin Prosperity Institute observation that "areas of Toronto with the fastest growing incomes have almost four times the amount of transit service seen in neighbourhoods where incomes are declining."[6]

Transit is just one example of the unequal distribution of public amenities, says University of Toronto geographer Alan Walks, contemplating the situation in the cramped confines of his office at the university's downtown Toronto campus. This inequity has been held in place partly by a controversial provision of Ontario's planning act known as Section 37, which stipulates that city governments can negotiate payments from developers to fund public amenities (parks, child-care centres, subsidized housing units, public art) in exchange for the city granting them release from restrictions in the official plan (such as limits on building height). Under Section 37, these public goods must be located in the same neighbourhood as the development. The result, says Walks, is that these spin-off benefits accumulate in gentrifying or wealthy neighbourhoods, to the benefit of populations who tend to be privileged already and to the exclusion of lower-income people who have been forced onto the periphery.

As *Toronto Star* columnist Edward Keenan expresses it, "the funds are not evenly distributed around the city. This presents a real fairness problem to the extent that, due to austerity measures imposed by low tax rates, Section 37 funding becomes virtually the only source of funding for things such as playgrounds and community centres."[7] In other words, if I'm a modest-income renter being displaced by a luxury condo development, the amenities offered by the developer won't benefit me: they will stay in the gentrifying neighbourhood and not move out to the suburban fringe to which I've been exiled.

Such a highly unequal distribution of resources has fuelled an understandable rage that Walks believes helps explain the seemingly unshakeable popularity enjoyed by the late former Toronto mayor Rob Ford (whose power base was centred in low-income sections of Etobicoke and Scarborough) in spite of Ford's scandal-plagued reign (2010–14) and his clear inability to offer policies that would actually help low-income people. In a paper on Ford's pro-automobile politics, Walks writes that "faced with a financializing economy of the core in which many residents in the deindustrializing . . . suburbs have little hope of partaking, it is not so surprising that many continued to be receptive to Ford's simplistic, populist story, even if they must embrace denial to accept it. The symbolism is often more important than the reality."[8]

So if you're an underpaid resident of the old suburbs with limited transit service who relies on an old beater to get you around,

Ford's railing against downtown restrictions on cars was likely to strike a chord. (The poorer, older suburbs have since then proven a reliable power base for the late mayor Ford's brother, Doug, who in 2018 used similar policy commitments and the same anti-elitist rhetoric of Ford Nation—an imagined entity rooted in the post–World War II suburbs that has spread across the province—to become premier of Ontario.)

Indeed, the solidifying sense that people banished to the old suburbs are being denied a stake in Toronto's booming economy has potentially explosive political implications. Lorinc sees Toronto's out-of-sight, out-of-mind high-rise suburban centres of poverty becoming like the *banlieues* of Paris, where a seething sense of discontent periodically erupts as rioting. He cites University of Toronto geographer J. David Hulchanski's 2010 study *The Three Cities within Toronto*, which extrapolates from current trends in income polarization to arrive at the conclusion that Toronto will eventually become a place "where poor suburbs surround a prosperous downtown and wealthy midtown enclaves" and the middle class have abandoned the older suburbs altogether.[9]

There is a rising realization that inner-city gentrification has created this massive social polarization, economic misery, and political anxiety by fuelling the inflation of property values that drives people of limited means out of functioning communities and into underserviced areas. It wasn't long ago, though, that the conventional wisdom was that gentrification is a uniformly *good* thing. Some exuberant prognostications about the social impacts of the urban gold rush began circulating around the turn of the millennium.

Enter Richard Florida

The chief proclaimer of the good news was Richard Florida, a writer and business professor who saw the migration of young, well-paid professionals into old urban centres—and the subsequent explosion in property values—as trends to be celebrated. In his influential

2002 treatise *The Rise of the Creative Class*, and in follow-up books, he offered the parallel shifts in the cultural and economic lives of old-economy cities (his primary case study was Pittsburgh) as evidence of the emergence of a new type of economy based on human ingenuity, a nurturing culture, and enlightened social values. This glowing picture of a culture-driven urban renaissance offered affluent newcomers to hitherto-faded urban landscapes plenty of opportunity for smug self-congratulation.

Though they've fallen out of favour in many circles (particularly among academic urbanists), Florida's ideas continue to have a formidable street-level impact in cities like Hamilton, where they've influenced where the battle lines have been drawn and how debates over redevelopment have been framed. Lauded by some and vehemently denounced by others, Florida's theories have had a polarizing impact, erasing much of the middle ground between pro- and anti-development partisans.

Florida's hypothesis hinges on a few unlikely statistical correlations. He observed, for example, that cities with large gay populations and thriving music scenes were much more likely to be magnets for new-economy enterprises and their workers (and therefore to experience steep rises in property values) than cities that merely offered traditional business and social advantages like a good port, a reliable transportation system, quality schools, and dependable health care. Why should proximity to gay enclaves and live music venues be a determining factor for where post-industrial economies take root? Because, answered Florida, the workers who keep the new economy running—the Creative Class, as he labelled them, always capitalized—need to be free of social straitjackets in order to thrive. "Creativity *requires* diversity: it is the great leveler, annihilating the social categories we have imposed on ourselves, from gender to race and sexual orientation," Florida wrote.[10]

Attracting these "creative" types to your city is indisputably a desirable thing because it signals that you are on the winning side of an increasingly stark and terrifying global economic divide: "The tallest spikes—the cities and the regions that drive the world economy—are growing ever higher, while the valleys—places that boast little, if any, economic activity, mostly languish."[11] In the new global economy, the rewards go to those whose contribution is "innovative" or "creative," and those people are very picky about where they pitch their tents. If your city doesn't make a convincing appeal to this group, it will be doomed to play host to the kind of old-economy activities that are sure to go underappreciated and undercompensated. Florida explained:

> The reality is that globalization has two sides. The first and more obvious one is the geographic spread of routine economic functions such as simple manufacturing or service work (for example, making or answering telephone calls). The second, less obvious side to globalization is the tendency for higher-level economic activities such as innovation, design, finance, and media to cluster in a relatively small number of locations. . . . There are still at most two dozen places worldwide that generate significant innovation.[12]

Florida did not believe that the tendency of the Creative Class to gather in a limited number of places (and therefore to drive real estate prices in those places beyond the reach of mortals) would be diminished by the ability of Wi-Fi-enabled creative types to telecommute or convene a meeting through Skype. That's because this new breed has a driving need to physically congregate with the like-minded.

Partly, that desire flows from practical considerations. Companies in need of venture capital, for example, must keep in mind that "only companies within a twenty-five minute commute of the [venture capital] firm's office are worthy of a high-risk investment."[13] But those sorts of dollars-and-cents calculations are really inseparable from a more general principle that today's high-octane, high-maintenance new-economy players can only do their best work in an environment that stokes their creative fires. Florida wrote:

Ideas flow more freely, are honed more sharply, and can be put into practice more quickly when innovators, implementers and financial backers are in constant contact with one another, in and outside of work. Creative people cluster not simply because they like to be around each other, or because they all happen to prefer cosmopolitan centers with lots of amenities, though both of those things tend to be true. Creative people and companies cluster because of the powerful productivity advantages, economies of scale, and knowledge spillover such density brings.[14]

In light of ongoing social trends with deepening chasms between Florida's Creative Class and the mere producers of solid goods or the providers of "simple" services—between the granite countertop people and those without dependable heating in the high-rises of Toronto's crumbling older suburbs—it's quite reasonable to read Florida's argument as a kind of cheerleading for an inequitable status quo. Those who are perched high on the "spikes" of the new order, we might infer, are there because the global economy naturally values their creativity, spirit of openness, and musical tastes—and not because the system is rigged to favour one group over another. Meanwhile, others "languish" in cultural and economic backwaters because they don't have the gumption or the skills to make it in today's pulsing creative hubs.

This is clearly the reading that motivated Chris Lehmann to assign Florida's concept of the Creative Class the position of Rich People Thing No. 12 in his book *Rich People Things: Real Life Secrets of the Predator Class*. A sly catalogue of concepts and commentators frequently dispatched to justify the dominance of the wealthy over the insecure, *Rich People Things* cast a satirical eye on "the vast array of comforting and comprehensive protections that allow the über-privileged to maintain their iron grip on almost half of America's wealth." Florida's signature concept is given a place within this pantheon because of its almost complete disregard, in Lehmann's view, of the role of political power in the creation of economic inequality within cities and between regions.

Lehmann acknowledged that Florida is far from alone among

American commentators in overlooking the fundamental role of class conflict and political power in shaping social and economic realities. Choosing to ignore the obvious, all of these ruminators must look for answers in unlikely places. The triumph of Florida and those like him, said Lehmann, is that "they have divined exotic new brands of class stratification that have almost nothing to do with material living conditions, and endowed them with strange and wonderful new powers to reshape the urban social contract, drive tax and investment policies, and even reconfigure the coordinates of the Western self."[15]

In Florida's case, said Lehmann, arcane statistical exercises have led to conclusions that apparently buckle when tested against common sense. For example, the proximity of so-called creative workers to gay communities and their high scores on Florida's Bohemian Index; Lehman takes this as indicative not of a fundamental shift in the values of today's information-driven industries, but instead as a marker of "the rather banal trend of younger workers thronging disproportionately to tech employers in big cities and bringing more tolerant social outlooks—and indie-scene-sustaining disposable incomes—along with them."[16]

In other words, this is only a coincidental relationship. There is no evidence that the ability to function as a hedge fund manager, a vacuum cleaner designer, or an IT person is dependent upon having an inclusive, liberal social outlook. That the two may coexist is most likely irrelevant, more plausibly explained by the idea that these industries—or more to the point, the workers who seek to be employed by them—are products of a socially liberal age. New industries are locating in heavily gay and/or bohemian cities because those new forms of enterprise arose in a time when bohemian values and a less intolerant social outlook had become (at least prior to the Age of Trump), the norm. The fact that social tolerance and high technology have risen to the fore at the same historical moment does not mean that one created the other.

Lehmann also pointed out that the creatives' apparent love of diversity seems much less a factor when one looks not just at whether new-economy enclaves overlap with gay neighbourhoods, but rather at whether they are likely to share their terrain with recent immigrants and poor minorities. In this context, Florida's own statistics, Lehmann wrote, undermine his argument. They show that while the latter sort of cross-class co-mingling does occur in large cities like Chicago and Los Angeles—which are big enough to accommodate separate and distinct minority-focused, low-wage service economies and predominately white high-tech industries— the same is not true of smaller-scale technology hubs. In those smaller communities, where there is economic and social homogeneity, the Creative Class seems able to survive just fine without the experience of "diversity."

Lehmann saw Florida's theories as dependent on overconfident extrapolations and sweeping generalization. He decried that "a class of workers whom Florida baptized into a great, all-purpose self-actualizing vanguard" is assumed to be culturally homogenous and to share a single set of social values and a common economic standing. In fact, Lehmann pointed out, while some of the people drawn to the economic opportunities in booming metropolises may be running their own start-ups or designing cutting-edge technologies, the vast majority are likely insecure wage slaves, without a spot on the property ladder and lacking pension plans, who function as "a corps of surplus service workers helping to make employment seem unduly scarce and wages artificially low."[17]

Perhaps the most vexing aspect of the notion of a Creative Class, however—one that came into sharp focus after the 2008 financial crash and the accompanying revelations of finance sector malfeasance—is the question of what exactly this Creative Class is creating. Sure, some segments of this "self-actualizing vanguard," to borrow Lehmann's sarcastic barb, may be developing apps to help you get to your bus stop on time or working on more effective asthma treatments or a cure for cancer. A thin slice may even be writing novels or making art.

But many of the sectors that Florida includes under the umbrella of the Creative Class—the wizards of high finance, for starters—practise some very dark forms of creativity. Some are dedicated to creating ever-more-inventive Ponzi schemes (like the subprime-mortgage caper that ruined countless lower-income families and came close to toppling the world economy in 2008) or figuring out how to compel garment workers in Bangladesh to work harder for less money. These activities are not incidental to the primarily city-focused new economy, but rather are some of its defining features. Florida's "higher-level" economic activities (finance, mass media) are perhaps better rewarded than "routine" manufacturing and service jobs partly because the former are involved with managing and maintaining a system that undervalues the contributions of the people who are in the latter category.

A wide range of city-watchers have also found fault with the Creative Class formulation on the grounds that its prescriptions for urban regeneration simply haven't worked. In 2004, two years after publication of *The Rise of the Creative Class*, Los Angeles–based urban scholar Joel Kotkin told *Metropolis* magazine that the notion of a Creative Class as the saviour of decaying industrial cities is fundamentally flawed because it "never addresses the issues of affordability." And a crisis of unaffordability in gentrifying cities will invariably undermine all the promised benefits (a diverse and welcoming society, a vibrant cultural life) that are supposed to flow to cities that cater to the hip and well-heeled. Kotkin complained that while Florida was advising desperate blue-collar burgs to cultivate the cutting-edge mystique of cities like San Francisco—a place he said embodies the "kind of genteel decline" afflicting cities so expensive that only the very rich can comfortably live there—he should have been telling them to seek salvation by taking on the less glamourous tasks of "reducing crime, improving transportation, providing education and public safety" and by focusing on their own unique and enviable attributes. "I'd say to people in St. Louis, Forget about being Soho. You're never gonna be Soho. . . . But you could be an affordable place where people can live in a great urban neighborhood near a beautiful Olmsted-designed park with an excellent art museum."[18]

Since then, the idea that Florida's theory largely ignores the poisonous effects of too much money has become something like conventional wisdom, borne out by the experience of cities across

North America. "Florida's formula has proven to benefit the already rich, mostly white middle class; fuel rampant property speculation; displace the bohemians he so fetishised; and see the problems that once plagued the inner cities simply move out to the suburbs," wrote Oliver Wainwright in the *Guardian* in 2017.[19]

Frank Bures, an early critic of Florida, added that many American cities that bought into the idea of art, culture, and the captivating veneer of hipness as keys to economic revival have overwhelmingly been disappointed. "Millions of dollars had been spent by hard luck towns across the Rust Belt in the hopes that a coffee shop, a bike path and a co-working space would restore their postwar industrial glory," Bures wrote in *Belt Magazine* the same year. "Yet for cities that took Florida's theory to heart, like Youngstown, Cleveland, or Duluth, the boom never really came."[20]

Despite taking serious flak from his detractors, Richard Florida has insisted that he's been misunderstood. In the revised edition of *The Rise of the Creative Class*, released a decade after the 2002 original and in the wake of an economic meltdown and increasing social tensions, he protested:

> Whereas some have dubbed the very concept of the Creative Class as elitist and accused me of privileging it over other classes, or derided me as a "neo-liberal" with a naively optimistic faith in the power of markets, I assure you that neither is the case. The key thesis of my argument is as simple as it is basic: every human being is creative. That the Creative Class enjoys vast privileges is true, but to acknowledge that fact is not to endorse it. The essential task before us is to unleash the creative energies, talent and potential of everyone—to build a society that acknowledges and nurtures the creativity of each and every human being. Creativity is truly a limitless resource; it is something we all share.[21]

With that, Florida acknowledged the widespread understanding that capital-C Creative cities are almost always atrociously inequitable. Conceding that "most of the [creative economy's] benefits have been enjoyed by a privileged economic and geographic cohort," Florida proposed that this be remedied through the adoption of a new Creative Compact "dedicated to the *creatification* of everyone."[22] This compact is essentially a multi-point plan for drawing a wider range of citizens into the orbit of this new economic system. It cites the need to more actively welcome new immigrants (whom Florida sees as bringing vast amounts of creative inspiration with them); to renew and reform the education system; to retool the social safety net to extend protections to people with precarious employment; to discourage wasteful urban sprawl; and to abandon the economic imperative to endlessly quest after growth. While proposing these reforms in response to the obvious economic and social disasters unfolding in North American cities does not exactly constitute a *mea culpa* (Florida insisted that his view was an egalitarian one all along), it does represent a distinct change of emphasis and offers some useful policy suggestions.

Florida ventured further down this road with the 2017 release of *The New Urban Crisis*, which suggested multiple remedies for the rampant urban inequality that Florida's critics claim he helped create. In that book, Florida decried the emergence of a "winner-take-all urbanism" and the widening of "deep divides [in] our cities and our society. As the affluent and advantaged return to cities, they colonize the best locations. Everyone else is then crammed into the remaining disadvantaged areas." In Canada, Florida said, this "ticking time bomb" requires that governments "invest in affordable housing, upgrading low wage service jobs, providing infrastructure to connect people and places to employment centers, and create a stronger social safety net" that can reunite the disaffected and discouraged urban poor with the mainstream.[23]

But are the later caveats sufficient to justify Florida's ongoing, enthusiastic embrace of the gentrifying class? Do they redeem his initial theory, despite its now glaringly obvious shortcomings? For that matter, does Florida's foundational premise—that incoming financial and tech workers have a "creative" outlook that's bound to be of benefit to the cities they emigrate to—stand up to scrutiny?

The Creative Class versus genuine creativity

Ask an artist and you are likely to get negative answers to all of the questions above. Many artists don't see themselves as social allies or kindred spirits of incoming new-economy workers at all. They complain that the newcomers—despite the spending money they may throw around in their new neighbourhoods—have smothered the creative impulses in their communities rather than enhanced them. Consider the cautionary words of Lawrence Ferlinghetti, who described how money chased away the artistic, independent spirit of San Francisco. Ferlinghetti, who died in 2021 at 101, was one of the original icons of the Beat Generation. A New York City exile who headed west in the 1950s, settling in San Francisco's North Beach area, he founded the City Lights bookstore, from which a literary revolution was launched, and helped to transform the city into a beacon for the sixties counterculture.

In 1998, Ferlinghetti—at nearly eighty years old—became San Francisco's first poet laureate, the literary patron saint of a city that had by then become a mostly unrecognizable mutation of its earlier self. In his inaugural speech, Ferlinghetti praised the city as "a frontier for free poetic life, with perhaps more poets and more poetry readers than any city in the world," but warned that "we are in danger of losing it. In fact, we are in danger of losing much more than that. All that made this City so unique in the first place seems to be going down the tube at an alarming rate."[24] He endorsed the observation of a writer for the *San Francisco Bay Guardian* that the city—which even this early in the new millennium had seen a 40 per cent rise in the gap between rich and poor over the previous two years—had been transformed from "a diverse metropolis that welcomed immigrants and refugees from around the world to a homogenous, wealthy enclave" where the people "who have been the heart and soul of the city for decades" can no longer afford to live.[25]

In an essay / short story / prose poem entitled "The Poetic City That Was," Ferlinghetti traced the steps of a painter whose path to San Francisco appears to mirror the author's own. When the painter arrives, in the 1950s, he finds a city with a kind of spiritual life that is lacking elsewhere:

> Fifty years ago the city seemed an ideal place for a poet and artist to live, especially one who considered himself a kind of expatriate. He was to learn much later how so many poets and artists in America increasingly saw themselves as expatriates in their own country, a country in which the "subjective," or the "inner self," was increasingly under attack in a ravenous consumer society. In fact, Henry Miller had prophesied it all in his *The Air Conditioned Nightmare*, written upon his shocked return to the U.S. after many years in France. "Another breed of men has taken over," quoth Henry, or words to that effect. Greed would be king, but that wasn't evident in 1950s San Francisco, as our anti-hero prepared to land on the Barbary Coast.

The artist—the subject of Ferlinghetti's prose poem—found "a big sunny flat for sixty-five dollars a month" and joined a movement of painters who "were dancing on the edge of the world." But events outside the sphere of ideas and imagination unfolded in different ways, and this creative paradise eventually became inhospitable to creators:

> Fifty years later, he awoke one fine morning like Rip Van Winkle and found himself again with his sea bag on his shoulder, looking for anywhere he could live and work. The new owners of his old flat now wanted $2500 a month, and his studio was $3000 plus. Many of his friends were also evicted, for it seemed that their buildings weren't owned by San Franciscans anymore but by faceless investors with venture capital. Corporate monoculture had wiped out any unique sense of place, turning the "island-city" into an artistic theme-park, without artists. And he was on the street.[26]

Not surprisingly, things got much worse after Ferlinghetti wrote those words in the early 2000s. City incentives to attract new employers enticed high-tech firms (which would otherwise have set up shop in nearby Silicon Valley) to open offices in the few segments of San Francisco that remained gritty and cheap. This led to an accelerated influx of high-echelon Creative Class types who were hungry for real estate. They worked alongside accomplices in the development industry, some of whom found clever ways around regulations that had allowed long-tenured residents to stay in their homes under rent control. Those developers, much despised by the poor, "invoked a 1986 California law known as the Ellis Act," explained Nathan Heller, writing in the *New Yorker*, "which permits evictions when landlords want to go out of business permanently. By repeatedly going 'out of business' and exploiting a loophole in the local condo laws, speculators have been able to transform rent-controlled buildings into market-value homes. From 1990 to 1997, there were twenty-eight Ellis Act petitions. . . . From 2006 to 2013, there were three hundred and seventy-four."

The deployment of this strategy led to scenes that seemed straight out of Dickens. In 2010, a community home for low-income single parents and their children named MommaHouse was shut down under an Ellis Act petition and its residents sent packing. Heller also reported on the efforts of a group of low-income activists to file charges of elder abuse against developers for throwing elderly and sometimes disabled residents (some who had lived in the same apartment since the 1970s) onto the street.

Cumulatively, these individual human tragedies have a huge impact on the character of a city. One of the most visible consequences is their contribution to the city's epic homelessness problem. (San Francisco has legions of people living on the streets and in parks.) But the poor are not the only victims of this vicious competition for housing. Per Heller:

> San Francisco today has the second-highest median income in the United States, but, even using that peg, middle-class San Franciscans can afford less than a sixth of the homes available in town. Every city on the up-and-up must contend with a gap between rich and poor. Yet few have also, like San Francisco, managed to immiserate a relatively well-heeled middle class.

Given this triumph of the moneyed over the majority, and in line with Ferlinghetti's observations, much of what made San Francisco unique seems to be hurtling towards extinction. "Artists, educators, and ethnic enclaves continue to get squeezed out of housing—pretty much the worst thing that can happen to a city's culture," Heller observed.[27]

Physical and metaphorical gentrification

Sarah Schulman describes a similar process of urban homogenization in her poetic and provocative treatise *The Gentrification of the Mind: Witness to a Lost Imagination*. As the title suggests, the book is concerned with more than the physical and economic process of gentrification that transformed the face of New York City between the late 1970s and the early 2010s. It also more metaphorically applies the concept of gentrification as a way of describing parallel shifts in less tangible aspects of reality: in social outlook, in artistic expression, even in the ways that people experience feelings of happiness.

Since the book largely explores the interplay between urban transformation and the AIDS crisis that took hold in the 1980s—(a crisis with which Schulman was deeply engaged, as an activist with ACT UP)—there's a major emphasis here on how the gay and artistic communities have become "gentrified." Having lost the memory of the determined, defiant opposition from ground level it took to force government to invest in medical research and treatment to contain AIDS—and how this struggle was a key part in the broader struggle for LGBTQ rights—the gay community is today much more likely to take a more conciliatory approach to the powerful, Schulman insists. The artists who tell this story are also less inclined to focus on how marginalized people confronted establishment intransigence. In Schulman's analysis, loss of memory is a key component of gentrification (both the physical and spiritual kinds): when the old tenants are gone, their history goes out in the trash by the side of the road, and is replaced by entirely different versions of past events.

Schulman's story begins, however, with the physical gentrification of the city, a process she defines with elegant precision:

> To me, the literal experience of gentrification is a concrete replacement process. Physically it is an urban phenomena: the removal of communities of diverse classes, ethnicities, races, sexualities, languages, and points of view from the central neighborhoods of cities, and their replacement by more homogenized groups. With this comes the destruction of culture and relationship, and this destruction has profound consequences for the future lives of cities.[28]

The planned replacement of one population with another is nothing new in New York. Schulman cites the story, for instance, of how the Bronx was essentially burned down in the 1970s so that real estate interests could collect the insurance money and rebuild and repopulate the area. Waves of gentrification before and since then can be traced back to provisions in the post–World War II G.I. Bill that gave incentives to (overwhelmingly white) veterans to move out of the city and into new suburban homes. This "white flight" ultimately led to New York's bankruptcy in the 1970s, as "the remaining poor, working-class, and middle-class residents simply did not provide a wide enough tax base to support the city's infrastructure." Although new city policies (such as offering developers tax breaks to convert low-income housing to luxury accommodation) introduced in the aftermath of the financial meltdown were ostensibly intended to close this funding gap, human services continued to be cut even as much of New York was transformed into a playground for the wealthy, awash in money.

Schulman notes the vicious coincidence of the AIDS epidemic striking just as gentrification was in full swing. In a chapter grimly entitled "The Dynamics of Death and Replacement," she describes how the mass death brought about by AIDS functioned much like the closing of traditional industries and the subsequent exodus of the workforce from industrial centres elsewhere. In places like Pittsburgh, former factory lands have been bought, developed, and resold as upscale residential neighbourhoods. A similar economic wave was activated in New York City: as more people died from AIDS, more apartments were made available and taken off rent controls, causing the speculators to pounce. The neighbourhoods with the highest recorded rates of HIV infection, Schulman observes, correlate directly with those that have undergone the most gentrification.

The death of industry, people, and imagination

Deindustrialization and disease are not the only disasters that have enabled opportunistic governments and business interests to jump-start gentrification. Peter Moskowitz, author of *How to Kill a City: Gentrification, Inequality and the Fight for a Neighborhood*, notes that Hurricane Katrina was used as the catalyst for the transformation of traditionally Black neighbourhoods in New Orleans into enclaves of wealthy white newcomers. In the aftermath of the 2005 mega-storm, redevelopment took a very specific form, with existing services such as schools being eliminated and tax breaks offered to the developers of luxury properties.

"Obviously, the city didn't plan for the storm," says Moskowitz, "but it planned right afterwards that the storm was a 'good thing' for the city. The governor at the time said that it took the storm of a lifetime to create the opportunity of a lifetime." The unplanned appearance of Katrina differs from the situation in New York, where "bankers and the government got together and literally planned how to deindustrialize so they could sell real estate." There, post-industrial redevelopment, Moskowitz explains, "was not some random occurrence" but a conscious plan to use changes to the building codes to force the shuttering of old factories and warehouses.[29]

Schulman's experience of New York's gentrification—post-AIDS epidemic and post-deindustrialization—seems completely antithetical to the type of creative flowering described by Florida. "As I watched my neighborhood transform," she writes, "it was quickly apparent that the newly rehabbed units attracted a different kind of person than the ones who had been displaced and freshly died. . . . [For one thing], the replacement tenants were much more identified with the social structures necessary to afford newly inflated mortgages and rents."

Far from being drawn to the city out of an appreciation for diversity and a need to broaden their horizons, these newcomers were colonists from the suburbs eager to uproot the existing occupants and impose a culture more flattering to themselves. She writes:

> The difference between refusenik Americans of the past, and the ones who created gentrification culture is that in the past young whites came to New York to become New Yorkers. They became citified and adjusted to the differences and dynamics they craved. This new crew, the professionalized children of the suburbs, were different. They came not to join or to blend in or to learn and evolve, but to homogenize. They brought the values of the gated community and a willingness to trade freedom for security.[30]

And so (to cite an example that Schulman finds particularly galling), affluent white people move to the city and bring their "foodie" culture that replaces real, family-run ethnic restaurants with "fusion" cafés where the food is not from any one recognizable place, and where the prices ensure that only the well-heeled invaders will dine there. In Schulman's neighbourhood,

> the corner bodega that sold tamarind, plantain, and yucca was replaced by an upscale deli that sells Fiji Water, the emblematic yuppie product. Habib's falafel stand, where he knew everyone on the block and put extra food on your plate when you were broke—was replaced by a "Mexican" restaurant run by an NYU MBA who never puts extra food on your plate.[31]

Perhaps more importantly, through the influx of rich people who need to make shitloads of money in order to pay the rent, a volatile, inventive urban mix has been superseded by a community of émigrés resigned to putting business before principle and artists more concerned with making the right career moves than with changing minds. The AIDS activists who demanded changes in public policies, the artists who brought about a cultural shift largely responsible for an erosion of prejudice against gay people—these sorts of rebels and misfits are less inclined to find (or afford) a place in this new environment. And that's bad for society, says Schulman.

> Urbanity is what makes cities great, because the daily affirmation that people from other experiences are real makes innovative solutions and experiments possible. In this way, cities historically have provided acceptance, opportunity, and a place to create ideas contributing to freedom. Gentrification in the seventies, eighties, and nineties replaced urbanity with suburban values from the sixties, seventies, and eighties, so that the suburban conditioning of racial and class stratification, homogeneity of consumption, mass-produced aesthetics, and familial privatization got resituated into big buildings, attached residences, and apartments. This undermines urbanity and recreates cities as centers of obedience instead of instigators of positive change.[32]

Gentrification goes global

Around the world, variations on this process have continued to unfold. In the London district of Islington—where British sociologist Ruth Glass observed an influx of middle-class professionals was displacing the working class, inspiring her to invent the new word *gentrification* in 1964—a new wave of "super-gentrification" has since ensured that people in that "middle-class professional" stratum are being priced out of the market. A 2013 report in the *Guardian* tells of young career people paying 1,000 pounds (around C$2,000) a month for a single room in a "flatshare," while homes that could be bought for 4,000 pounds in the late 1960s are now selling for up to 5 million pounds.

Teachers, mid-ranking civil servants, doctors, lecturers and jour-
nalists—who have traditionally made up the Islington 'chattering
classes' can no longer afford to put down roots. . . . By the end of
the decade, families who do not qualify for social housing will
need to earn £90,000 a year just to afford to rent in the area,
while house-buying will be out of reach for most.[33]

This phenomenon of super-gentrification is being driven by an
influx of financial sector workers, an impressively well paid international elite who control global money markets from only a handful
of financial capitals across the globe. But since Islington is simultaneously the site of a significant quantity of public housing, the new
domination of the private housing market by ultra-wealthy bank
employees has led to a striking study in contrasts in this community.
Writes Carole Cadwalladr in the *Observer*:

> Britain has been suffering the consequences of the financial crash,
> and in Islington, it's being played out on the streets. It's where the
> bankers who presided over the system live side by side with those
> who are now paying for it: the poor.[34]

The inequality is seen in the reality that a neighbourhood filled
with upscale delis where a loaf of bread costs five pounds also produces some of the country's grimmest statistical social indicators.
Islington has the fourth-highest level of child poverty in the country; a third of its children live in overcrowded conditions; 40 per
cent of older people live in poverty; it has the lowest life expectancy
in London and the highest number of serious mental health issues
and depression in England.

Let's move across the channel and overland to Berlin, where an
abundance of cheap rental accommodation and studio space had
attracted an immense artistic community. Although Berlin has no
significant financial sector to drive up housing prices, other factors
have ignited a rapid gentrification that's enraged locals and led to
explosive social conflict. Berlin's reputation as "the coolest city
in the world" has both inspired a gigantic spike in tourism (with

overnight stays rising from 13 million in 2004 to 27 million in 2013) and attracted the attention of overseas real estate investors. With turbulence in financial markets making real estate one of the safer places where global investors can park their cash, and newly relaxed German purchasing regulations facilitating the process, Berlin has been the target for a multitude of foreign investors. Some buy properties to rent out on Airbnb; others aim to flip them to fellow foreign speculators.[35]

Long-time residents were not amused. "Their solution to this vicious cycle of hipster-driven gentrification is to surround themselves with graffiti saying stuff like 'No tourists, no hipsters, no yuppies, no photos,' and chasing you with dogs if they see you pointing a camera toward them," wrote journalist Matt Shea. Protests against gentrification and the evictions it had produced became increasingly violent. A rally against the eviction of a family who couldn't afford their raised rent attracted five hundred people and resulted in fifteen cars being burned and ten police officers injured.[36]

Meanwhile, as urban activists vent their rage, speculators get craftier. Some have been using "eco-scams": appealing to local councils' desire to go green by promising to retrofit buildings for energy efficiency, and using this pretext to hike the rent, sometimes by as much as 300 per cent. Some owners have invoked their plans for green improvements as a means of removing tenants, but have not followed through on the renovations after they found new tenants willing to pay the higher asking price.[37]

A hurricane hits Hamilton

The collision of Richard Florida's luminous predictions with this growing global catalogue of gentrification-driven disasters gives a context to the mixed response to Hamilton's own version of the urban gold rush. Let's return to that gathering of diverse downtown stakeholders one evening at the Sky Dragon Centre—the event that eventually devolved, as Kevin MacKay recalled in chapter two, into a free-for-all of flying insults and accusations. Evidently, the people participating in that melee brought radically divergent perspectives with them, drawing upon distinct historical touchstones, political ideas, and social goals, and possibly upon entirely different ways of perceiving what was happening on the landscape around them.

Many lower-city Hamiltonians (including the newcomers) would interpret the whole package of changes underway in their city—the renovations, the new construction, the influx of Torontonians, the freely flowing cappuccino, the evictions, the rising prices, the speculation, the morphing of artistic spirit into something increasingly driven by the quest for profit—through the lens of the Creative Class and its boundless promise of urban salvation. You can hear strong echoes of Richard Florida's steadfastly upbeat outlook, for instance, in the words of Keanin Loomis, president and CEO of the Hamilton Chamber of Commerce, who wrote in the *Hamilton Spectator* that "a large part of Hamilton's renaissance is driven by the fact that people are flocking to live in real, livable cities again" and that "Hamilton's livability is driven by history and culture."[38] Florida himself had urged Hamilton's decision makers, in his address to a 2008 Chamber-organized gathering, to focus on the amenities that attract creative workers, in order to maximize the city's stake in an innovation-driven regional economic boom.[39]

But by the time that gentrification shifted into high gear in Hamilton, there were enough stories circulating, from various global outposts of the new knowledge economy, to suggest that Florida's Creative Class theory was either dangerously oblivious to the vulnerability of the poor in supercharged post-industrial cities, or worse, that it was some kind of scam to provide cover and justification for the pillaging of working-class neighbourhoods by realtors, financiers, and their new-economy co-conspirators. In the latter interpretation of events, all that gushing over arts festivals, galleries, live music, and fancy bars and restaurants is just an elaborate distraction from the reality that low-income people are being mugged by the agents of speculative finance and then dumped onto the street.

Still, gentrification is often seen as an entirely good thing, in part because of the enduring and seductive idea that newcomers are doing something virtuous by bringing new value to derelict areas. The notion that gentrifiers bring culture to a cultural void or establish communities where before there was only empty space or decay, explains Peter Moskowitz, creates a psychological "bubble [that] is necessary to maintain this fiction that you are doing a good thing by building a house on top of the waste of Detroit, or on top of where a Black family once lived in New Orleans. You are helping the world by doing this. It's a completely attractive thought for anyone who is complicit in the process."[40]

The assumption that many of the newcomers investing in downtown Hamilton inhabited this kind of bubble of self-congratulation might go a fair way to explaining the bafflement and incredulity that greeted the hostile anti-gentrification theatrics that took place in the city over several years. Here, two completely opposing viewpoints collide. The mainstream opinion is that new investment downtown is breathing life into a city where rigor mortis had clearly set in. In the other corner are people who are aware of the devastating consequences of urban revitalization elsewhere, and view all that euphoric rhetoric about the wonders of the Creative Class as a loathsome lie.

It seems natural that the latter view would produce the kind of destructive spectacles that have by now become a part of local lore. To recap: first there was the plastering of doors and storefronts with posters emblazoned with slogans such as "Fuck your boutique—Defend Hamilton." Later, masked individuals hurled obscenities and unsavoury objects at the Try Hamilton real estate investors' tour of the East End in 2016.[41] This was followed, in 2018, by a group of black-clad, masked people—carrying a banner reading "We are the ungovernables"—parading down Locke Street and smashing windows of businesses (most notably, an upscale donut shop, which after the attack had lines around the corner as locals waited to purchase pastries in an expression of sympathy for those at the receiving end of this gesture).[42]

The Locke Street donut riot put in motion a chain of escalating events that generated considerable heat for the Tower, despite the group's denial of direct involvement in those now legendary moments of window smashing and trash-can throwing. The police, eager to demonstrate that they were on the case and confident that those declarations of innocence wouldn't ring true in the court of public opinion (and possibly an actual court), arrested Cedar Hopperton,[43] a habitué of the Tower who had previously been incarcerated after an episode of property destruction near the G20 summit in Toronto in 2010,[44] and charged him with conspiracy. The Tower also attracted the attention of neo-Nazis (this being the Donald Trump era, when far-right provocateurs on either side of the border have felt comfortable coming out of the shadows and into daylight) who sought to extract their own public relations advantage from the Tower's growing name recognition by smashing up its Cannon Street home. This prompted the building's rattled owner to evict his anarchist tenants (who subsequently relocated to Barton Street).[45] The City of Hamilton, meanwhile, in an ill-informed and quickly reversed move, made its own statement on the trashing of Locke Street by declaring the anarchist movement's circled A on a black background a hate symbol and moving to ban its use.[46]

In a thoughtful and unusually cool-headed post-riot analysis, author and civic commentator Simon Orpana ventured that one positive aspect of these distasteful dramatics is that they confronted Hamiltonians' iron-clad denial that gentrification could ever have a downside. Previously, "attempts to raise awareness about the threats of gentrification," wrote Orpana on the Raise the Hammer website, "were all but shut down amidst a chorus of scorn and censure. City-boosters were miffed at what they perceived as a group of 'outsiders' from the university (which is where some, but by no means all, of these critiques originated) intervening in the struggles of Hamilton to emerge from decades of obscurity and hardship."

As the machinery of the real estate industry constructed a "cult of Hamilton," which had the impact of ensuring that "ordinary, stigmatized 'dirt' was transformed into marketable, fetishized 'grit,'" contrarian perspectives were painted as unpatriotic. "This was finally Hamilton's moment to shine after decades of obscurity and hardship, struggle and stigmatization," continued Orpana, "and activists concerned about gentrification were dismissed as wanting to 'keep Hamilton poor.'"[47]

In the intervening years, the negative consequences of gentrification—displacement of poor people, overzealous policing, the criminalization of poverty—have become acceptable topics of conversation in polite company. The *Hamilton Spectator* carried a story, for example, about lawyer Peter Boushy, acting on behalf of client Dwight Perry, who joined in a constitutional challenge of the Ontario Safe Streets Act, under which panhandlers who don't pay fines (which, almost by definition, they can't afford to pay) can be sent to jail. Perry had amassed over $20,000 in tickets for what he and his lawyer see as a victimless crime. When Perry doesn't get any money when he asks a passerby for change, "he wishes them a good day anyway. No harm. No foul," the *Spectator* story reads. Boushy adds that his client's extra income from panhandling, which augments his $313-a-month welfare payment, is key to his survival. For this, he should not be ticketed and threatened with jail. "It's just fundamentally offensive, if not morally grotesque," the lawyer remarks, "when people in a position of power pick on the poor."[48]

Who's picking on the poor?

The police practice of targeting people who take to the streets to supplement their incomes is a long-simmering issue in Hamilton. It has created a web of conflict involving vulnerable people and their advocates, local businesses, and residents, both newly arrived and long-established. Sometimes those groups play unexpected roles. Although it may seem logical to assume that newly arrived gentrifiers will want to purge the poor and disadvantaged in their midst, that assumption may not capture the complexities of these conflicts or lead to durable solutions.

Writing in *Briarpatch* magazine, Hamilton anti-poverty activist and writer Sarah Mann advanced the idea that what's primarily responsible for the vigorous application of laws such as the Ontario Safe Streets Act is pressure from community organizations in gentrifying neighbourhoods. Mann wrote that sex workers and drug users, in particular, are seen as "undesirable" people who diminish the quality of life and restrain real estate prices downtown. She recalled that, following a well-publicized Hamilton gallery exhibition that featured surveillance camera images of assumed sex workers standing on corners and urinating behind buildings, the tone of discussion at a meeting of a community association in the Landsdale neighbourhood was close to hysterical.

The neighbourhood gathering "provided a forum for the scapegoating of sex workers and drug users as the causes of the community's crime problem," wrote Mann.

Posters and a petition were circulated to advertise the meeting. "Drug dealers and Prostitution," read the bold lettering. "Working to get them off our streets and out of our community." Community members at the meeting were visibly hostile, describing sex workers as predators of children, dangerous and violent criminals, and insane drug users who, if you talk to one, will "stab you with an AIDS needle."

Response from *Briarpatch*'s readers was divided. While many supported the proposition that video surveillance and police street patrols downtown amounted to an assault on the most vulnerable in Hamilton's poor neighbourhoods, others insisted that framing tensions downtown as a struggle between wealthy, self-interested gentrifiers and the city's most disadvantaged citizens was misleading and overly simplistic. Several correspondents identified themselves as downtown residents from low-income backgrounds who expressed resentment that Mann would dismiss their complaints that the sex trade and drug use threaten their safety and well-being.

"It's tiring checking the park for discarded needles and broken glass before it's safe to let your kids play," wrote one local. "It's tiring to have to take your stroller onto King Street in the morning rush hour because there's been another bar stabbing and the sidewalk is closed off. . . . It's tiring to hear your neighbours say they have had their clothes stolen as they hung out to dry." Another resident complained that the article ignored the violence that sex workers experience at the hands of pimps and customers, and bemoaned the author's "disregard for other marginalized groups who share space with prostitutes and drug users."[49]

The persistence of tension in downtown communities over street-level sex work prompted the Social Planning and Research Council to undertake—in 2015, five years after Mann's story was published—a series of consultations in the Sherman neighbourhood. Intended to find common understandings and identify potential solutions, the project included meetings with local residents as well as focus groups among women with a past or present involvement in the sex trade. Part of the project's mandate was to take a harm-reduction approach that would address both sides' daily concerns, as well as seek to establish mutual understandings that could provide the basis for resolving grievances.

The community's preoccupations centred on public safety. The SPRC report noted, for instance, that "many people expressed fear for women, particularly young women who some think are being groomed to become active in sex work. They also worry about the stigmatization of women living in the area who are often approached and propositioned by potential johns. It was also noted that johns have been seen taking pictures of women in the area."

The focus group of women gathered at the Sex Trade Alternatives, Resources, and Services (STARS) drop-in centre approached things from a different angle. They were largely concerned with the need for ramped-up services—such as addiction treatment, crisis and support lines, and more pay phones on the street—as well as more adequate social assistance to make sex work less of a necessity. They also proposed that specialized training for police might help de-escalate encounters with law enforcement on the street.[50]

While Mann's article in *Briarpatch* framed the community hostility towards sex workers as a consequence of gentrification (and, by implication, the influx of Creative Class migrants from Toronto), SPRC senior social planner Deirdre Pike, who worked on the Sherman consultations, sees an entirely different dynamic at work. "When I was leading a conversation on sex work in the community," she tells me, "that first night, [long-term residents of] the neighbourhood were like, 'These hookers, we've got to get rid of them,' and it was a very negative thing. The next meeting, there were some new folks at the table—they were new to the neighbourhood. They had seen sex workers on the streets in Toronto, and they came with a more progressive view than people who were already here.

"I think Hamilton is an awesome place," she adds. "But I also think that people moving in from Toronto is a really good thing. I've seen them influence neighbourhoods in a really good way."

The role of artists on Hamilton's gentrifying landscape is another case where the reality is more complex than it's sometimes made out to be. Consider, for instance, that Hamilton's artist district on James North long predates even the suggestion of gentrification. Consider also that a significant segment of the street's arts practitioners identify much more strongly with the poor residents around them than with the forces of high finance.

Boyle Heights: A cautionary tale

Hamilton is far from the only place where artists have been accused of complicity with real estate speculation. So perhaps it's wise to backtrack and look at how the issue of artists' role in gentrification has played out elsewhere. Across the globe, the term *art-washing*—at first used to describe the practice of large corporations placing ads in galleries—is a label for artists' role in glamourizing neighbourhoods that are targets of gentrification.[51] Probably the best-known flashpoint over art-washing is Boyle Heights, a poor Hispanic neighbourhood in East Los Angeles. Known as the Ellis Island of the West Coast, Boyle Heights had throughout its history been a point of reception for new immigrant groups (much like James North in Hamilton). Since World War II it had attracted a growing population of Mexican Americans, who brought with them a rich culture and set of traditions that have helped define the neighbourhood.

Over the years, multiple other Mexican communities in L.A. have experienced displacement by forces beyond their control. In the late 1950s, Mexican Americans' properties in Chavez Ravine were expropriated (with minimal compensation) to make way for the L.A. Dodgers' baseball stadium. Some homeowners were forcibly removed by police. More recently, predominantly Hispanic neighbourhoods like Silver Lake and Echo Park have been bought up by rich white people and transformed into enclaves of high-rise condos.[52]

Around 2015, it looked like the same fate awaited Boyle Heights. Prices in the downtown art district had begun climbing enormously, prompting gallery owners to look towards that bargain-basement barrio across the L.A. River. Conflict soon erupted. In 2015, a mobile opera called Hopscotch, whose patrons paid $150 to ride limos to performance sites across the city, made a stop at Hollenbeck Park, where many of Boyle Heights' community festivities are held. An organization called Serve the People, who were distributing free food at that spot, were outraged. The group rallied Boyle Heights residents and a high school marching band, who came to drown out the performance.[53]

The same year, the owner of the new Maccarone gallery in Boyle Heights told the *New York Times* that the neighbourhood "still has a dangerous quality—I like that. I like that we spent a fortune on security." The condescending, nay, racist nature of that remark galvanized the efforts of groups like Defend Boyle Heights (DBH) and the new Boyle Heights Alliance Against Artwashing and Displacement (BHAAAD), which launched a campaign demanding that the new art galleries leave Boyle Heights immediately.

According to journalist Alexander Nazaryan, some of the new galleries did indeed harbour the kind of colonial outlook that opponents described. "Maccarone is not the only gallery that treated Boyle Heights like a dystopian landscape with no culture of its own, no pride of place," he wrote in *Newsweek*. But BHAAAD and DBH have targeted arts organizations *generally*, even denouncing one group, Self Help Graphics and Art, that has deep roots among poor Hispanics in Los Angeles. The Self Help space is "richly adorned with prints by Chicano and Latino artists," wrote Nazaryan, "including works that explicitly addressed immigration, drug violence and indigenous culture. It was like the [white, upscale] galleries of South

Anderson only in the most literal sense, in that it displayed art, some of which was for sale. That art, though, could be bought for as little as $50. Some of it was made by high-schoolers."[54]

Defend Boyle Heights justified its targeting of Self Help with the reasoning that, in an era when affluent, white gentrifiers have already started to take over the neighbourhood and inflate rents, you can either be (to paraphrase George W. Bush) for us or against us—there can be no middle ground. In a blog post explaining its disruption of a community meeting at Self Help, the activist outfit posed the rhetorical question: "If gentrification is a class war, which side are you on? Are you serving the people, defending the people? Or are you pushing people out?"

Citing the lasting influence of Richard Florida's Creative Class ruminations on Los Angeles's planning principles, DBH made clear that its primary target was an "outside group of creatives and opinion-makers" whose promise of an "influx [of] 'new money and energy'" had persuaded developers and planners to build "infrastructure to lure in outsiders to under-resourced, primarily people of color neighbourhoods rather than focusing on the needs of the existing community. This idea borders dangerously close to eugenics."[55]

But beyond that group, DBH and allied organizations also targeted local non-profits they saw as insufficiently committed to the fight to drive out gentrifying galleries (a goal that has been, to some degree, successful; repeated demonstrations have pressured the gallery PSSST to pull up stakes only a year after arriving in Boyle Heights).[56] The community-based Self Help Graphics and Art (which DBH acknowledged as a "40 year-old Chicanx artist nonprofit") found itself in DBH's crosshairs because it was seen as a collaborator with outside arts groups (apparently, it had provided some logistical support when Hopscotch, the mobile opera, stopped in Boyle Heights) and for its general lack of enthusiasm for DBH's analysis. In particular, DBH disrupted Self Help's community meeting on artists and gentrification when it got word, from someone inside the meeting, that the event was attended mostly by artists and that the "dialogue was already painting the artist [as] . . . free of culpability."[57]

Like the Tower in Hamilton, DBH was not shy about denouncing a range of "progressive urbanists." The L.A. organization's twelve-page statement also condemned, for example, a community development agency called the Leadership for Urban Renewal Network (LURN) on the grounds that its executive director, Rudy Espinoza, has "openly expressed support for redevelopment and 'urban renewal'"—a sentiment that the activists evidently interpreted as being soft on gentrification.

And with that casual aside, a whole new debate opened up. Espinoza responded, via the internet, with his own manifesto, entitled "On Defending Boyle Heights," in which he characterized the street-level collective as "disrespectful and misinformed" and doubled down on his choice of terminology: "After long discussions . . . our team . . . decided to not shy away from the word 'urban renewal'; we wanted to 'reclaim' these terms and fight for ways where a community could be invested in to support existing residents, not displace them," he wrote.

Yes, Espinoza did oppose gentrification, which he described as "one of the mutations of capitalism . . . that feeds off irrational real estate speculation and combines racism and colonialism to drastically change lives of people who have invested their whole lives into creating a place for their families." But his prescriptions for countering the process—enumerated under the heading "My 'theory of change'"—involved a transfer of power to existing residents rather than simply the expulsion of intruders (which he said would only serve to maintain the old neighbourhood status quo). He described the neighbourhood's predicament not as an either/or situation where repelling the advance of outsiders will equal victory, but as a long-standing crisis that could only be resolved by finding creative means of constructing a new reality.

Alongside gentrification, said Espinoza, Boyle Heights struggles with existing evils including lack of credit or even access to banking services (which drives people to payday lenders charging as much as 500 per cent interest, ensuring that "every time we earn a paycheck, we get poorer"); a desperate shortage of affordable housing; lack of jobs; poisoning by fast food; and the lack of property ownership by community members (most residents are renters at the mercy of self-interested landlords).

He said that LURN (which has since changed its name to Inclusive Action for the City) was developing a whole slate of solutions to counter these scourges. They were working to tap unconventional funds for microfinance loans for people who are undocumented or have bad credit scores. They were researching community land trusts and similar instruments for neighbourhood ownership of land. They were pushing the city to decriminalize street vending so more people can make their own living. The one certainty, he said, is that things can't stay the same. Espinoza wrote:

> Things are not okay. It's not okay for me that people live in over-crowded housing, it's not okay that people are afraid to call their landlord if there is a problem for fear of a rent increase, it's not okay that our entrepreneurs don't have the resources that others have to hire more staff, renovate their spaces, and stay in their community. I believe we need more investment in our community, BUT I'm equally passionate about making sure that people that live here now have an opportunity to enjoy new investment.[58]

There are several clear parallels between Boyle Heights' battles over gentrification and the corollary set of events in Hamilton. One of them—beyond the similarities in the rhetorical style and tactical choices of the anti-gentrification cadres—is the role of artists as a lightning rod for conflict. In both locations, a cluster of street-level activists have taken Richard Florida's musings on the Creative Class as a key to explaining a devastating surge of displacement of existing residents and—having accepted artists as the flag-bearers for an encroaching army of realtors, finance industry employees, and prosperous professionals—committed themselves to an undifferentiated campaign of denunciation and harassment targeting artists *as a class*.

Artists: The foot soldiers of gentrification?

In Hamilton, as in Boyle Heights, some of the arts-related enterprises that have moved in are opportunistic, opting to sell expensive adornments to wealthy(ish) people from lower-priced premises that come with an edgy, urban cachet. But Hamilton also has its own versions of Self Help Graphics and Arts: artists and gallery operators who reject the Floridian narrative that's been imposed upon them, identifying and interacting more with their lower-income neighbours than with comfortable art collectors. Non-profit, community-oriented art spaces have been operating on James North long before anyone thought gentrification was possible here.

So, when Bryce Kanbara (a founding member of Hamilton Artists Co-op in 1975, who now runs the similarly public-spirited You Me Gallery) found an anti-artist, anti-gentrification sticker plastered on his window one morning, "it was kind of ironic," he says. "The one that was stuck on my window was 'You may own your own building but you don't own the neighbourhood,' or something like that. I just left it on because I thought it was kind of neat." He found it ironic because of the assumptions expressed in that sticker about the financial position of artists. It's correct that he does own the James Street North space that's home to his You Me Gallery. But, he says, "I don't make any money on the gallery."

Still, even while he disputes being characterized as a marauding fat cat bent on neighbourhood domination, Kanbara can appreciate the validity of the phantom sticker plasterers' underlying concerns. Around the time that You Me opened in 2003—the same time Florida's writings were making a splash—some artists were "naively" flattered to think that they had a starring role in the process that Florida described. It didn't take them long to figure out, however, that "the Creative Class wasn't artists as we know them. It was more commercial artists and new media people," says Kanbara. And while people in that niche are inclined to pursue glamorous and lucrative careers, and the social influence that comes with those things, the artists in Kanbara's orbit have always had distinctly different goals.

The Artists Co-op (now Hamilton Artists Inc.), which Kanbara co-founded in 1975, consisted of "a group of artists who thought it was important to reflect the local reality and to be connected with the neighbourhood and try to promote art very locally," he says. This often took the form of Hamilton-themed exhibitions. Kanbara, who also served as the co-op's first administrator, recalls, as an example, a lunch-bucket show, where "we put out a general call to the community and people made, or adorned, lunch buckets: used them as planters, painted them, crocheted them, made them out of bread." It was a way of celebrating the local culture, at a time before representations of blue-collar life had any commercial value.

Kanbara has carried over this "people's art approach," in a certain way, to his current venture, the You Me Gallery. Several exhibitions featuring portraits of people in their homes—Muslim men and Hindu families at dinnertime, urban Indigenous people at home downtown—exemplify a desire to "create some sort of interaction amongst diverse communities," says Kanbara. "We're doing these community projects to try to break down the barriers between communities. It's my feeling that you have to have personal engagement for those barriers to start coming down."[59] So, rather than any desire to make a buck off its status as part of Hamilton's newly glamorous arts community, Kanbara insists that the point of You Me is much the same as when Hamilton Artists Co-op first opened up: it's about understanding what's happening in real life, how the lives of diverse groups of people impact the urban fabric around them.

Community engagement is also at the heart of things at Centre[3], a non-profit that's helped anchor the James North art scene since founders Colina Maxwell and Katherine Zarull opened its doors in 2004. Originally called the Print Studio, its spacious, three-storey premises provide exhibition and studio space to artists working in a range of media, while giving artists who specialize in print making access to both digital and traditional, low-tech equipment.

Print making, says Centre[3]'s Ingrid Mayrhofer, is also an inherently "democratic" medium that's especially well suited to collaborations with community members without fine arts backgrounds or aspirations to work as professional artists. She recalls one project where the surface intention was to teach a group of older women print-making techniques to use in the creation of practical items like gym bags, laundry bags, and placemats. The deeper social goal, however, was to facilitate social interaction: these image-adorned goods were incorporated into information packages distributed to other seniors.

Mayrhofer recalls that one of Centre[3]'s most successful community efforts was a training program for at-risk youth, originally a collaboration with the Good Shepherd agency, which runs a youth hostel directly behind Centre[3]'s James Street building. Good Shepherd was looking for ways to make it easier for street-centred young people to finish high school, and the board of education (which has since taken over the program) made that possible by agreeing to grant a school credit to those who completed print-making training at Centre[3].

"For the board," explains Mayrhofer, who came to Hamilton in 2004 to take a job at McMaster University's Art Gallery, after having spent about a decade at the Toronto art collective A Space, "it's been more successful than what they could have done in the schools, because the youth like coming to the studio. It's a different kind of environment. We had a really high rate of retention: one year, we started off with twelve students and actually finished with fifteen kids going through the program."

Some graduates of the program "became really good print makers," and in addition to being able to sell their printed T-shirts at pop-up shops during Art Crawl, some were offered occasional employment at Centre[3]. Mayrhofer says the most lasting benefit of the program, however, was that it helped build the confidence required to explore other possibilities. "One of the stronger motivations" for the students, she says, "was to have a place where they felt grounded, where they could express themselves and follow whatever creative itch they had. That built a bridge for them to get into something else, to look for new opportunities."

In addition to bringing people from the neighbourhood into its facilities, Centre[3] sometimes took its ideas and expertise out into the surrounding community. When Hamilton hosted a segment of the 2015 Pan Am Games, for example, Centre[3] staff co-ordinated a project in which artists populated derelict storefronts along Barton Street with installations commissioned for the event. Mayrhofer says much of the work provided "a critical examination of the games, of the spectacle of the games and how it treats audiences." She says that it was made free to residents of this low-income neighbourhood "so they didn't have to pay admission to go into a strange building."

Regardless, "some of the more hard-core anti-gentrification activists, who don't even live in the area, were saying, 'Oh, it's lipstick on a pig and artists are conspiring with the city to make Hamilton look better,'" thereby enabling the local bureaucrats and the business establishment to attract more investment and fuel gentrification. Mayrhofer insists, however, that while ideologically driven activists saw the artists as pawns in a larger game controlled by the real estate industry and the politicians, long-time residents of the neighbourhood welcomed the resulting improvements in their daily lives. "When we started cleaning the buildings up and taking out weeds between abandoned buildings," she says of the Barton Street storefront project, "people appreciated it. They appreciated that their neighbourhood got some attention, that someone was there to make it look better."

Mayrhofer believes the reason artists have been painted as complicit in gentrification is because anti-gentrification forces have bought into Florida's ideas about the function of creatives on morphing urban landscapes. But she says artists themselves refuse to be defined by that view of the world.

"Most of us here are not fans of Richard Florida and his Creative Class," says Mayrhofer. "We are the creative producers, and whatever that Richard Florida strata is all about, is not us. I read one of his books from front to back and he didn't mention artists once." The most cogent definition of a member of the Creative Class may be someone, Mayrhofer offers, who can afford to *purchase* art, although that's not necessarily a strike against them. "I have nothing against people who buy art. But if that's as creative as they get, then let them buy art and shut the fuck up."

Artists: Whose side are they on?

Exactly what political role cultural producers play on the urban chessboard is a contentious question. Some Hamiltonians I've asked (aside from the ones who are openly hostile towards those they might define as "arts industry fucks") have grumbled, off the record, about how artists tend to be individualistic and opportunistic, which may make them unreliable allies for people engaged in social justice struggles. Still, it's more common to hear (especially from artists themselves) that cultural creators have a clear affinity with people lower down on the economic ladder. The two groups share certain life experiences—having to live on next to nothing, and being motivated more by ideas and feelings than by the pursuit of material wealth—which would tend to make most artists more simpatico with the common folk than with the Tesla-driving, country-club-going crowd.

There is, however, a third option: perhaps cultural workers, like many other people, have allegiances that lead in multiple directions—perhaps they are not bound by a few tightly defined social compacts, but instead are part of a more expansive web of relationships. And perhaps observing things this way might help make the case, in turn, that envisioning a city that works for everyone might require that we move away from drawing rigid battle lines and towards the concept of pursuing "the common good."

A couple of encounters with recent émigrés to Hamilton suggested to me that artists find themselves living in proximity to different groups (the rich and the poor, the privileged and the disenfranchised) at different times, according to different circumstances. This might occasionally allow them to act as interlocutors between competing social groups, between people who normally seem disconnected from one another. Perhaps more importantly, though, the presence of artists—who mostly live like the poor but sometimes enter the spheres of the advantaged and influential—should remind us that we are all members of the same society with a stake in its success and that, at some point, our apparently divergent social interests intersect.

This idea rose to the fore for me during a visit to an old industrial building in northeast Hamilton. Known as the Cotton Factory, it produced boat sails, tents, awnings, and other cotton products for several decades following its construction in 1900. In its day, the building at 270 Sherman Avenue North was not only a model of imaginative design (with pleasing ornamental features such as a gigantic turret out front), but also the embodiment of an unusually enlightened approach to labour relations (with tennis courts for workers in the central courtyard, a soccer field behind the building, and tea carts that brought refreshment to the labourers). Once situated within a bustling, mixed neighbourhood of residential, industrial, and commercial buildings, it is currently a few minutes' walk from a semi-revived strip of cafés, galleries, and shops on Barton Street, but also (and more strikingly) adjacent to mostly empty industrial lots alongside a wild and overgrown former railway right-of-way. The Cotton Factory was saved from the wrecker's ball when Rob Zeidler bought it in 2014 for just under $5 million (representing perhaps half of the cost of fully reanimating this place, given the need for major investments such as a million dollars' worth of new windows).[60]

One radiant summer day, as sun streamed through those massive windows, Rob Zeidler (son of the celebrated architect Eb Zeidler, who designed Toronto's Eaton Centre and Hamilton's McMaster University Medical Centre) was preparing to welcome potential new tenants to an open house event. The guests who arrived when I was there were sharply dressed, well-coiffed youngish people, who I'm guessing were entrepreneurs of one type or another. Zeidler confirmed that he was indeed aiming to rent to people who run commercial enterprises, but there was also—and this is the unusual twist to this story—space for those less financially secure creatures known as artists (actual artists, not Creative Class poseurs). How much rent you pay here depends upon what you do. Though Zeidler doesn't like the word *subsidize*, in reality that verb goes a long way towards defining the first group's relationship to the latter.

"The long-term vision," Zeidler explained, "is to have a mix of people who are working in creative industries who can afford to pay market rent, and artists who cannot afford to pay market rent. This isn't one of those places where a landlord fills up the place with artists to make it cool, and as soon as it's cool they get rid of all the artists." Zeidler borrowed this idea of lowering the rent for worthy tenants from his sister Margie Zeidler, who runs the building at 401 Richmond in Toronto, where the mission is to provide afford-able space for socially oriented enterprises (full disclosure: Between the Lines publishing is one of those enterprises).

The Cotton Factory is a for-profit business, not a charity. ("It's healthy to make money," says Zeidler. "If your building doesn't make money, sooner or later you don't own it, and the next person who owns it will kick all the artists out and destroy everything you've created.") But the owner insists that this business is unlike conven-tional real estate companies that "have only one metric, which is 'How much money can we make?'" His non-pecuniary goal is that the mix of talent and world views among tenants, along with certain of the building's design aspects, like the common kitchenette, will nurture "a sense of community" at the Cotton Factory, so that peo-ple get to know each other and share ideas. "In my perfect world, you will walk down the halls and everyone has their doors open," he says. Encouraging that spirit of community is "a very conscious thing and something we've put a lot of thought and effort and time into."

But a sense of community also tends to arise spontaneously in Hamilton, according to Adrian Ellis, a composer of music for film and television, who moved to the city with his wife, Susanna Milenkovic, a digital marketing specialist, in 2015. Adrian sug-gested a meeting at the Relay Café ("Saving the Day Since 2008") on Concession Street. This bustling little place sits right across the road from a Halal meat market and a tad down from the Salvation Army's Hamilton Laotian Corps, landmarks indicating how this suburban thoroughfare has moved away from the monochromatic, Wonder Bread version of itself that existed thirty years ago.

Adrian likes it here. Motoring down the highway a few years back, in search of a place to live, "the minute we rounded the 403 past Highway 6 and I saw Cootes Paradise [marsh], then when we drove through downtown, it was love at first sight," he says. "I was like, 'This is just a fantastic place.'" Since then, his primary take-away from living in Hamilton for years is that it's a lot easier to make social connections here than in self-conscious, segmented Toronto. Susanna is involved with Concession Street Business Improvement Area and Adrian helps out with a big food drive organized by musicians around Christmastime. But aside from these kinds of institutional engagements, what makes it easier to feel connected here is Hamiltonians' apparent inclination to approach people when they see something needs to be done.

Adrian became aware of this after buying a barbecue and "stupidly thinking that this massive box would fit in the back seat of our sedan, which it didn't." When a "gentleman with a pick-up truck said, 'Do you want me to help you take that home?'" the recent transplants from Toronto half suspected (and this is big-city conditioning at work) that the passerby was intent on pilfering their purchase. But no—the Good Samaritan gesture was for real. The stranger put the barbecue in his pick-up, drove it up to Adrian and Susanna's home, and politely refused their offer of compensation once it was unloaded.

"We've experienced that kind of thing over and over again," says Adrian, citing another case that unfolded after a neighbour living close by fell on hard times and had to sell his house. The neighbour moved away abruptly, leaving behind "an enormous amount of animals which had been living in this chaotic home." So Adrian and Susanna joined forces with another neighbour, a fellow animal-lover, to remedy the situation. "Our little project was rescuing these cats and getting them rehomed, essentially," recalls Adrian. "Which is nothing like I would experience in Toronto, in the sense of being able to think, 'Oh, we actually did something as a little micro-community.' I feel more connected to the idea of community here than I ever have in any other city."

This sense of belonging—and of being able to contribute, in whatever way, to some expression of the common good—seems partly to grow out of a few common traits the newcomers share with long-time Hamiltonians, but it also exists despite some clear differences between them. Adrian says that he and Susanna can relate to the struggles of a large number of people in their neighbourhood who live on modest incomes because, as freelancers, their work is precarious and not hugely lucrative. On composition projects, says Adrian, he's "often working for minimum wage or less."

And although these new Hamiltonians' progressive political outlook generally meshes with the political culture of the community around them (Hamilton's urban core and its older, postwar suburbs consistently elect NDP representatives, for instance), when you get into the finer points, some sharp distinctions emerge between downtown Toronto socialists and their residually blue-collar Hamilton brethren. In Hamilton, says Adrian, people with their sympathies on the left tend to focus on workplace and economic issues like "working conditions, fair treatment, and fair wages," while their cosmopolitan Toronto counterparts are more concerned with diversity and cultural inclusion. More generally, Adrian says that Hamilton strikes him as a more insular place—you're more likely to find people here who have spent their entire lives in the city and have little wish to leave. Outsiders may mistake this insularity for xenophobia, and occasionally that impression may, sadly, be correct.

Greater than the sum of its parts?

Those are two sample scenes from the emerging Hamilton—one in the old city's industrial heart, the other almost due south of there, in a post–World War II vintage suburb overlooking the core from atop the escarpment. Both seem to support the idea that the old us-versus-them understanding of gentrifying cities doesn't always have to apply, that the standard narrative can mutate and evolve. In the first case, business owners are being asked to pay a portion of their rent to make it possible for people from a different economic bracket to keep living and producing in the same building in the same city—almost like an informal tax. In the second case, two freelance media types move to Hamilton, and rather than aiming to remake their new home in the image of the place they came from, they quickly learn to love the existing culture (or most of it, at least) in their adoptive hometown. Although it's surely unwise to extrapolate too much from two isolated conversations, a common element in these two stories is that it's possible for newcomers to act out of more than a sense of self-interest, that they can quickly develop feelings of affinity with the people in this new place and a sense of duty towards the community.

Is it possible that the era of polarization is yielding to a more inclusive, complex understanding of the city? In his analysis of the Locke Street riot on Raise the Hammer, Simon Orpana floats the controversial idea that militant anti-gentrification rhetoric and theatrics may have been a necessary corrective to the simplistic cheerleading for new investment—a shrill, piercing cry that (at least partly) managed to shatter the city-boosters' persistent denial that new investment and migration could be anything other than positive. Prior attempts to raise the negative impacts of redevelopment had been consistently dismissed as the whining of people bent on keeping Hamilton poor. "Could we identify this failure of discourse," asks Orpana, "as possibly contributing to the kind of blockage and frustration that might lead a handful of angry, idealistic protesters to lob rocks through the windows of a purveyor of premium donuts?"

Orpana does not believe that breaking windows is an effective means of resolving the negative impacts of urban redevelopment. But he does see events on Locke Street as providing a useful illustration of how public opinion has been polarized—either you oppose gentrification or you buy a four-dollar donut to express your disgust with the vandals; either you embrace artists as part of a shining new order or you despise them for their role in priming the landscape for redevelopment. This ultimately sentences Hamiltonians to remain boxed in by the "forced choice between 'keeping Hamilton poor' and embracing contemporary gentrification."

What gets lost when urban issues are framed as a "choice between exclusionary binaries," continues Orpana, are a huge range of potential solutions that might flourish on a landscape where more than just either/or is possible.[61] Finding other options, writes

Orpana, is made easier by looking at Hamilton's history, which contains multiple examples of efforts to preserve and protect "the commons"—the resources that sustain the common good, that are assigned for common use.

Hamilton's relationship to this idea of the commons goes back to its original inhabitants. The Dish with One Spoon agreement shared between the Attawandaron and their neighbouring Nations established the imperative to communally use this region's land and its abundant resources. Today, Orpana continues, a substantial, residual commons (recreational areas, health facilities, and other everyday expressions of the public good) exists as one of the "legacies of industrial capitalism." These services were nurtured during the industrial heyday of Hamilton because they were part of "the life-support systems necessary for the maintenance of a healthy workforce." Industrial trade unions, in Orpana's view, were also dedicated to preserving the commons: in the case of the Nine Hour Movement, formed in Hamilton in 1872 to fight for a shorter work week, the particular form of commons at the centre of their struggle was time.

Once again, as crises of homelessness, social polarization, and poverty emerge from what some envision as Hamilton's renaissance, a renewed focus on the commons is necessary. In fact, that's already happening, writes Orpana. A range of citizens are

> creating co-ops, collectives, and land trusts, and reinvigorating neighbourhood organizations as modes of realizing our shared stewardship of the city, and the strength and dignity we cultivate when we work with others to assert our common interests. They are continuing the practices of mutual aid, hospitality and generosity that have characterized this area's culture for centuries.[62]

True enough, there are many people in Hamilton who never bought into that binary thinking or the caricatures that accompany it. Some are attempting to draw inspiration from the city's history; others, seeking something new. They've been hard at work for years, staring down tough odds and absorbing repeated defeats in pursuit of the occasional victory, trying to map out a path to a place where equality has tangible form, where everyone can enjoy the benefits of the city's advances. Their commitment seems unlikely. The odds remain difficult. Cause for optimism remains rare. Like others in cities around the globe, there are advocates for the common good who are motivated by an attachment to a particular place and a sense that things can be better.

A Blue-Collar Legacy— for Better and for Worse

"HAMILTON'S ALWAYS BEEN a working-class city, so you get this kind of gruffness, but there's this warm, fuzzy underbelly to it," says Mark Furukawa, who came to the city in the early 1990s against the advice of his concerned, confused friends, and has remained here as the proprietor of the James North countercultural hub Dr. Disc. In Hamilton, says Furukawa, "people seem more genuine than in other places, in my experience. If people think you are a good egg, you are welcomed with open arms. Hamilton has this underdog mentality, where we all try to stick together. When you come to Hamilton, I think you get that very quickly—that people are genuinely caring and inclusive."

If Hamilton had an astrological sign, it would be Gemini: animated by two personalities, often at odds and sometimes irreconcilable. There's the warm, neighbourly persona that revealed itself to Furukawa after he'd stayed here long enough to prove that he wasn't out to fleece the locals and then high-tail it back home. But Hamilton has also been identified with mobsters, bar fights, street crime, racist skinheads, biker gangs, and an assortment of other threatening forces that have flourished, at various points, amid the crumbling housing stock and beneath the canopy of tainted air.

Ironically, this negative image of Hamilton once made it possible to afford a roof over your head if you were poor. "When Toronto discovered us, that changed everything," says Jeff Neven, who runs the Indwell social housing organization. "Prior to that, there was a stigma attached to Hamilton, particularly the lower city. And that stigma protected the affordability of our housing." Not only is that stigma now shattered, but many of the formerly offputting aspects of life here have been recharacterized, within the romantic narrative of the real estate biz, as positive things. A culture once dismissed as unsophisticated is now hailed as authentic; the shadow of industry is no longer dirty and déclassé but part of the local flavour.

Yet as much as this idea of a city having a recognizable character is prone to manipulation for commercial gain, it's also reasonable to suggest that Hamilton has a genuine civic persona—a real and substantial psychological profile, distinct from the flimsy sloganeering and casually tossed clichés—and that it likely has an influence over how life is lived here. Common histories and shared experience help mould local communities and their institutions in both positive and negative ways. And if you accept that premise, well, that leads to a host of questions for a city that's searching for a sense of itself and a new path into the future. Can history be the basis for a roadmap forward? Are there unique aspects of Hamilton's past that can help it avoid the worst aspects of gentrification that sullied other post-industrial landscapes? What sort of entrenched characteristics are best left behind? What kinds of dreams stand a good chance of taking root on the local soil?

Many of the people interviewed for this book—people who've been trying to envision an egalitarian, inclusive new city emerging on the vacant land and acres of parking lots where sprawling factories and thriving commercial districts once stood—answer those questions in a strangely hopeful manner. Strange in the sense that those same people will also offer a depressingly long list of obstacles to positive change, from a general societal shift towards self-absorption and isolation, to the influence of big money over planning, to unsympathetic responses from higher levels of government, to a history of lost opportunities and dysfunctional decision making at the municipal level. But in the face of all that, they also say that communities in Hamilton regularly exhibit an uncommon tendency to pull together and look out for the vulnerable. There are many ideas as to why this is the case. One you're likely to encounter frequently is that the "all for one" sentiment is a vestige of the city's history of blue-collar toil, hard-fought union battles, and associated triumphs and tragedies. Sadness, hardship, and struggle have found their way into the soil, and they have a palpable impact on the city today.

A historic tipping point in 1946

To get a more detailed sense of how these values have been transmitted from the past into the present, and to cast about for ideas on their implications for Hamilton's future, let's venture up to the eastern edge of the Mountain, the postwar suburban frontier atop the Niagara Escarpment. We'll visit with Bill Scandlan, who had witnessed the birth of Hamilton as a rock-solid union town and participated in the more general transformation of the city that flowed from that. Not so many years ago, the most influential institution in blue-collar Hamilton was the United Steelworkers' Local 1005, and the most formative historical moment, by common consensus, was the great Stelco strike of 1946. Scandlan was involved with the union and participated in that historic strike.

Scandlan passed away in September 2019, at ninety-five years old.[1] At the time of our interview, he was ninety-one, highly convivial and still sharp. He was eager to reflect on his days within the labour movement and on how he carried that experience out into his work in the community. Scandlan had been my parents' city councillor for some of my youth (he spent twelve years in municipal politics) and—before retiring in the 1990s—had served on a number of local boards.

These roles were outgrowths of his earlier vocation as a union official with the United Steelworkers. "I spent thirty-three years as a staff rep and the last ten years I was an area supervisor," he said. Scandlan learned about politics and administration through trial and error and hands-on experience. He had a particular expertise in pension finance (vividly on display when he took a call from the Canada Revenue Agency during our interview) that he acquired not at college but through contract negotiations and by picking the brains of the insurance actuaries hired by the union.

Scandlan lived in a nice neighbourhood of well-kept ranch houses and expansive, neatly groomed lawns. There was an older-model car in his driveway that he regretted he was no longer allowed to drive. His home spoke of a lengthy retirement and an earlier working life played out in the kind of unassuming suburban comfort that I would associate with this area from having lived fairly close by as a kid. (Our house, in an older segment of the neighbourhood, was decidedly more downscale.) But that day, Scandlan talked not so much about the good years that industrial workers enjoyed in places like these throughout the heady 1950s, sixties, and seventies. Instead, the conversation veered more often towards the lean times that led people to dream of something better. His description of growing up poor conjured an image of life that seemed a million miles removed from this quiet street of prosperity and contentment.

During the Depression "there were seven of us and my mother had fifty dollars a month to pay for rent, fuel, clothing, food, and everything else," Scandlan said, sitting at his kitchen table. "I remember my mother, when she made a big pot of stew, taking some of that to the neighbour next door because her husband was away on a [railway] section crew and she had no money and two kiddies there. She was crying because she didn't know what she was going to have for supper. My mother takes some of this big stew that the seven of us were going to have and shares it with them. We hardly knew them, but they were hungry and needed help and that was the way my mother was."

Scandlan would see the same spirit of sharing expressed during the landmark Steelworkers strike of 1946, a monumental stand-off that would fundamentally change how business was done in the city. Scandlan had been set on the road to union activism in 1942 when, at the age of eighteen, he landed a job at Stelco. After a brief departure to train for the army, he returned to the foundry and soon found himself playing a novel role in a drama that seized the emotions of the city and even the country.

"You have to remember," he told me, "it was just after the war and here come all these guys who had come back crippled—you know, all kinds of hell they went through, and then they come back and get told everything is going to be the same. You know: 'Back to the dungeon.' They resented it. And there was great sympathy [among the public] for the vets."

Recalling the 1946 strike in their captivating graphic history *Showdown: The Making of Modern Unions*, Rob Kristofferson and Simon Orpana portray the summer-long stand-off as a make or break moment, the one last chance for leaving the bad old days behind. Before the war, labourers at Stelco had worked up to twelve hours a day, five and a half or six days a week, in intensely hot, noisy, and smoky conditions. Accidents were commonplace and foremen had free rein to bully and often extort the mostly Italian and Eastern European workers who were given the low-skilled, low-paid jobs that came without any form of job security.

"Men who wanted to keep their job," the authors wrote, "often had to slip the foreman a pack of cigarettes with a few dollars tucked inside every payday, or leave a bottle of whiskey on his desk." There was even one story of a labourer who, on payday, had to "take his boss home, put a bottle of wine on the table, and leave him there with his wife for a couple hours."

Unionism had gained some footholds slowly and by increments. The Independent Steel Workers' Union—formed in response to a 33 per cent wage cut for sheet mill workers between 1929 and 1933— staged a ten-day strike in 1935. It won wage increases but failed in its quest to have Stelco recognize the union. A year later, Stelco workers sought representation by the Steel Workers Organizing Committee, an affiliate of the U.S.-based Congress of Industrial Organizations (CIO), leading to the formation of the later-to-be-famous Local 1005 at Stelco. While labour peace prevailed through World War II, the federal government of W.L. Mackenzie King passed order-in-council PC 1003 in 1944, legalizing unions in workplaces where the majority had voted for them. Consequently, numerous unions were certified and negotiated contracts at workplaces throughout industrial Hamilton—including at Stelco, where Local 1005 signed its first contract.

But with the end of the war, businesses and government tried to roll back those advances. In July 1946, King signed another order-in-council stating that the government was taking over the steel industry (though the companies remained privately owned, profit-making entities) and outlawing strikes. Workers in industries across Canada and the United States went out on strike that year to consolidate their former gains. (At Stelco, Local 1005's demands were for a forty-hour work week, union recognition, and mandatory contribution of union dues from the workers' wages.) The battle at Stelco became a symbolic struggle and a bellwether for the prospects for trade unionism in the post–World War II era.[2]

Bill Scandlan recalled that—as Local 1005 stared down a Stelco management determined to vanquish the union—the Steelworkers were buoyed by the support of a wide network of sympathizers. In the searing summer of 1946, workers from Westinghouse and Firestone, who were themselves out on strike, picketed in support of the Steelworkers, and donations rolled in from other unions, international and national, because "unions across the country knew that this was the strike for unionization in Canada. If Stelco fails, all else fails. So they contributed. If you got fifty or a hundred bucks, that was a lot." Farmers donated produce to support strikers' families, businesses chipped in by providing services, and brigades of union "moochers" would "go 'round to the various stores for the sandwiches. We had a crew that walked down Barton Street and King Street to the butcher shops to ask for baloney or whatever the hell they could get, and another went to Brown's Bakery for day-old bread."

A rented basement below a store at Barton and Ottawa served as a union welfare office where provisions would be bagged and distributed to keep steelworker families afloat while management tried to wear down their resolve. Ottawa pressured the mayor to read the riot act so they could send in the RCMP and the army to disperse the strikers, but Mayor Sam Lawrence, "an old-country labour guy from the stonecutters' union and, of course, a great friend of Hamilton working people," showed his support on the picket line instead.

For his part, Scandlan, then a vice-president of his local, was put in charge of the entertainment committee (an area he knew nothing about) "so that [they] had some morale boosting." As he described it, "We organized a Friday night variety show and got talent. There's all kinds of talent people have that you don't know about: someone plays the fiddle, the guitar, the mouth organ, or whatever." A highlight was a three-day stopover by the son of a high-ranking union officer who had become an opera singer with New York's celebrated Metropolitan Opera. Scandlan recalls finding him an accompanist who normally played during lunch hours at Woolworths and worrying that a singer from the Met might not want to work with a pianist who could only play by ear. "He was good," Scandlan said of the pianist. "But for an opera singer?" Still, they practised together a bit and in the end their collaboration was "beautiful."

The novice entertainment director felt similar trepidation when "someone suggested [they] get a hold of Pete Seeger." Clueless about how to track him down, Scandlan and his committee ultimately acquired the celebrated folk singer's telephone number through the director of the rubber workers' union and simply "picked up the phone and called him." Seeger agreed to perform, flew into what was then the Malton airport outside Toronto, and arrived in Hamilton to give a performance at the picket line, outside the main gates of Stelco, just as rumours that police were getting set to bust up the strikers' line had started to make people uneasy.

"It was one hell of a crowd," Scandlan remembered. "When we got it all set up and we got Pete up there, there were about twenty-five thousand people, enough to close the street. At that time, the streetcars ran, and they just couldn't go—there were just so many people. It was a warm August night, and all along where the hot mill was, the scabs off-shift were sitting out there because it was hotter than hell inside. And they could hear Pete Seeger up there, singing 'Roll the Union On.' 'If the scabs get in the way, then we'll roll over them,' and the whole crowd singing along with Pete. It was quite an evening."

In a city where pro-union sympathies ran high (Ontario Provincial Police officers brought in to break the strike were refused accommodation everywhere in Hamilton), the heart of community support ran along Burlington Street, close to the steel mills. "There were a lot of Italian people who lived along there," recalled Scandlan. "Every Friday, they set up these tables and ran a spaghetti and meatball dinner for the strikers. The women cooked the stuff and they set these tables up and everybody enjoyed it." Hamilton's Italian population had a special stake in the strikers' cause because of the treatment Italian workers had typically received. Opportunities for promotion were reserved for employees of British heritage, while Italians were given the worst jobs and often treated with contempt. "Over the Depression years," recalled Scandlan, "people used to line up to get a job. The company people would come out and say, 'You, you, and you.' They'd go to work and if you complained, the boss would say, especially to the Italians, 'Hey look, you dago, there's ten more like you out there. If you don't do what I say you're gone. I've got ten more who can replace you.'"

The eventual victory by the union brought some fundamental changes to the tone and substance of workplace relations. Stelco president Hugh Hilton (who "was like Winston Churchill in his features" and notable for his "off-with-your-head attitude," said Scandlan) stepped down, leaving room for a more enlightened new guard. Animosity yielded, as Scandlan remembered it, as management realized that "without the workers, they don't make a dime—the Steel Company is a piece of scrap," and as the union recognized that "the management we had in there were decent people. There was that kind of respect showing."

The Stelco strike of 1946 was history-making in many respects. As Kristofferson and Orpana document in *Showdown*, the dramatic ways in which the confrontation was played out left a colourful mythology for future generations. Beyond the picket lines on land, there were both airborne and naval skirmishes. When Hugh Hilton attempted to bring in strikebreakers and supplies by boat, for example, his forces were interfered with by strikers in a speedboat (the *Whisper*, allegedly once owned by a rum-runner). And when the union attempted to drop leaflets by plane for the strikebreakers in the plant, a Stelco plane flew into the path of the union's aircraft.

More to the point, the Stelco strike also changed the face of labour relations in Canada. Kristofferson and Orpana contend that not only did the strike lead to a more secure workplace, better pay, and benefits such as insurance and pension plans, but it also helped change the social climate in a way that made new government programs like unemployment insurance, old age pensions, and universal health care possible.[3]

From the picket line to the arena of politics

Bill Scandlan also believed that the ascendency of Local 1005, as a result of the Stelco strike, changed the way that Hamilton functioned as a community. Working people won greater representation in civic institutions, as labour officials ran for public office, labour organizations endorsed other sympathetic candidates (such as sportscaster Vic Copps, who became enormously popular as mayor in the sixties and seventies), and working-class people took a hand in steering local agencies.

Scandlan himself ran for city council in 1964 and was one of six successful labour candidates (along with three school board trustees). Around this time, the newly minted politician and other members of the city's Labour Council noticed that although "there would be appointments for all kinds of community positions, there was never a labour appointee. It was always somebody's friend" who was picked. Having observed that "if you had a baseball team or a hockey team it would always be our guys—the moms and dads—who came out to help," the trade unionists decided to put this spirit of volunteerism to work in other spheres. Labour leaders approached members who had distinguished themselves in the union setting and encouraged them to serve on the parks board, the library board, the hospital boards, and other municipal bodies.

"The parks board, for example, what the hell is that for? Well, the parks are for kids. And who's got kids? We do." Scandlan says the exercise unleashed new energy. "We knew people who could do the job. The fellow who wrote our paper, *Steel Shots*, a monthly paper all about grievances and settlements, we asked him to go the library board, and he did. He was on it about six months and the chairman of the library board comes to me and he says, 'Holy Christ, where did you find that guy?' I said, 'Why?' He said, 'This guy's wonderful.' He had all kinds of ideas about what the library board should be doing. They were pleased as punch with him."

Scandlan himself went on to sit on the board of the Art Gallery of Hamilton (AGH), the Community Living board (for people with disabilities), McMaster University's board, and the Chedoke-McMaster hospital board, in addition to helping to found the community information services agency. At McMaster, Scandlan worked with others to insert labour studies into the curriculum; it later became a degree program. The focus on contributing to post-secondary institutions, Scandlan explained, was an outgrowth of the Hamilton Labour Council's broader understanding that access to education was a crucial means for working-class families to escape the restrictions of their traditional social roles and broaden the range of opportunities available to their children.

"We wanted our kids to go to university because, in the old days, Mom and Pop probably only went to grade four. If the son or daughter gets to high school that's wonderful, but when a kid finally gets to university, they're really on cloud nine. They feel so good not only because they've accomplished something, but because the world needs them and their country needs them. Our philosophy was 'Let your brain take you as far as possible.' And there should be no financial barriers. In the old days, it used to be the doctor or lawyer profession was passed down from father to son. Because who else could afford the tuition?"

In this and other ways, Scandlan said union activists not only affected change locally but also introduced new ideas that had national impact. An example is the Steelworkers' blood bank, introduced in the early 1950s, ten years before Canada had medicare. It all started with the plight of one individual person, the aunt of a union officer who "was going for serious surgery and required several blood transfusions. But they had no money and no coverage of any kind. She would need at least twenty pints of blood and it was twenty dollars a pint." When the officer raised the matter at an executive meeting, Scanlan recalled thinking of the massive participation in blood drives that happened during the war. "I thought, if we did it in wartime, why the hell can't we do it now?"

Scandlan hatched a plan that would wind up helping many more than just this one person in need. "I went to the manager in our plant and said, 'I have a favour to ask.' I told him the story and he said, 'That's too bad.' I said we're going to get blood from volunteers—we'll put up a flyer and people can give blood at the hospital. He said, 'That's goddamn noble. Good for you.'" After a bit of back and forth, the union persuaded management to spring for two hours' pay for volunteers who went to the hospital to give blood at shift change. Soon there was too much blood for the needs of the nearby Hamilton General Hospital, the original intended recipient, and the Steelworkers' volunteer blood bank began supplying all the city's hospitals. A trucking company that had provided transport during the 1946 strike voluntarily hauled the blood to the hospitals. "We advertised," Scandlan continued, "and we had people from unions and non-unions saying, 'Could we get some blood?' and we just said, 'Sure.' We said we'd turn nobody down. That's how we established the Steelworkers' blood bank. The Red Cross took it over and after that they started doing it across the country."

This characteristic of looking well beyond the shop floor and into the community, says Don Jaffray of the Social Planning and Research Council, made the Steelworkers a key ally for any group working for the poor and forgotten in Hamilton. Today, Jaffray concedes, although "the Steelworkers have a great legend, they don't have the power to mobilize like they used to," given the massive losses of employment in steel production. Still, before the steel industry melted down, the Steelworkers' influence lasted for decades. They were well organized, well heeled, and always highly attuned to the plight of people living on the margins or encountering difficult circumstances.

"I think the Steelworkers somehow found closer affiliation with people who struggled," says Jaffray, himself a former steelworker, "maybe because there were a lot of injured workers among them and families who had lost people because of a high incidence of cancer in the industry. They seemed a little more sensitive, a little more attuned, to families who had hit the wall."

Today, although new unions have risen to the fore, Jaffray believes that the expansive spirit of an earlier age has been replaced, to a noticeable degree, by a creeping tunnel vision. The largest unionized group in Hamilton today is the hospital workers. "When they do a charitable drive, they think about the health charity. And the big educational institutions, there's a lot of unionized staff at those places, and they think mostly about educational investments."

Jaffray says this tendency feeds into a trend where the powerful fundraising machines in the health and education sector have eroded the power of community-wide, collaborative efforts like the United Way to funnel funds to a wider group of recipients. "The big, institutional charitable trawlers are very high-tech and highly skilled and they've got a very clear product to pitch. Their message reaches into a lot of families. People say, 'That health issue—that's me. That poverty issue—that's not me.' People are drawn to investing in education and in health. But investing in poor people doesn't really compete."

Jaffray tempers his clear frustration with Hamilton's post-industrial unions with a measure of diplomacy. "There's a lot to be said for the more professional unions: the teachers' associations, the health worker unions. They have some very talented people. But they don't seem to be reaching the whole spectrum of community issues that the Steelworkers did."

Enter the beatniks and the hippies

That Steelworker-inspired, community-centred ethic shows up in places you might not expect it; not just in social service work but also in the arts community. A case in point is a now-defunct organization called Hamilton-Wentworth Creative Arts. Influential in the 1970s and for a while beyond that, they staged the annual Festival of Friends (held one weekend in August in Gage Park), ran an art gallery and a coffee house, managed a stable of musicians, and had a small record label and a publishing arm that included a monthly newspaper called *Random Scan*.

Creative Arts played an important role in the city's bohemian subculture, which, on the surface, seemed worlds apart from the mainstream blue-collar, Steelworker culture, with its practical and regimented outlook, its conformity and tough-guy veneer. But one clear point of connection is a veneration of the idea of community and a "one for all, all for one" ethic. Time for another personal disclosure: I had the good fortune of being hired as a reporter with *Random Scan*, Creative Arts' tabloid, in the late seventies (having left—but not quite graduated from—high school). That gave me a chance, like probably dozens of other young people who drifted in and out during that era, to develop some basic craft in a creative field and to have exposure to an actual audience. It also provided the opportunity to get to know, to a limited extent, the firebrand couple who ran Creative Arts, Bill and Lynne Powell.

Bill, whom we heard from in chapter one, passed away in 2015, shortly after being interviewed for this project. His lineage as a Hamilton notable went directly back to the labour aristocracy that transformed Hamilton in the wake of the 1946 strike. His father, Bill Powell Sr., who had been chief steward at the all-powerful Steelworkers' Local 1005, was one of that handful of labour candidates elected to council alongside Bill Scandlan in 1964. He had also been head honcho of the regional conservation authority and served as mayor in the 1980s. Bill the younger brought to the scene a kind of bohemian variant of the civic boosterism his father embodied.

Bill Jr. was bearded, bearish, and blustery; a heavy-smoking, type-A extrovert who was typically sighted swaying to the rhythm just off stage at the Festival of Friends or introducing a new act at the Knight II coffee house. Lynne stayed more in the background but was spoken of as the person who kept the whole locomotive on the rails. Quietly good-humoured, seemingly unflappable, and apparently blessed with a supernatural administrative acumen, she was responsible for all those unglamorous essentials like grant applications and payroll. She also helped typeset the newspaper and cooked the chili at the coffee house.

Years later (well, decades, actually), I called Lynne and Bill to ask if we could meet to discuss where their enterprises fit within the larger story of Hamilton. Lynne told me that Bill hadn't been well and that his memory was sometimes fuzzy. When Bill came to the phone, he was philosophical: "I'm seventy-six now and things fall apart." When I visited their tidy, suburban bungalow in Dundas, they provided a few more details on the precise type of hell the two of them had been through over the past four years. Bill had broken his hip but had been made to wait a very long time for a replacement because his cardiologist wouldn't clear him for surgery. In the interim, he was on heavy pain medication that put him "right out of it" and at one point made him berserk enough to lunge at a hospital orderly. Eventually, Bill had the surgery and came off the drugs. At the time of our conversation, things seemed to be looking up. Bill was going with Lynne to a local gym each day to work out, partly to try to regain some of the muscle mass he had lost while his hip was out of commission. Another one of Bill's daily rituals was watching a favourite cowboy show that played on the Aboriginal Peoples Television Network. They had four small dogs (three of them chihuahuas) that barked manically when a stranger would come to the door. Although Bill's health would take a turn for the worse in the coming months, there was a definite upbeat feel to the conversation that afternoon.

Lynne had to fill in a few of the details for Bill—What year did this happen? What particular piece of real estate were they occupying at the time?—but both reconstructed the history of their quixotic enterprises with equal enthusiasm. Their parade of recollections began in the 1960s with the Ebony Knight coffee house, a performance/crash space located at the corner of Caroline and Main Streets in "a monster of a house," recalled Bill. "We rented half of it and hippies rented the other half. At one time there were twenty-two people living and working in the coffee house. It was a crash place for anybody coming through. Brownie McGhee came and stayed for a week. Joni Mitchell stayed there for a short period of time. So did Murray McLauchlan. He lived in my closet. True story."

Open from roughly 1963 to 1968 or '69 (these are the details that become more elusive as time passes), the Ebony Knight, in Bill's retelling, attracted not just wandering musicians but also visual artists, curious academics from across town at McMaster, and fanatical chess players. "We had one guy who was a Canadian master," said Bill. "He'd come in, hit the clock, and play twenty-three games of speed chess and win them all." Although the Ebony Knight could be seen, in hindsight, as a prototype of the kind of arts establishments that today's civic leaders welcome to the downtown core—the ideal of a "creative hub" that urban visionaries have come to embrace as a key to reanimating Rust Belt communities—in the sixties a very different dynamic was at play.

In a typical blue-collar Ontario town of the time—the kind of place distinguished by towering stone churches and sullen, windowless beer parlours with separate entrances for gentlemen and ladies and escorts—hives of bohemian exuberance were greeted, at best, with suspicion. "First we were a curiosity," recalled Bill. "Then we were feared. The Mounties would drop in regularly but they never found anything, not even a roach. That's because we had a deal [with coffee house guests] that if you want to smoke, you smoke out there. If you've got a stash, you go to stash it out there. I didn't want it on my property because it would have been the demise of something very, very good."

Lynne met Bill when the effects of entropy had taken hold and the Ebony Knight was on the verge of closing. Having moved to Hamilton from the even more conservative Paris, Ontario, Lynne had married a banker, had a daughter, and then divorced. She was working at a bank and one day was invited to a lunch that her manager had convened to celebrate the Grey Cup. One of the other guests that afternoon was Bill Powell, whom Lynne knew as an occasional customer, notable for his beard. Not long after (Lynne pegged it as the summer of 1971), Bill, Lynne, and her young daughter formed a new family unit and Lynne—who had grown up in a strict Seventh Day Adventist family where listening to Elvis Presley was considered a sin—found herself on the yonder side of the social divide that seemed to define the era.

"We were hippies," she said. "Although I went to work every day in an office, I'd come home at night and put on my peasant dress. We lived in a bus, and right by it was a big tent run by a gentleman by the name of John Dee. He ran theatre in the tent in the evening, and in the lobby of the tent we put art." Still, Lynne was not your typical hippie. Her business background and practical outlook would have a noticeable impact as the couple began launching the myriad grassroots artistic ventures that would ultimately coalesce as a kind of local arts empire. Years later, Lynne says her success in overseeing the left-brain functions of Hamilton-Wentworth Creative Arts was partly the result of having been mentored, in her pre-hippie days, by Ellen Fairclough, "a really great lady" whom Lynne worked for at an institution called Hamilton Trust and Savings. Fairclough, who had been Canada's first woman cabinet minister, "taught me a lot," recalled Lynne. "She taught me about being organized and doing things right. I've always prided myself on having good practical skills like budgeting. I think that's why we always kept on top of things financially."

When Lynne was pregnant with their son, the Powells forsook the bus and the tent and opened up the Canvas Gallery (named after the canvas you make tents from rather than the canvas you paint on) and the Knight II coffee house in a three-storey apartment building on Augusta Street. They bought the building with a down payment consisting of a hundred of their own dollars and contributions from four friends. They did well enough that they decided to buy a second building. But that didn't work out so well. When interest rates climbed above 20 per cent, the whole enterprise teetered on the brink. Fortunately, another big-hearted friend came to the rescue.

"There was a really wealthy friend of ours," said Lynne, "and he went down and talked to John Sheppard, who at that point was the vice-president of finance for Dofasco." The resulting chain of events proves that it's good to have friends in high places. "He said to John, 'This young couple are working hard for the arts and they really deserve a break.' And John said, 'Who has their mortgage?' I think it was Canada Permanent at the time. So he said, 'Yeah, I know them.' And he calls the president of the bank or someone like that, and basically says, 'Lay off these people. They are trying to sell the building and they will pay you back.' That saved our bacon, and we were able to go back to running our business."

With disaster averted, things really took off after the city (which had been lobbied by arts groups to institute a showcase for their work) suggested that the Powells apply for some of the funds that the provincial government had just made available for cultural events. Lynne put a budget and a proposal together and hit the jackpot. The result was the inaugural Festival of Friends in 1977, programmed in partnership with London, Ontario, impresarios John and Joanne Smale, who had deeper connections on the Canadian music scene. The festival has run each year since then, although, since Bill and Lynne retired, under different management and with a different focus and an out-of-town venue. Lynne also takes pride in having run a handful of other festivals in later years—an environmental festival, a multicultural festival, a medieval festival, and others—and never losing a dime on any of them.

Hamilton as a long-standing artistic hub

Though Bill and Lynne Powell were arguably the city's highest-profile arts impresarios in the seventies and eighties, they were by no means the only people promoting culture in this blue-collar town. Hamilton has a long and rich history of involvement with the arts, both high-brow and populist. Look around downtown and you'll notice that the Art Gallery of Hamilton sits smack dab in the centre of town, on a prime chunk of real estate that sprawls between the central thoroughfares of King and Main Streets, facing city hall on one side and Jackson Square on the other. You can take this as evidence that Hamilton has long dreamed of being more than just a steel town.

Those aspirations have survived and sometimes flourished as the years flew past. The AGH came into being in 1914 following the donation of a group of paintings by Hamilton-born and internationally recognized artist William Blair Bruce—a gift that came with the caveat that the city must provide a suitable exhibition space. At first, the AGH collection (which has since grown to include over ten thousand works by the likes of Canadian painters Alex Colville, Tom Thomson, Emily Carr, and Norval Morrisseau, alongside international artists) languished for several decades in a dingy set of rooms in a library on Main Street. In 1953, in the midst of the post–World War II boom that promised to bring life's finer things to the masses, the AGH relocated to a new, purpose-built art deco building close to the McMaster University, sparking a major fundraising effort by the gallery's Women's Volunteer Committee and enabling, in turn, the acquisition of over a hundred works between 1954 and 1975.

The gallery opened its current building in 1975, one of the few happy outcomes of the city's problematic Civic Square urban renewal scheme. In its new location, the AGH made some new friends, including Joey and Toby Tanenbaum, who in 2003 donated more than two hundred works of nineteenth-century European art to the gallery.[4] The AGH is not, however, the only local institution to benefit from the largesse of prosperous art collectors. The Herman H. Levy Collection at McMaster University is named after a prominent Hamilton jeweller and diamond seller who liquidated the family business in 1960 to devote himself to acquiring art. In the mid-eighties, Levy gifted McMaster's art museum with over 185 European and American works, including paintings by Camille Pissarro, Claude Monet, and Vincent van Gogh.[5]

Hamilton's unlikely role as a home to internationally significant collections of fine art, says Rosemary Donegan, curator and former board member at the Hamilton-based Workers Arts and Heritage Centre (WAHC), is largely a testament to the success and influence of the city's entrepreneurs and industrialists. But this is matched by an equally vigorous pursuit of artistic expression by Hamiltonians from more humble backgrounds. A website called Building Cultural Legacies Hamilton provides a catalogue of some of the artists, galleries, and community groups—many of them specifically focused on reflecting the concerns of working people—that have made their mark in the Steel City across multiple decades.

Consider, for example, Paul Cvetich, a brewery worker turned sculptor whose *Day of Mourning* memorial, a powerful tribute to workers killed and injured on the job, stands at the corner of Main and Bay Streets. Cvetich is without question a product of Hamilton's artistic milieu: he received his training from McMaster University as well as from the Dundas Valley School of Art, a legendary local hub that has provided classes and exhibition space for artists at all levels (while often challenging community tastes and standards) since the early 1960s.

A long list of private galleries, co-ops, and artists' organizations have nurtured Hamilton's arts scene and provided support and spotlights for the city's artists. Hamilton Artists Inc. (discussed earlier in these pages) has been a fixture on James North since the 1970s. The Photographers' Union, meanwhile, took shape in 1982 to advance the work of documentary and art photographers from a home on Napier Street. Though its tenure in the city was short—founder Lynne Sharman moved the organization to Thunder Bay after four years—its lasting contributions include the organization of a conference that led to the formation of the Native Indian/Inuit Photographers' Association, which has retained its connections to Hamilton.

There is also the hybrid creature (part historical museum, part art gallery) known as the Workers Arts and Heritage Centre. The product of several years of collaborative planning by a group of labour historians, artists, and community and union activists, WAHC opened in 1996 on Stuart Street, in the old Custom House, a historic North End gem that required two million dollars' worth of renovations to return to a habitable state. In its role as a museum, WAHC presents exhibits documenting the lives and experiences of working people and major events in the labour movement history. (It also fulfills this function through its Workers' City website, which provides photos and materials for a series of self-guided walking tours focused on various aspects of Hamilton's blue-collar history.) In 2007, WAHC made good on its promise (alluded to in its name) to provide arts programming, opening a main gallery that features exhibitions of contemporary art with relevance to working life and working people.[6]

Counterculture meets blue-collar culture

The egalitarian, unpretentious attitude that distinguishes a sizable segment of Hamilton's artistic and cultural activities, past and present, was also woven into Bill and Lynne Powell's flagship project, the Festival of Friends. The festival clearly reflected the character of the community where it was born. In its musical program and in the accompanying countercultural trappings (health food concessions, craft stands, and so on), the Festival of Friends wasn't substantially different from a multitude of smaller folk fests that formed a cross-Canada circuit. But those other events were typically admission-charging ventures targeting a community of acoustic music fans who sought the company of the like-minded. The Powells saw their festival as an offering to all of the people of Hamilton, a public gathering built on a core value of openness to people across social, economic, and cultural divides and accessible to people of all ages.

"We were always pressured to charge admission and we always said no," recalled Lynne. At one particular time "[the city] said, 'You should put in a beer garden because this will make money for you,' and we said no, because we didn't want to separate families. Our laws are so strict in Ontario that you can't just wander around with a beer. So dads and moms might be in here and the kids are out there, and we didn't want that." And when stray kids did start hanging around, looking like they might make trouble, the organizers didn't shoo them away but gave them T-shirts and assigned them tasks as volunteers. "Our whole idea was to try to be as inclusive as possible and to appeal to people's best behaviour and their better instincts," said Lynne. Though it may have assumed greater significance through the misty lens of nostalgia, what the Powells remembered most fondly, looking back on events from the living room of their bungalow, were the platoons of young people gathering garbage after the musicians had all assembled onstage for the ritual crooning of "Good Night, Irene," the festival's nightly farewell anthem. They also expressed some amazement that, despite the size of the event, no one was ever arrested at the Festival of Friends.

Not that that it was never a possibility. Bill remembered one tense afternoon of discussions with the chief of police, who had brought a generous supply of cops and police wagons to Gage Park after learning that fifty or so members of the Satan's Choice motorcycle gang were motoring up from Niagara Falls. Bill recalled requesting that the police park the wagons outside the park (or rather: "I told the police chief, 'Get your fucking stuff out of here and take them to that empty lot over there'") and mobilizing volunteers to fence off an impromptu motorcycle parking pen.

Bill remembered the events that followed with an unlikely combination of Steelworker bravado and flower-child idealism. "Okay," he began, "so they are coming down Lawrence Road and everyone is shitting a brick. I come walking up the alleyway and they come in the driveway. I say, 'Who's in charge?' They say, 'Frenchie is.' 'Okay, Mr. Frenchie, this is the deal. I want to welcome you. I want to make you all welcome. Just a few rules—nothing that's hard to do. Number one, I've got a compound the guys built for you right over there. And you'll get a board to put under your kick stands so the bikes won't topple on the ground. All I'm asking is that you strike your colours and put them in your bag and I will put two guards on the compound so no one but Choice people can get in. We'll look after it and hopefully we'll see you not only this year but next year as well.' Anyhow, it worked."

So Altamont was not replayed in Hamilton. Bill said this was no surprise to him, given the spirit of kinship that descended upon Gage Park each year at festival time. "We had parking lots and we should have created the worst traffic jam in the fucking world," he said. "But the people would pull out and they would wait for the other guy to get through, and the cops would say, 'We emptied the park in fifteen minutes.' I said, 'Yeah, because they were in a mood to co-operate and share.'" Bill saw this spirit of friendliness as almost a supernatural force: "You could feel the vibes in Hamilton," he said, using a flower-child idiom that I wouldn't have associated with Bill when I knew him in the seventies. "As our advertising started, you would feel the vibes lift. And then for two weeks after [the Festival ended], they were floating on it."

It's easy to write off this description as a kind of euphoric hyperbole arising, perhaps, from the passing of time or from the effects that a years-long medical nightmare had on Bill's recollections. But most people who were there would likely agree with the basic point underlying Bill's rhetorical embellishments: that the park felt thoroughly safe when the Festival of Friends was on. And this, it must be said, represented a remarkable state of affairs in east-end Hamilton during the 1970s. This Haight-Ashbury scenario of peace and love in the park provides a stunning contrast to the bleaker reality of daily life in the city.

It's not hyperbole to describe Hamilton in its industrial heyday as a place seething with violence. There were stabbings and shootings outside the most notorious bars and random ambushes in many neighbourhoods after dark. Gangs—the Parkdale gang, the Sherman gang, the Barton-Sherman gang—were well known, with their exploits routinely making it into the pages of the *Hamilton Spectator*. Even leaving aside the legends of Johnny Papalia, who had run a cross-border crime syndicate from central Hamilton, and the biker gangs holed up in militarized fortresses by the waterfront, industrial-age Hamilton could easily have provided the setting for one of Martin Scorsese's darker cinematic imaginings.

Reckoning with hate, death, and indifference

When I brought this reputation to Bill's attention, he did acknowledge that violence was a part of life in Hamilton, but he downplayed the idea that it was a defining factor for the city. Still, his reminiscences were peppered with tales of physical threat. He talked of having to defend himself from an attempted mugging while supply teaching shop class—before his arts enterprises could pay the bills—at Scott Park high school. (The kids "resented authority and they were from split homes," he explains. "Their strength was in the gang they belonged to, and in that situation, it matters who is the toughest. Fortunately, I was pretty big.") On another occasion, a handful of guys drinking in a North End bar had read a story in the *Spec* quoting Bill, in his painter persona, saying "We are all magnolias." They stormed up to the coffee house wanting to beat up the guy who talked about being a flower, but were repelled and ejected by the resident beatniks. There is some humour to be found in that account, but none whatsoever in the tale of Bill's artist friend Phil Stone, who died in 1975 after being gay-bashed by a gang of thugs.

"They threw him in front of a bus," Bill recalled. "He went to the hospital but they wouldn't serve him because of the way he was dressed, all painted up and with belts this wide and boots this high. He was a gentle, gentle man. He lived with us for a while. They threw him in front of a bus, and the nurses wouldn't treat him because they thought he was a kook, so he went home and died." (Published reports have it that Phil died by suicide after the beating).[7]

The dark side of the old Hamilton—a city where prejudice and violence were never far below the surface—still exists. Consider the chilling similarities between Bill's story of the death of his artist friend Phil (and the role that institutional indifference played in it) and another tragedy that made its way into the headlines over forty years later. On December 2, 2017, nineteen-year-old Yosif Al-Hasnawi, who had begun medical studies at Brock University, was shot outside the Al-Mustafa Islamic Centre as he tried to stop two young men from accosting an older man. Witnesses reported that, when paramedics arrived, they accused Yosif of "acting," did not treat him, and at one point even shook him.[8] The young Good Samaritan, as bystanders described him, died during the prolonged trip to the hospital.

The paramedics were later fired and Yosif's family launched a ten-million-dollar lawsuit against Hamilton's police, the paramedic service, and St. Joseph's hospital.[9] At the criminal trial of paramedics Christopher Marchant and Steven Snively, eventually found guilty of failing to provide the necessities of life, expert witness Dr. Patrick Croskerry testified the first responders were influenced by eight "subconscious biases," including one that often comes into play when authorities deal with people from minorities or marginalized groups.[10] In this more recent tragedy, the victim is not a gay artist but a young Muslim man, but the other details are uncannily similar to those in the story told by Bill Powell: both incidents began with an explosion of violence against someone who looked somehow different from the majority culture, and in both cases, the victim's death was apparently hastened by a casually dismissive response from people entrusted to help save people's lives.

How much of the stone-age mentality of the old Hamilton survives in the new, post-industrial city? Does that tragedy outside the Al-Mustafa Centre, for example, suggest that a significant segment of the authority figures in Hamilton still carry with them ingrained racist assumptions that make them unfairly suspicious and disbelieving of non-white citizens? This question had also entered the public discourse in 2016 when former Ward 3 councillor Matthew Green, Hamilton's first Black city councillor (and later NDP member of Parliament for Hamilton Centre), brought a complaint against an officer who stopped to question him as he waited for a bus home from work.[11] Green insisted that he was the target of "carding"—or racial profiling—by police. Although the complaint was eventually dismissed in court, there remained two irreconcilable versions of events throughout the case: while the constable testified that he was merely checking on Green's well-being, Green himself stated that he was aggressively questioned until the officer realized he was speaking with a city councillor.[12] The role of police in the city's race relations re-emerged as a point of contention late in 2020, when a group of eighty to a hundred protesters demanding that the police budget be cut by 50 per cent and the funds be reallocated to public housing camped out for fifteen days in front of city hall.[13]

Although racist motivations may be difficult to prove at an institutional level, there are hard numbers indicating that these attitudes are alive and well on Hamilton's streets and within its communities. *Maclean's* magazine parsed the stats and found Hamilton to be the third-worst Canadian city for hate crimes in 2017—only slightly behind Sarnia and Thunder Bay, where an epidemic of violence against Indigenous people has become one of that city's primary claims to fame. That year, there were 16 hate crimes reported in Hamilton for every 100,000 residents.[14] Many Hamiltonians say their city's reputation as a hive for white supremacists was cemented in 2001, when Hamilton's Hindu temple was burned down in an arson case that would take over a decade to solve.[15]

A long and disheartening record of hate-driven incidents has left a lasting mark on this place. But what distinguishes the present from the past, says Deirdre Pike, a frequent columnist for the *Hamilton Spectator* in addition to her work with Hamilton's SPRC, is a new commitment by a formidable segment of the population here to confront intolerance and attempt to run it out of town. To make the point, she invokes yet another recent incident with depressing similarities to the 1976 attack against Phil Stone, save for the note of redemption at the end.

"There was a particular incident with a gay restaurant owner being beaten by an eighteen-year-old high school student," Pike recalls. The man had been targeted as he left his restaurant and was badly injured in the subsequent attack. But rather than eliciting a shrug, the attack galvanized the community. "The city looked at itself and said, 'What the hell?'—including the mayor, who called a meeting one Saturday morning" where a range of people made the commitment to change conditions to pre-empt future homophobic violence. Pike says she was "very moved by what happened that morning" and began working to make Hamilton a more hospitable place for LGBTQ people. For example, she's since been invited to local high schools (including the one attended by the attacker) to lead sessions on LGBTQ issues. Both Catholic and public schools have set up positive spaces for LGBTQ students, where none existed before. "I've seen a lot of positive change over the past two decades, and that's been great," she says.

The same resolve to deal with hatred head-on, Pike recalls, was evident in March 2018 when a white supremacist group that calls itself the Sons of Odin announced they would march in downtown Hamilton. "We had the Gandhi Peace Festival outside city hall and we heard there was going to be this [white supremacist] rally, so the Hamilton Faith Communities in Action made sure that we all showed up to say, 'Here we are. You can spout your hatred, but here's how many more of us love.' That's a kind of Hamilton response I've seen over and over again: 'You can spew your hatred. We're going to show up with love.'" Though the Sons of Odin were a no-show (they relocated their event to Niagara), a big contingent from the churches and the labour unions went ahead with their Hamilton rally regardless.

But subsequent events clearly show that the war is far from over—that the worldwide resurgence of the far right has been expressed particularly forcefully in Hamilton. In June 2019, Hamilton's Pride Day celebrations in Gage Park were marred by violence after a group of homophobic demonstrators carrying banners emblazoned with slogans such as "The wicked shall be cast into Hell" and "Liberal commies and homo fascists are destroying Canada and our children" attacked a group of counterdemonstrators.[16] The latter had held up a portable barrier in an attempt to keep the homophobic group's signs out of view, while other Pride Day participants converged on the area and held their own signs and used noisemakers to drown out the hate peddlers. The far-right group then became violent. Video of the scene showed the far-right demonstrators punching Pride supporters and one pro-Pride person being smashed in the face with a helmet.[17]

The resulting public furor focused as much on the response of police as on the violence of the far-right agitators. There was consternation when police, rather than making it a priority to charge members of the anti-Pride contingent, moved quickly to arrest transgender activist and Tower habitué Cedar Hopperton (who had previously been charged with conspiracy in relation to the Locke Street riot) for parole violation. This occurred in spite of statements by multiple people that Hopperton was not at Gage Park during the Pride festivities.[18] Police eventually did charge one of the anti-Pride demonstrators—a twenty-seven-year-old from Kitchener named Christopher Vanderweide, subsequently known as "Helmet Guy"—with two counts of assault with a weapon for bashing his victim in the face with a helmet.[19]

Complaints about police went beyond their apparent eagerness to focus on pro-Pride forces' role in the confrontation, while seeming lackadaisical in pursuing the people who committed the actual violence. The *Hamilton Spectator*, for instance, suggested that police also seemed unwilling to take action that would have prevented the incident. "When you watch video of the conflict," reads a *Spectator* editorial, "you cannot help but feel that something went wrong with police crowd control in this case. . . . Assuming police personnel were in the area, why didn't they stop the advancing protesters before they got to the Pride celebrations?"[20] Two city councillors also called for an independent review of police actions on Pride Day and afterward.[21]

The violence that descended on Hamilton's Pride Day fits with some observers' impression of the city as, increasingly, a magnet for imported right-wing extremism. The ritualized presence of racist, Islamophobic, and homophobic "yellow vests"—who, for much of 2019, were camped outside Hamilton City Hall on Saturdays—sends a disturbing message that intolerance is flourishing in Hamilton. "People who practice the faith of Islam now on Saturday don't walk in front of city hall," said Kojo Damptey of the Hamilton Centre for Civic Inclusion, quoted by CBC News. "Think about that for a second. The place that's supposed to be the beacon of safety of everyone in our city, people can't walk there on Saturday morning."[22] Similarly, Matthew Green worried that "we have a very real and present problem . . . We have people coming in from across the country seeing Hamilton as fertile ground for a new neo-Nazi movement. And the response politically has been lacklustre."[23]

All of this leads to a composite portrait of Hamilton as a confusing place with contradictory public faces and conflicting social outlooks, where each one is struggling to gain the upper hand. The contest is played out in a range of social settings, not just at confrontational public demonstrations. Deirdre Pike is angry, for example, that some social service organizations continue to discriminate against LGTBQ people. But she says those intolerant attitudes coexist alongside a striking sense of concern among many in the community for people who have been marginalized. The central presence of the church in Hamilton has left some baggage—"This city has all these pockets holding on to old beliefs around homosexuals and Black people and people who don't believe in Jesus"—but at the same time it "has always led to good responses to people in poverty, because at least there is that kind of charity in Hamilton. It's not the fullness of what justice needs to be, but there is a good sense of charity here." There's also been an openness to reflection and change. The church-led charities that impose their own discriminatory moral codes on clients contrast with others, like the Catholic-affiliated Good Shepherd social service agency, which "is now recognized as being one of the most welcoming places for LGBTQ people," says Pike.

Pike says how you view Hamilton will likely come down to what aspects of Hamilton's splintered personality you've had most experience with. For example, when she secured employment in Hamilton in the early 1990s, after losing a job in the tiny burg called Hanover, Ontario, "at first it was, 'Oh crap, I have to come to Hamilton.' But eventually, it was amazing," she recalls. "I got to join a women's choir *filled* with lesbians, whereas normally I would think I was the only one that ever existed. If you're from here, you might think, 'This is the worst, most homophobic place in the world,' but if you have a good experience, it's something else."

The broader point here is that the emergent Hamilton is a difficult place to read, likely because the old Hamilton it grew out of was also contradictory to the point of incoherence: capable of inspiring both vast affection and bitter disgust from its residents. This yin/yang thing moves through just about every aspect of Hamilton's civic life. People will tell you that Hamilton was a very churchy place in profoundly good yet profoundly repressive ways. That it had its own authentic culture and homegrown bohemian tradition, but that non-conformists were often persecuted. That its unions were committed to raising up the poor and comforting the afflicted, but that the brutal aspects of life and work in an industrial town also made this a place of frustration and intolerance—a tough, dangerous town of brawls in many of its bars and victimization on the streets.

What will rise from the rubble of the past?

With a new reality now under construction amid the ruins of the old industrial order, the complicated nature of Hamilton brings the lesson that simple nostalgia won't help much with the quest to refashion this community as something better and more humane. Sure, the past can provide inspiration and a foundation for moving forward. But some things you've got to let go of. And there are new ideas that you've got to embrace.

Wayne Lewchuk, a labour studies professor at McMaster University, brings this kind of dual vision to his examination of how global economic transformation has changed the way people spend their working hours and how this, in turn, has impacted the lives of individuals, families, and communities. This is an especially important subject in cities like Hamilton, where the whole economic basis of the community has been turned upside down. Lewchuk is an expert on the present-day phenomenon of "precarious employment," the successor to the old "spend-your-whole-life-in-one-factory" model upon which the post–World War II economic order in blue-collar cities like Hamilton was built. His work includes a leading role in a McMaster-based research consortium that brought a group of scholars into partnership with Toronto's United Way to study the impacts of precarious employment in the GTHA. He has an acute understanding of how the reordering of workplace norms (notably, the demise of the full-time job and the rise of the "gig economy") has triggered huge, often destructive changes in the way people live their lives. Those wrenching shifts have brought instability, financial hardship, and constant time crunches for individuals, in turn straining the larger community bonds.

Yet Lewchuk isn't advocating a return to the past. He notes that life in the old, solidly blue-collar Hamilton was far from perfect. And some key changes have arisen through those years of post-industrial dislocation that should be recognized as improvements over the old status quo.

In conversation in his office at McMaster's leafy campus, the labour studies professor offers that the main social good that's been lost with the passing of the industrial age is a widely felt sense of commitment to the community—an aspect of that thing that unionists refer to as "solidarity." But here's a paradox: that uplifting spirit was born of a material environment that, in some respects, was inhumane. To make sense of the ledger—to measure how the current, post-industrial reality stacks up against the past—Lewchuk believes you have to begin by understanding the contradictory nature of the traditional industrial workplace. Though work in the old factories and on assembly lines was physically punishing and sometimes lethal, Lewchuk says it offered some intangible—almost spiritual—rewards.

"There is no doubt that people who were working in the steel mills were exposed to horrendous health and safety issues," he says. "For some of them, it shortened their lives. So yes, the working conditions could be dirty and hot, and the air was often uncomfortable. But there was also an incredible sense of community. I know this from having worked on the line for over a year [in a car plant in Windsor]. Sure, your body is getting the crap beat out of it, but in your mind you know you are part of a community. It's lovely to collectively struggle against management—you don't always win, but solidarity is a good feeling."

This sense of kinship has dwindled as employers have moved, typically, from a long-term commitment to their workers to a preference for hiring people on short-term contracts. This is the definition of "precarious employment." It is a condition that affects not only minimum-wage retail clerks called in to work shift by shift, but also more glamorous classes of contemporary toilers, from contract university lecturers to newspaper editors or IT consultants who may make decent wages but have practically no job security.[24]

That lack of security has far-reaching impacts, both inside and outside of work. For example, although the modern workplace is generally considered safer than a vintage steel foundry, where hazards do exist, insecure workers are generally ill-equipped to mitigate the risks. "People in precarious jobs," says Lewchuk, "are often working with no proper training, in positions where they can't simply put up their hand and say, 'Excuse me, I think this job is killing me.'" There are also broader social consequences, since today's lack of job security has proven fairly effective at whittling away at the bonds of community that Lewchuk associates with the old factory floor. Simply put, people who are preoccupied with what the future may hold once their contracts run out develop a kind of tunnel vision. The age of precarious work brings a whole range of anxieties that make it difficult to look beyond yourself and your immediate family.

"In the seventies world," Lewchuk explains, "the men had jobs at Stelco and Dofasco and those jobs were good enough to support a household. Not necessarily a great standard of living, but those households were not going to fall apart. They probably had some kind of supplemental health benefits and some kind of drug plan, so they were insured against those risks. Now, you may have people making the same amount of money per year as those Stelco workers back in the seventies, but they probably don't have pension plans so they have to find that money themselves. They don't have a drug plan or a dental plan. So if Johnny needs braces or gets his teeth knocked out, that comes out of your budget. There's this unpredictability in life that creates lots of stress, and I think that means that people have become less weighted in the community. They are concerned about themselves. They are not safe. And if you are not safe then it's hard to be generous and engaged in your community, because you are worried about your standard of living and protecting yourself from all those uncertainties."

This, of course, is in addition to the more direct, fundamental impacts of stress on the individuals experiencing it. "With all the mental stresses of work and not knowing how long you're going to have a job," reports Lewchuk, "we've seen mental health issues go through the roof."

Life after lunch buckets

One person who's had a ground-level view of how the changing workplace has impacted workers' daily lives and social outlooks is Bryan Adamczyk, a one-time blue-collar employee at Stelco who would later become a Steelworkers union staffer. In the latter position, he represented a diverse membership ranging from hotel and retirement home workers to the University of Toronto's administrative, IT, and support staff.

His trek from the certainties of the industrial age to the brave new workplace of today began in 1976, when he was hired at fourteen dollars an hour to work at a small, specialized Stelco plant that had just opened out on Appleby Line near the QEW. Originally hailed for its advanced technology, the plant has since fallen under the wrecker's ball and is now the site of a parking lot. Adamczyk took an interest in the union and soon became a shop steward, working to advance the interests of a behemoth Steelworkers organization that represented 24,000 members in Hamilton, about 13,000 of them with the powerful Local 1005 at Stelco. But as the 1980s rolled in, the sense of strength in numbers—of being part of something massive and unstoppable—began to crumble. Adamczyk describes a perfect storm where a flood of steel from offshore (as a new globalized economic regime brought down trade barriers) combined with advances in automation to seal the steelworkers' fate.

"Once things went global and the steel industry down in the U.S. died in the eighties, it was just a matter of time before we got it too," he says. Adamczyk concedes that inefficiency and feather-bedding was one factor leading to Stelco's decline: "I never worked in the big plant, but back in the day [if you worked there] you could walk around all day with a shovel in your hand and nobody would ask who you were or where you were going, just because the place was so big," he says. Still, he believes that targeted, reasonable reforms could have been made that would have enhanced productivity while retaining employment. Selling Stelco to U.S. Steel in 2007, a move that Adamczyk describes as the final "kiss of death" for Local 1005, was likely the worst of all options, as the idle Stelco lands now attest.

Today, the Steelworkers union has about 5,000 paying members in Hamilton from across all economic sectors, only about 650 of them in the once-mighty Local 1005 representing industrial workers. Adamczyk believes that the drop in numbers has profound implications for the city. "When I came on staff [in 1987], and even when I was an activist in the local, there was a culture that as Steelworkers we got involved in the community," he says. "We were always the ones that led the pack with regard to health and safety and a lot of issues in the community. But we're not big players anymore like we used to be."

Still, in times of change "you have to move on," says Adamczyk, and that's just what the Steelworkers (like other once-blue-collar unions) have done. As employment has shifted, the Steelworkers union has taken on the task of representing legions of workers whose daily routines have nothing to do with steel. And so the United Steelworkers' diminishing presence in industrial Hamilton is offset by a rising regional influence that's largely centred in the service sector. Adamczyk, for example, works out of the Steelworkers' Toronto office. His old job was to represent staff at the University of Toronto; at the time of our conversation he was organizing low-wage, precariously employed workers such as retirement home and hotel staff and security guards.

Though he spends his work days in the Greater Toronto Area, helping to spread the Steelworkers' protective blanket across new groups of workers, he continues to live in the Hammer—"I'm proud of that name," he says—in a recently redeveloped neighbourhood of tidy houses, late-model cars, and well-groomed lawns near to the now-repurposed Hill Park high school. I remember this area from my childhood as a community of cramped, dishevelled "wartime houses" (single-storey wooden homes, hastily constructed after World War II for returning vets) with a reputation as one of the toughest parts of the city, beset by poverty and gang activity. "Yeah, that's the story," Adamczyk confirms. "I know an old guy who used to live here in the sixties who said the cops would be afraid to come here after dark."

Though Adamczyk seems to favour the contemporary remake of his neighbourhood over the *West Side Story* version spoken of by old-timers, his appraisal of how workplace relations have changed over the same period is far more negative. His work with mostly immigrant workers in hotels and retirement homes, for example, appears to conform to the letter to Wayne Lewchuk's assessment of how precarious employment negatively affects the way of life and the health of the contemporary worker.

"A lot of the women [who work in retirement residences or hotels] will have two or three jobs," says Adamczyk. "So they'll be one place a couple days a week and then someplace else. It's very hard for them to plan their future. It really hit home when we had a strike at a hotel. You have people who are making twelve or thirteen dollars an hour and they've got maybe two or three jobs. Maybe one is in a hotel in the north of Toronto, and then they have to travel to a hotel downtown later in the day. They've got to take public transportation a long way and that eats into your wages. Some people, I just don't know how they manage it. It seems to be the nature of the industry. At one retirement home, we've got a lot of casual workers who work under twenty hours a week. There are only six full-time people. Some are registered nurses who have to be on site, and there's another couple people in food services. But the personal support workers are all casual and part-time."

Despite the hardships—and despite the chastening recognition by people in low-wage jobs that "there are lots of people who would be willing to take your job in a heartbeat"—Adamczyk says he's encountered many workers, particularly immigrants, who are willing to take major risks in order to fight for a more just workplace. On the other hand, he says, that rebellious, determined spirit seems much less common among the better-educated people the Steelworkers represent in academia.

Universities are "probably the worst environment I've seen with respect to bullying," says Adamczyk. He views these places as rigidly hierarchical, where policy and behaviour are generally dictated by professors who have special status, exceptional power over their subordinates' prospects for professional advancement, and often cannot be reprimanded. "Here's the problem: you can have a prof being a son of a bitch to one of our members, but because they are high profile and because they bring money to the university, they can't do anything to them. They just can't."

What compounds the problem and is "most frustrating for us," says Adamczyk, is how little resolve to push back against employers—a quality that was in plentiful supply on the grimy old foundry floor—has made its way into this more genteel workplace. "There are still a lot of people, if they have a problem they would go to the employer or go to the professor, rather than go to the union. It's still a paternalistic type of relationship. They feel like they are going to get more mileage out of going to the employer. They identify more with the employer than with the union that represents them."

While workers occupying those widely different strata of today's polarized economy face different challenges in their workplaces, Adamczyk believes they all are affected by one overarching reality: that economic expectations for the majority have declined since the golden age when he started at Stelco for fourteen bucks an hour. Early twenty-first-century Canadian workers may, in general, have far greater levels of education than their predecessors. Technology may have given them vastly expanded entertainment options as they ride the bus to work or retreat into their electronic cocoons after they've returned home. And these things may be considered social advances. But in purely financial terms, Adamczyk believes that many present-day workers—especially young people—have been pushed back into a far worse position than the one faced by their predecessors.

"The good side," says Adamczyk, of the way things used to be "is that people could afford to buy a home—the middle class was strong. It was never a problem getting a job. You could start out at Dofasco in the morning. If you didn't like it, you could walk across the street and get hired at [International] Harvester or Stelco."

The ability to buy your own home—Adamczyk's primary barometer of economic well-being—is increasingly out of reach for many younger people. The union rep doesn't have to look far to find some striking examples of this.

"I don't think my kids are going to have the same standard of living that I had," he says. "There's a whole generation that's struggling. They've got degrees, a good education, but can't find a decent-paying job in a field they'd like to work in. I have three kids. My eldest is my daughter who has a degree from Brock University and is working at McDonald's. My son has gone back to Mohawk College. My other daughter has a university degree from McMaster and is working in an office making fourteen dollars an hour and having to drive back and forth each day from Oakville. She and her boyfriend are moving into an apartment and have to share with a third person to help pay the rent. My kids right now, when I look at them, I don't know whether they'll ever be able to afford a home. That's a tragedy."

Foundations for an economic resurgence

That's the bad side of things for people growing up in the wake of Hamilton's industrial collapse: many of the new jobs have little security and don't provide enough income to cover the rising costs of things (particularly a house) that were once considered essential to a middle-class existence. On the other hand, counters Lewchuk, things were never as bad in Hamilton as they might have been, or as bad as they were in other industrial cities that simply rusted away. Hamilton's proximity to Toronto, along with the fact that it possessed an advanced social and educational infrastructure, meant that new economic opportunities eventually began to offset the job losses in heavy industry.

"When you take a look at Hamilton," says Lewchuk, "you can

see that it's not falling apart. It's certainly had some bumps, but there's been a transition. For one thing, there's the potential to tap into aspects of Toronto's economy. And there's been a transition from the big employers like Stelco and Dofasco to a whole range of more specialized high-tech employers. Some of those new jobs are good jobs, although there's also a little more fragility because these tend to be smaller companies."

Like other former industrial powerhouses in the United States, Hamilton's status as a regional centre has meant that new employment in health services and education (particularly through the expansion of McMaster University and Mohawk College) have helped offset lost factory jobs. Those positions tend to be unionized. Lewchuk points out that twelve hundred formerly non-unionized support staff at McMaster, for example, are now represented by Unifor, the contemporary descendant of the Canadian Auto Workers. This has changed the composition of Hamilton's labour movement: while unions were once overwhelmingly male-dominated, women now make up the majority of unionized workers in the city, and they've brought new approaches and perspectives that influence how those organizations work. In this respect, at least, Hamilton is a more egalitarian place than it once was.

Moving towards this new reality wasn't as difficult a process for Hamilton as it was elsewhere. Even when Stelco was sheering off vast numbers of jobs in the eighties and nineties, there were factors that buffered the shock. Since Stelco had stopped hiring new workers years before, the later rounds of mass layoffs impacted "mostly older workers," says Lewchuk. "If they did have households and families, their kids were further along and their mortgages were closer to being paid off." This was less catastrophic than the scenario unfolding in Windsor. "When Chrysler hit the wall in the seventies, you had a lot of younger workers—probably in their twenties and thirties—who had maybe just started a family and gotten a mortgage. You saw a pretty large amount of bankruptcies and a lot of people having their houses foreclosed."

This is not to downplay the hardship that also descended upon a large number of Hamiltonians. Probably the people worst hit by

Stelco's demise, says Lewchuk, were the widows who depended on their steelworker husbands' pensions and supplemental benefits, which were reduced or eliminated after U.S. Steel took control of the company in the 2000s.

Adamczyk similarly recalls that the onslaught had varying impacts on the people in its path. Some older workers, he concedes, did have nest eggs and other interests and were able to reboot their lives. "One fellow," he remembers, "had a hobby farm and decided, 'That's it for me.' I'd see him occasionally at the farmers' market." In other cases, "some found jobs through word of mouth. One guy I knew, his health wasn't the best, so he ended up getting a pension from the compensation board. Another fellow had a real estate business on the side, so he ended up doing that full-time."

But Adamczyk says some ex-steelworkers' stories were much harder. Especially badly hit were a small subgroup of workers who spoke Italian, hadn't learned much English, and faced the daunting task of learning a new language late in life in order to become re-employable. Outside this group, there was enough misery to go around: "A good portion fell on hard times. For every person who loses a job, we're talking about a family of several people who are going to have a hard time. Hamilton really went down on its knees."

The inner city becomes a haven for the poor

The collapse of manufacturing didn't only force workers to find new livelihoods—it also compelled the city as a whole to find a new economic raison d'être. With the urban core already weakened by a steady exodus to the suburbs from the 1950s onwards, the erosion of the blue-collar economy further depressed land values and diminished downtown Hamilton's appeal. Ironically, this became the inner city's competitive advantage and its economic saving grace during the bad years. What made the old Hamilton attractive—just about the only thing that would convince people to move there—was that it was cheap. So people with low incomes and disabilities who were being squeezed out of rapidly gentrifying Toronto, for example, often relocated to Hamilton. Government policies encouraged the trend.

"In the eighties and nineties, when I was growing up," recalls Matthew Green, the downtown councillor turned member of Parliament, "upper levels of government tried to keep the city afloat by providing centres for social services. This, of course, attracted populations that needed social services. There was a lot of concentrated social pressure from other communities that pushed Hamilton in this direction. The idea was that, rather than have a lot of social services in Oakville or Toronto, they would just give somebody a bus ticket and say, 'Go to Hamilton, where the cost of living is lower and the services are greater.' We did a great job of providing services to people throughout the eighties and nineties."

Jeff Neven, executive director of the social housing organization Indwell, agrees that Hamilton's new identity as a sanctuary for the poor arose partly because growing suburban municipalities elsewhere in Ontario insisted on developing as uniformly affluent communities. "You take a city like Milton," remarks Neven. "Do you know how many social housing units they have for families in Milton? There are a hundred thousand people living in Milton and nine social housing units. Do you think that there are only nine families living in poverty in Milton? No, that's not the reason. The reason is that we have cities that have no concern for the poor or for people who don't have the same income or employment advantages as others."

The migration of many low-income, service-dependent people to Hamilton occurred alongside other social and political trends. The fraying of Canada's social welfare system led to an increased social polarization that became obvious in Hamilton's downtown communities. "Repeated cycles of neo-liberal austerity, the stagnation of wages, the stagnation of Ontario Works [social assistance] and Ontario disability payments," says Green, created "what I would call an ecosystem of economic violence on the working class"—one that became clearly visible on the urban landscape. Having more people surviving on less money triggered "a flight of inner-city financial institutions, so now not only are you low-income, but you also can't access banking services. That means you have to go to secondary markets like payday loan companies" that charge punishing interest rates and fees. Thus, the dire conditions created by government belt-tightening became even worse.

The impact of this cycle on areas like Ward 3, east of Hamilton's central core, was to replace the old mix of neighbourhoods that had been "intentionally designed to be mixed income . . . where literally every other street has different housing stock to cater to different economies" with enclaves of concentrated poverty. "Beautiful old Victorian homes were turned into rooming houses," says Green, and storefronts became occupied by businesses like those usurious loan operations. On the flip side, the remaining wealthy or middle-class people in much of downtown Hamilton moved out to newer car-dependent, shopping-mall-focused suburbs, places that Green describes as "suburban ghettos for the rich, where people are so poor, all they have is money."

Green's own story is also typical of young Hamiltonians in that period. As the downtown became impoverished and the future was suburbanized, an eighteen-year-old Matthew Green (having grown up in a postwar suburb on the Mountain) decided there were few opportunities for him in Hamilton and left for Costa Rica, then to study law and political science in Nova Scotia, then to live in Germany. When he returned home in 2004, before launching his business as a personal trainer and later taking the leap into politics, he was surprised to discover that Richard Florida's ideas about a Creative Class colonization of old inner cities had begun to take root in Hamilton. A sudden sprouting of "high-end German car dealerships" was, for him, the first sign of what would later be revealed as "a generational shift" away from suburban life and back to a preference for an urban style of life.

During his time as Ward 3 councillor, Green spent some of his workdays mediating between recent émigrés from Toronto and longer-term, lower-income residents who experienced tensions, he recalled, "not so much around income but around expectations" about what form city life should take. Unsurprisingly, many of the biggest problems in Green's ward sprang from the epidemic of displacement that unfolded as downtown Hamilton's attractiveness to outsiders grew and real estate prices soared. Newer residents sometimes got upset about the remaining rooming houses in their midst; longer-term downtowners were concerned that the services and businesses they depended on were disappearing.

The roots of—and remedies to—displacement

Like Matthew Green, Alan Whittle grew up on Hamilton Mountain and left the city to study elsewhere. He's similarly acquired a longitudinal view of how the stable, industry-driven status quo of the 1950s, sixties, and seventies gave way to the current conditions of social division and economic disparity. Partly, these cleavages are a result of broad changes across Canada and beyond, but given Hamilton's history as a solidly blue-collar town, those changes have had an especially dramatic impact here.

Whittle is director of community relations and planning at Good Shepherd, an organization that operates social housing projects across Hamilton (as well as in Toronto). The largest of Good Shepherd's handful of Hamilton developments is a 161-unit King Street complex consisting of two modern mid-rise buildings separated by a shady, tree-lined parkette—a little urban oasis of picnic benches, flower gardens, and ornate brickwork. The site, which was once home to Sir Allan MacNab's sister and a military barracks during the War of 1812, also houses the organization's administrative offices. Here, Whittle unfolds the story of how changing social conditions transformed his employer from an agency on the fringes to one that is vital to many Hamiltonians' survival.

An urban planner by training, Whittle is responsible for bringing new social housing plans to fruition—a task that involves finding and purchasing suitable properties, securing funding and support from different levels of government and partner organizations, and assembling the required architectural and construction talent to bring the projects to fruition. The fact that his job involves planning large-scale housing developments to serve as long-term accommodation for a range of people (rather than running short-term, emergency housing as Good Shepherd has done in the past) is itself an indicator of how profoundly Canadian society has changed. The vast demand for subsidized housing, and the inability of agencies like this to keep up with that demand, indicates how widespread and mainstream the threat of homelessness has become over the past few decades, and how thoroughly the old middle-class dream of owning a piece of property has been eroded.

The Brothers of the Good Shepherd, as they were originally known, opened up shop in Hamilton in 1961. (Founded in Albuquerque, New Mexico, in 1951, the Brothers were an offshoot of the far older Hospitaller Order of Saint John of God, which, as far back as the early 1500s, founded hospitals across Europe and in the New World settlement of Louisbourg when it was under French control.) When the Brothers began working in Hamilton, "they served skid-row alcoholics and that very stereotypical kind of man of the time: the Brother who founded the order referred to them as Knights of the Road," recounts Whittle. "In 1961, they were seeing probably not even a dozen men a night, and they were all men."

In the thick of the postwar industrial boom, even men in dire straits could find rooms in rundown parts of town, as well as casual work that made it possible to survive. "Hamilton in particular was the kind of place that, if you had a strong back, you could get some kind of work, although not all the time and likely not well paying," says Whittle. This is not to suggest that poverty had been eliminated during the age of industry-driven prosperity: with a lack of supports for seniors and people with disabilities, for example, losing your health or growing old was very likely a ticket to misery. But the risk of finding oneself without the basics of life generally remained confined to a smaller group of people, says Whittle, even into the 1970s, when the Brothers' newly opened dining hall, "designed to hold seventy or eighty people, as it does today," was considered busy if it served twenty or twenty-five people.

The situation had changed dramatically by the late eighties, and not just because of the decline of the industrial economy. New groups of people faced the threat of homelessness: women escaping domestic violence, who were now less likely to be compelled to stay at home to suffer further injury and perhaps death; and deinstitutionalized psychiatric patients, who were sent en masse into the community with inadequate supports. These crises unfolded against the backdrop of a general economic squeeze involving rising prices, falling wages, and plummeting expectations, which arose in large part from the evaporation of well-paying industrial jobs. Suddenly, food banks became commonplace in Canada and widespread hardship was almost normalized.

Good Shepherd's creation of its Non-profit Homes division in 1989 was a recognition, says Whittle, of a structural shift in Canadian society requiring long-term solutions rather than temporary emergency fixes. The need has increased steadily since then. When Whittle was first hired by Good Shepherd in the early 1990s, the organization had between sixty and seventy staff; today, it has close to six hundred. And despite the efforts of organizations like Good Shepherd, the housing crisis continues to deepen, moving well beyond people who are in crisis or who need special supports, affecting people whose employment provides an income that used to be—but often no longer is—sufficient to afford a decent place to live.

As a society, "we need to build more housing," says Whittle. "And not just for people who have good jobs at banks and insurance companies. What about the person who makes the coffee for them at Tim Hortons each morning? Where are they going to live?"

A lack of affordable housing, growing economic disparity, lives of hardship unfolding alongside lives of privilege—these conditions are hardly unique to Hamilton, although they seem more visible in a city with such direct experience of deindustrialization and its aftermath. The recent history of Hamilton seems like a case study in how some massive global forces (the decline of manufacturing, the rise of precarious work, governments' adoption of austerity policies, to name a few) have brought uncertainty and instability to one particular place.

The Hamilton social planning council's Don Jaffray notes another component of that recent realignment of the world order that's had a noticeable impact on Hamilton: the replacement of national and even locally owned businesses by multinational corporate entities with the reach and resources to compete in a global marketplace. These mega-corporations can be counted on to be much less socially invested in the communities where they operate. Jaffray says the significance of this fact was driven home to him after a conversation with a former United Way director who described how the organizational structure of the annual fundraising campaign had changed.

Until recently, explains Jaffray, Hamilton's big industries were owned and operated by people who actually lived in the city: they were local businesses, albeit on a grand scale. This brought a certain sense of obligation, a feeling of investment in the community, and a concern by companies with the way they were perceived by local residents. The corporations were deeply involved in the city they called home. Dofasco sponsored the Dofasco men's choir and ran inspirational radio and TV ads with the tag line "Our product is steel; our strength is people." Stelco supported the symphony. Jaffray says the same corporate engagement made the United Way a huge moneymaker before the industrial apocalypse arrived.

In the earlier era, the United Way had been led by a "campaign cabinet" responsible for designing and deploying "a strategy to raise six, seven, or maybe eight million dollars," says Jaffray. "There would be eleven people in this cabinet—eleven men. And those eleven men were the CEOs of the eleven biggest industrial corporations, basically along the waterfront. This was the early eighties and it was like that for years. Those eleven CEOs would sit down with the United Way and say, 'Okay, what's your target?' And then they'd say, 'Our corporation will make a donation, and our corporation has a big union—so you go talk to the union leaders and the union is sure to co-operate. Everyone agrees that this is good for the community.' And so essentially workers from the industrial sector all agreed to a payroll deduction."

It was a very effective system, but with the meltdown of the old industrial order it collapsed. "Those eleven guys are all gone now. It used to be that ninety per cent of what the campaign raised was on the strength of the commitment of those industrial leaders, in partnership with the labour leaders. The other ten per cent came from special events and bake sales—community stuff. Now it's flipped. The community stuff has become ninety per cent of the campaign, and the United Way has been losing ground annually for a number of years."

Jaffray remembers witnessing an ominous forewarning of the current situation in the early 2000s. "John Mayberry, who was the CEO of Dofasco, got up one year at the United Way campaign celebration," Jaffray recalls. "We'd finished the campaign and we all wanted to feel good about it, but John Mayberry did something I've never seen anyone do before or since. He kicked everyone's ass. He said, 'You people aren't paying attention. You don't understand.' He must have known he was going to retire. He said, 'I'm from Hamilton. I live in Hamilton. But that's not the way that business is going. That means you're going to have to change your strategy. Think about that. Good night everybody.'"

Today, it's tougher to get a commitment to community work from remote entities that know Hamilton almost entirely as numbers on a balance sheet. In today's world money travels around the globe with a few keystrokes that can be entered in any anonymous location far from the site of the eventual impact. Decisions get made by remote control, in places well removed from where things actually get made. "The people who run things never come to Hamilton," Jaffray says. "They've never worked in Hamilton, and they're not about to move here. This place doesn't even register on the map for them."

So Hamilton got hit from all sides. Not only was much of the city's economic purpose yanked away. Not only did legions of once-secure workers find themselves adrift in a new, alien world, suddenly unable to make a decent living. Added to that was the unravelling of local support systems that, alongside similarly eroding government safety nets, had helped Hamilton weather tough times in the past.

But Hamiltonians are nothing if not adaptable and tenacious. The collapse of the old order created a surge of misery that's still evident in the midst of the current civic renaissance—with the campsites of newly homeless people, for example, at times on view a stone's throw from recently gentrified neighbourhoods.[25] Even so, many people in this city are struggling to revive Hamilton's historic community cohesion and social concern, so that the new, emerging Hamilton will not become just one more place where money prevails and the poor are left behind. In recent years, Hamilton has been a kind of laboratory in which civic organizations, drawing support from both multi-generational Hamiltonians and newcomers alike, struggle to find ways to make the city's long tradition of concern and compassion a viable force within this brave new world. The goal is the creation of an integrated city where everyone, from whatever economic level or social background, can thrive and contribute. Successes have been few and mostly tenuous. But the idea that something better is possible, as we'll see in the final chapter, persists.

CHAPTER FIVE

Slogging towards Tomorrow

B Y 2005, HAMILTON was indisputably in a state of crisis. Amid the full effects of industrial decay, combined with continual, cumulative cuts to the social safety net, a palpable despair had set in across the city. But this dire moment also spawned a nascent sense that things could be better. What galvanized many Hamiltonians' resolve to launch a counterattack—to look for ways out of this deepening malaise—was a single statistical marker indicating that further downward momentum would, essentially, foreclose on the future.

"A report went to city council showing that a quarter of all of Hamilton's kids were growing up in poverty," recalls Tom Cooper, director of the Hamilton Roundtable for Poverty Reduction. "Our community by and large found that unacceptable and wanted something done about it."

Although no one could point to what specific measures would be required, there was a clear sense that solutions had to go well beyond crisis management. "There were great organizations in our community helping people living in poverty with their daily crises," continues Cooper. "There were food banks and shelters and numerous social service agencies. What we didn't have was a more holistic look at what we needed to do as a community and a society to reduce poverty over the long haul."

Enter the Hamilton Roundtable, a new entity that would draw on the perspectives and expertise of people from government, the non-profit sector, business, the churches, and perhaps most importantly, individuals who have themselves experienced poverty. The Roundtable's goal, says Cooper, was to mine these multiple insights to arrive at some big-picture solutions. The focus would be much more on root causes than on symptoms.

This approach had several interlocking aspects. One of the Roundtable's essential activities has been to promote a deeper understanding within the broader community of how difficult it is to break free from the cycle of poverty and of how many people "are languishing in situations they can't move out of," says Cooper. To this end, the Roundtable created a speakers' bureau that brings Hamiltonians with first-hand experience of poverty to events where they can help educate other citizens. It has also worked with the board of education to create educational materials "to teach students about the root causes of poverty and what we can do as a society to break some of those cycles." Cooper sees this kind of work as a necessary precursor to driving policy change: governments are only likely to improve the lives of people experiencing hardship if there is a widespread public understanding of why that's important.

The Roundtable has also functioned as a kind of street-level policy factory, making the case for both big and small initiatives that could chip away at the existing crushing rates of poverty. Part of the focus has been local, with the Roundtable encouraging the city to apply its budgets and planning powers in ways that benefit lower-income residents and, in doing so, to road-test new ideas that other municipalities might also adopt.

Still, even the nimblest, most creative municipality can only hope to make changes at the margins, given that higher tiers of government have overwhelming control over the big policy levers and have far greater budgetary clout. Says Cooper: "We've often talked about the importance of provincial social assistance reform.

The need for living wages. The need for a national housing strategy. Without those types of investments from senior levels of government, there's only so much that we can do locally, although we've certainly tried."

I am speaking with Tom Cooper at the Roundtable's offices in a concrete tower called Century 21, one of the first embodiments of Hamilton's embrace of urban renewal back in the 1960s, at first envisioned as a magnet for prestige businesses but now occupied mostly by non-profits and government agencies. He expresses some satisfaction at the ways his organization had been able to nudge various government and non-governmental actors to take meaningful action. This is a couple years before the election of Doug Ford's scissor-wielding, poor-bashing Progressive Conservative government, when the momentum is still clearly moving in the right direction.

The Roundtable is one of a cluster of organizations that don't view the challenges and possibilities facing Hamiltonians within the polarizing framework set out by Richard Florida. As we've seen earlier, the debate over the fate of changing inner cities has devolved, over several decades, largely into a screaming match between those who accept the urban theorist's initial euphoric propositions—that an influx of professionals with hipster sensibilities will benefit everyone by injecting new life into dying cities—versus those who vehemently reject those ideas. The latter camp (the headline-grabbing "anarchist" provocateurs in Hamilton or their counterparts in places like Boyle Heights in Los Angeles) are so suspicious of anyone whose enthusiasm sounds remotely like Florida's that they will identify the promotion of any kind of development (more efficient transit, neighbourhood improvement projects) as adjuncts of a stealth plot to advance gentrification and displace the poor. Florida's ideas about a Creative Class have often been used as public relations cover for predatory behaviour by real estate speculators. Therefore, these highly visible anti-gentrification campaigners tend to believe that only continued stagnation and neglect will provide security for the poor in places like Hamilton.

Groups like the Roundtable, on the other hand, see the chessboard quite differently. Their approach is defined not by the hypothesis of a Creative Class nor by a reflexive reaction against it. They don't accept that the city's problems are rooted in a basic struggle between gentrifying newcomers and the established poor. On the contrary, they say that growing poverty poisons the community for everyone, and so citizens at all economic levels have roles in finding solutions. In particular, groups like the Roundtable do not dismiss political institutions as being ineffective or in the pocket of the real estate industry. Consequently, they seek institutional solutions to the shameful conditions of poverty and inequality that exist in the city.

Despite the long odds, they've had some successes. At the time of my discussion with Cooper, there had been some significant achievements at the local level. The Roundtable had pushed the city to introduce a half-price Affordable Transit Pass for low-income working people, which helped several thousand people facing the catch-22 of having to spend a significant part of their incomes to travel to low-paying jobs. This program, Cooper believes, would make life easier for a far greater number of people if it were made available to all low-income people, including children.

Hamilton had also served as ground zero for a "living wage" movement that spread to some thirty communities across Ontario. It was in Hamilton that people first started seriously discussing the idea that employees should be paid wages they can actually live on, creating a groundswell that spread across the province. The movement subsequently informed the former Liberal provincial government's decision to raise the minimum wage to fifteen dollars an hour.[1]

"We've had a number of firsts here in Hamilton," says Cooper. "Our public school board became the first elected body in Ontario to officially endorse a living wage for their employees [although city hall did not]. Our Chamber of Commerce has signed on as a living-wage employer, which is kind of unprecedented, because usually business voices are pretty reactionary around these issues. But our Chamber of Commerce has actually taken on a leadership role. We've had small businesses, non-profits, and faith groups signing on as living-wage employers."

What is the curious cross-sectoral appeal of the living-wage issue, with non-profits and business groups equally eager to get on board? Cooper says part of the reason businesses supported the initiative was practical self-interest. "There's a strong business case to be made," he explains. "When living wages are paid, organizations become more efficient. There is less absenteeism, less turnover. Workers who are paid more feel valued and are willing to put in extra effort."

But is there something particular to Hamilton that would predispose local businesspeople to see their own fate bound up with the quest to raise the poor out of poverty? Here we return to the proposition that the collective legacy of hardship in this community (the memory of families suffering the consequences of industrial accidents, workplace-related disease, layoffs, and so forth) makes empathy the default response for many people around these parts.

Cooper reveals that one of these typically Hamiltonian stories influenced his own choice of livelihood. Having worked as a political staffer and then leaving, disenchanted, Cooper says his decision to move into anti-poverty work was almost certainly influenced by the memory, from his teenage years in the 1980s, of his own family's struggle to survive when his father was let go from International Harvester. It's a reasonable assumption that many others who grew up amid the uncertainty and hard knocks of blue-collar life—regardless of whether they moved on into business, management, the professions, or politics—would carry the same engrained understanding of the need to advance the common good and, especially, to look out for the most vulnerable.

Cooper sees this attitude as a motivating force behind several local initiatives that address poverty. At the level of local politics, some Hamilton city councillors committed to turning part of their local ward money over to student nutrition programs (which, in other countries, he notes, are universal benefits that city politicians wouldn't need to underwrite). Similarly, Hamilton mayor Fred Eisenberger's dedication of fifty million dollars to a mayor's anti-poverty initiative, unique among Canadian municipalities, shows that reducing economic inequality is seen in this city as a *local* challenge, as much as it is a matter for higher levels of government.[2]

So Hamilton's municipal government took whatever steps it could to halt a descent into deepening poverty, all the while waiting for senior levels of government to get on board. Eventually, the resolve to do something meaningful seemed to percolate upward. Although the Ford government in Ontario would later take several steps backward, in the mid-2010s senior levels of government moved away from the crushing austerity that had sentenced a quarter of Hamilton's children to a life in poverty. Governments were finally demonstrating, as Cooper expresses it, "a willingness to invest in people again that wasn't there previously."

In 2016, for instance, Justin Trudeau's federal Liberal government introduced a new, more generous, and tax-free Canada Child Benefit weighted towards providing greater assistance for children in low-income families. The CBC described the benefit as "one of the most ambitious social policies to be implemented in Canada in decades," which "is expected to push tens of thousands of Canadian children above the poverty line."[3] The federal government also signalled its intention to re-engage with the issue of affordable housing (after a decades-long absence) with the 2017 announcement of its National Housing Strategy. The $40-billion, ten-year plan includes the creation of a housing benefit program to assist up to 300,000 households with housing costs, as well as a $16-billion fund to build 60,000 new affordable housing units and to repair 240,000 more. Although some advocates were at first disappointed that funding would not be released until 2020, following the 2019 election (which effectively made implementation of the strategy contingent upon the federal Liberals being re-elected), the funds have since started to flow.[4]

There was even evidence of a quantum shift in the way that governments think about poverty. In 2017, the province's governing Liberals launched a basic income pilot project, with test programs running in Hamilton, Lindsay, and Thunder Bay. It was built around the notion that to achieve economic mobility and take control of one's life, a minimum financial floor was required (for single people, that was determined to be $17,000 annually). In other words, a person has to be able to afford the necessities of life, to experience a basic financial security, in order to move to a higher economic niche by getting more education or landing a better job.[5] Unfortunately, this program was announced late in what turned out to be Premier Wynne's final term in office. When the Ford Conservatives took office in 2018, they broke a campaign promise and cancelled the basic income program before the pilot was completed. This move bitterly disappointed participants who'd believed that they had been moving towards a better, fuller, and more promising life,[6] and even provoked opposition from a hundred business CEOs, who petitioned the Ford government to reverse the cut.[7]

Despite more recent rollbacks, it's clear that some of the earlier measures to combat poverty had an impact. A direct result of the Canada Child Benefit is that "families with children experiencing poverty are going to be significantly better off than they were previously," says Cooper. Ontario's increased minimum wage also contributed to a reduction in rates of poverty.

Of course, good news is often not quite as good as it first appears. Cooper points out, for instance, that profound shifts in the nature of work still create vast pressures in daily life—especially for people struggling at the lowest income levels—that aren't captured in the official stats. The trend towards precarious employment now forces many lower-income people to cobble together multiple jobs in order to make ends meet. This creates a crushing stress at odds with the picture arising from outwardly robust employment figures and seemingly more comfortable family incomes.

Other confounding factors have worked to negate some of the hard-won gains of the mid-2010s. The most obvious one is that fickle beast called politics. In Ontario, a government that had belatedly gotten serious about narrowing the vast chasm between rich and poor was replaced by an incoming regime with a transparently brutal approach to social policy. (We'll get to a more detailed accounting of the Ford government's cuts later in this chapter.) The real-life effects of gentrification have also undermined advances made by the poor. Minimum wage and child tax benefits may have risen, but in booming Hamilton they are often more than offset by large rent increases, driven by increases in property values that incentivize landlords to find loopholes allowing them to raise rent or to clear out low-income people to make way for better-off tenants. The result of this process for people with modest incomes is to either face unmanageable accommodation costs or find a place far from the city centre that entails a gruelling commute to work.

Despite this clearly negative trend, Cooper believes that it is still possible to manage the city's gentrification-driven growth in a way that brings benefits to everyone. "I think for the vast majority of Hamiltonians, they see the opportunity for new investment as a positive thing. But it has to be handled well and we have to ensure that people aren't left behind by it. There have to be policies and planning decisions that protect public spaces and affordable housing. And that has to be intentional."

Hamilton, he says, still has the potential to become a model for an egalitarian form of civic renewal. "My utopian dream of Hamilton is that it becomes a place where everyone feels they can be a part of their neighbourhood and their community, where everyone feels welcome, everyone has a home, nobody is going hungry. I think that is realistic, but we have to make important investments today to make that a reality tomorrow." On the other hand, says Cooper, "if we're not careful how we manage change, more people will get left behind."

A marathon battle over transit

One particular public investment that highlights the ability of civic amenities to either promote social equality or, conversely, to enhance the privileged position of the well-off, is transportation. In Hamilton, the debate around transportation has been dominated by a seemingly endless political battle over the adoption of a light rail transit (LRT) line downtown. At a basic level, embedded in transportation decisions are some obvious social outcomes: new highways, for instance, will benefit people who own cars and live in more far-flung suburbs much more than they will benefit the poor, who are likely to gain more from investments in a reliable transit service. Beyond this rudimentary logic, how a transit system is designed—whether it is intentionally constructed to make the amenities of the city accessible to rich and poor alike; whether it is conceived of with broader social goals in mind—will determine whether transit acts as an agent for more egalitarian development or serves as a prestige project to polish the image of a gentrifying city.

The story of Hamilton's on-again, off-again LRT initiative is tangled and fractious. Long after the provincial and federal governments had agreed to spend billions to cover the entirety of project costs—and while other Ontario municipalities (Ottawa, Kitchener-Waterloo, suburban Toronto) were hurtling headlong into construction of their own LRT projects—local Hamilton politicians were playing a protracted game of political ping-pong that forestalled the laying of even a single metre of track. The project was first proposed in June 2007 when the province announced a $17-billion plan to build multiple rapid transit lines across the GTHA.[8] But it didn't get a thumbs-up from all the necessary parties until eleven years later, in 2018, when the incoming Conservative government at Queen's Park announced (to the surprise of many people who expected them to reverse the previous government's support for LRT) that the province would provide its share of the funds. The rejoicing gave way to disbelief a year later—a few days before Christmas 2019—when the green light turned red and the province withdrew its funding. Hamilton's mayor fumed that the province's reversal was a "betrayal" of Hamilton and characterized the premier's earlier assurance of support for the project as "a lie."[9]

The story doesn't stop there. A task force set up to examine the best transit alternatives to LRT in Hamilton kept light rail among its favoured options. The federal government reiterated in October 2020 that it still wanted to see the rail line built. LiUNA commissioned a study showing the province had overstated the project's costs, and subsequently offered to contribute its own investments alongside government contributions. By November Premier Ford had backtracked, describing the Hamilton LRT as "a good project" and suggesting that if Hamilton's council supports it, it should prob-ably go ahead. There were a few new developments since then but no resolution; by the time of this book's publication, Hamilton's LRT remained in a state of tortured limbo.[10]

Ironically, for years before the province's 2019 withdrawal of support, the provincial and federal governments had both been fully onboard with the Hamilton LRT. The obstacle throughout that period had been the ongoing unwillingness by a majority of Hamilton city councillors to endorse the project and agree to accept the province's money. Even more ironic, says Raise the Hammer publisher and LRT advocate Ryan McGreal, is that "the biggest obstacles to the [provincial] Liberal party approving LRT in Hamilton seems to have been Hamilton Liberals," including former mayor and Liberal federal member of Parliament Bob Bratina, a leading LRT skeptic.[11] This non-partisan lack of enthusiasm for LRT is partly explained by the fact that the LRT line (as well as a second proposed route, later dropped from the plans) runs entirely below the Mountain, inexorably separated from the vote-rich suburbs where the private automobile remains king. Along with the geo-graphic divide, there's an associated cultural reason to oppose LRT: the new train could easily be seen as a pet cause of newly arrived, New Urbanist hipsters with romantic visions of downtown life that don't resonate much in the land of sprawling lawns and two-car driveways.

Later on, the LRT became a convenient political football. Later-stage expressions of anti-LRT agitation on city council, says McGreal, can be explained as the reflexive opposition by an informal right-wing bloc (which coalesced after the 2014 municipal elections and a 2016 by-election) to any policies proposed by a progressive government at Queen's Park.[12] Ex-councillor Matthew Green agrees, telling me that later attempts to delay and obstruct LRT approval can be seen simply as gamesmanship by "a partisan Conservative caucus who wanted to take potshots at the [then Liberal] premier."

There were also, to be sure, solid reasons for downtown pro-gressives—that is, people concerned with social equity and the deepening divide between rich and poor—to be suspicious of the

LRT. One is the prospect that the new rapid transit line, planned to run between McMaster University in the west and the decidedly modest neighbourhoods near Eastgate Square in the east, would accelerate the process of gentrification by providing a new wave of ex-Torontonians with a fast link between the previously untouched East End Hamilton and downtown Toronto, where many of the newcomers work. Were this to happen, "there are some very real concerns that property values are going to increase to the extent that the people who have lived in the East End of Hamilton for most of their lives may no longer be able to afford to live there," says Tom Cooper.

Another potential problem, in the eyes of anti-poverty advocates, is that the LRT—a flashy prestige project—would distract from the needs of the disadvantaged. "We sometimes forget what our real priorities need to be," Cooper continues. "An LRT is important, but there's something much more important, and that's ensuring that we can pull nearly a hundred thousand people experiencing poverty in Hamilton up to a better quality of life for themselves and their families. Some of our members have said to me, 'It will be great to have this world-class transit system so I can get to the food bank and back.'" But if that's all the LRT is good for—if an impressive new piece of physical infrastructure is put in place but inequality remains intact—then everybody will have missed the point.

On the flip side, experience elsewhere proves that it's possible to use big public works projects as a lever to achieve social goals—they need not be mutually exclusive. Cooper points to a device known as a community benefits agreement (CBA), pioneered in Los Angeles and recently attached to the construction of the Crosstown LRT line along Eglinton Avenue in Toronto, that's designed to direct some of the economic spin-off generated by these massive public investments to the people who live nearby. Toronto's Crosstown line has provided benefits to the traditionally working-class and multicultural Weston–Mount Dennis neighbourhood, for example, mostly in the form of job training and employment opportunities. An agreement with the provincial transit authority Metrolinx, as the *Toronto Star* reported, "has brought local hiring and procurement.

Young people from newcomer families are getting good jobs in the construction trades, and local businesses are getting contracts for everything from catering to communications." A new maintenance facility in the neighbourhood is also expected to provide ongoing employment for local residents.[13] Jobs, training, and the construction of affordable housing are among the types of benefits that are typically written into CBAs.

The underlying concept that mega-spending on public works can simultaneously support enlightened social policy is also seen in New York City's approach to the redevelopment of a Brooklyn neighbourhood known as East New York. As gentrification threatened to displace residents of this traditionally low-income community, the city sought to use its control over transit planning as a means to ensure that more subsidized housing is constructed, so that a big chunk of lower-income East New Yorkers could stay put even as wealthier residents moved in. City planners understood that by building a new subway in East New York and rezoning the area as mixed commercial and residential, they were creating the conditions for developers to make unthinkable amounts of money. So they attached a quid pro quo: in exchange for this municipal commitment, developers must agree that half of the six thousand new homes they plan to build will be affordable for low-income people. In this way, the provision of transit became an instrument of progressive housing policy.[14]

Back in Hamilton, the city's former director for the LRT project, Paul Johnson (who's since been relocated within the municipal bureaucracy), wielded a policy weapon with a little less heft than a subway line, but his goals didn't differ much from those of the transit and housing mandarins of New York City. A heavy-set football enthusiast with a grown-out brush cut, at the time of our discussion Johnson occupied a modest office on the second floor of Hamilton's GO Transit terminal—the former TH&B (Toronto, Hamilton, and Buffalo) railway station, a compact art deco gem decked out in dark wood trim, marble floors, and a tasteful, rounded ceiling.

Johnson has never strayed far from this place—you could say the TH&B station is close to the epicentre of his world. "I'm born, raised, educated, and shaped by this community," he says. "This is my home." He grew up on the mostly upmarket west Mountain, close to the Mountain Brow, and attended schools that I also recall having friends at in my youth. Johnson studied history at McMaster, then got a job at Wesley Urban Ministries, the downtown social service agency where he had volunteered as a kid. Moving up the ladder to the executive director's position at Wesley, he oversaw the building of five dozen units of affordable housing in the 1990s.

The history degree remained helpful in his work as a transportation planner because "context is everything, and history allows you to understand context," he says. Meanwhile, both his bona fides as a hometown Hamilton boy and his experience in social services inform his vision of the social role of public transit. To summarize: transit has the ability to put the poor on a more equal footing with the rich, to make the city a more egalitarian place by allowing people at all economic levels to live in neighbourhoods throughout the city (rather than ghettoizing them in their own enclaves) and to be able to travel freely to employment, education, and recreational opportunities wherever they may be.

What is the model for this more inclusive city? Partly, it's the Hamilton that *used* to exist. Where Johnson lived as a kid, he says, "we were on a street of modest suburban homes, but around the corner from us were the million-dollar homes on the Brow. And then behind us were lower-income rental units. So there was this whole mix of people, and I think it made the neighbourhood stronger."

The equalizing impact of good transit

Johnson doesn't claim that rapid transit in itself could resurrect the more socially integrated city that he remembers from his youth. The LRT plans only envisions a fourteen-kilometre corridor of rail that doesn't touch on the vast suburban tracts where most Hamiltonians live. Still, the LRT was conceived of as the spine of a much larger (101-kilometre) network of interlocking transit routes (such as express bus routes) set to take shape in Hamilton over the next twenty-five years. Johnson believes that replacing the current inadequate bus service with something faster, more efficient, and more complete will make it the common-sense option for going about your business, regardless of what segment of society you're from.

"The more rapid and reliable your transit is, the less stress you are going to place on the people who need to move around," he says. "And those who need it come from all sorts of different backgrounds. I may hop on it to get to a meeting at McMaster or the East End of the city, or to go to a Ti-Cat game after work and then get back home. Others may take it to get to school or to work or to get their kids to child care or whatever it is."

When transit develops this kind of broad appeal, there will no longer be a stigma attached to taking public transportation. When two people get on at the same stop, speculates Johnson, "the fact that you are headed off to Bay Street in Toronto to trade millions of dollars and I'm headed down to a trade school to get back on my feet after losing my job, who cares? We'll have a bit of an idea which direction we're headed in, but other than that, we're just two people starting their days."

Johnson predicts that the association of public transit with economic class (which has stayed strong in car-worshipping cultures like Hamilton's) will be further eroded as the population ages and more people find themselves unable to drive to doctors' appointments or social engagements. In other words, having a dependable and extensive transit service will become essential to keeping seniors healthy and socially engaged. And that's just one more reason why "we have to stop looking at transit as a social service and start looking at it as a critical piece of infrastructure in the community. In the same way that we should all have access to turning on the tap and having safe drinking water, we should all be able to access affordable and reliable ways to get around the community," Johnson insists.

Clearly, though, good transit is of essential importance to people living on low incomes. For one thing, it offers a possible remedy to the displacement of low-income people from gentrifying downtown communities. As the value of Hamilton's inner-city real estate reaches previously undreamed-of heights, it's logical for planners to look to more remote areas, where land prices are more affordable, as the site for future social housing projects. But catapulting people out of the inner city and into the disconnected suburban hinterlands is really no solution at all.

"You can't say to someone, 'We're going to build more affordable housing in this area' [far from the downtown core] but then have no transit links," says Johnson. "In that case, you are also saying to that person that you've got to have a car, which is an expense which could push them over the edge. You aren't really making that place affordable at all."

By contrast, developing affordable housing throughout a metropolitan area that has good transit links allows people more choice over where they will live. "You should be able to say, 'If I want to live on the south Mountain or in Dundas or in Ancaster or in the downtown core, there should be opportunities at varying income levels so I can be a part of that community.'"

This transit-centred approach to city planning addresses not only the need for a broader mix of housing over a wider geographic span, but also the need to make future employment opportunities accessible to more people. In the coming years, says Johnson, a lot of new jobs are anticipated in Hamilton—"Even at the entry level, these are businesses that offer jobs with decent wages and decent benefits and the prospect of a career"—but they'll be located in areas like the forthcoming economic development zone surrounding the airport and the Red Hill business park, which are difficult to travel to if you don't have your own set of wheels. And so, much in the same way that the city built multi-lane crosstown thoroughfares to get people to work in the era of heavy industry, the city must now build rapid transit connections to outlying industrial parks as a way to "help people move up by accessing the right kind of employment that provides the right kind of income," Johnson proposes.

To say that rebuilding the transit system will give people from across the income spectrum access to housing and jobs in the suburbs is not to say, however, that it's necessary to cede the inner city entirely to the better-off newcomers who have been scooping up

Hamilton's old Victorian houses. One of the key rationales behind those LRT plans was to increase density downtown, and the strip of land where the LRT was to (and still may) run will keep that zoning as a higher-density transit corridor, even if the LRT is ultimately quashed. The effect of the new zoning will be to allow developers to construct higher buildings (possibly with a quotient of affordable units) without having to do legal battle with neighbourhood associations that are likely to resist the shift away from a uniform landscape of low-rise dwellings and retail outlets. Even if the LRT is never realized (perhaps replaced by express buses on a dedicated right-of-way), the new zoning may still encourage builders to increase density.

Transit as a lever to increase affordable housing

Johnson believes that higher densities will allow for a greater range of construction at different price points. There's a continuum of affordability, he says: some people can afford virtually no rent (and therefore require almost completely subsidized housing), while others might be able to afford $400 or perhaps $900 a month, but can't find anything available on the private market that matches their budgets. Increasing density along transit routes will allow for economies of scale that should (theoretically, at least) translate into greater numbers of more reasonably priced units. Alongside the central, east-west (although perhaps now LRT-less) transit corridor along King and Main Streets, "I think you will see opportunities for an interesting housing mix. I don't think it will be all condos," says Johnson. "You can have apartments, maybe six to eight storeys, and then further east you can have things like stacked townhouses—say, eleven-hundred-square-foot townhouses, stacked on top of each other—which would be a great thing for families, and affordable." In fact, the prospects for more affordable units being built in this central corridor, paradoxically, got a new boost after the province appeared to have blown up Hamilton's LRT plans. A group called King Street Tenants United called for the ninety properties that were expropriated for use as LRT facilities to be turned over to the city and used for affordable housing, a proposal endorsed by Mayor Fred Eisenberger.[15]

Encouraging a mix of construction geared to different levels of affordability is in line with the recommendations of researchers at Ryerson University's City Building Institute, who concluded that the GTHA's housing crisis could be effectively addressed by dealing with the "missing middle"—that is, mid-density housing that lies somewhere between the two extremes of single-family dwellings and high-rise apartment towers. In nearby Mississauga, for example, some 174,000 "relatively affordable" homes could be added to the market by situating medium-density developments around transit hubs and on underused strip mall and shopping plaza lands.[16]

In Hamilton, boosting density would also be a smart choice in places where there were never any plans to run an LRT; for instance, further north, along Barton Street, the once-thriving commercial strip now lined with mostly papered-over storefronts and empty lots. The recent shift in retail business away from brick-and-mortar stores to online ordering appears to have sealed Barton Street's fate, making it nearly impossible that this storied thoroughfare will ever return as a shopping destination. But it could have a new life as a higher-density residential strip with social and commercial ameni-ties mixed in. Johnson also points to downtown properties owned by public agencies—schools, hospitals, empty lots—as logical can-didates for medium-density redevelopment. It should be standard practice, he says, for civic agencies to reach across their jurisdic-tional divides and explore how they can "stack" different functions onto one piece of land.

"If we build a recreation centre," says Johnson, "have we thought through whether housing can be built there as well? Have we thought about whether a medical facility can be added or some other type of amenity? For a long time, we just said, 'Here's a plot of land and we need to build a school, so let's build a two-storey school.' But maybe we could really use some affordable housing in this community, so what if we built a five-storey facility there? We'd have our two-level school, but we'd also have housing. Or could we ring the school with some townhouses?"

This is the kind of integrated thinking that *New York Times* columnist David Brooks claims has already given Canadian cities' anti-poverty efforts a leg up over those of their American counterparts. Brooks writes that many Canadian communities have bought into the idea that "a problem as complex as poverty can be addressed only through a multisector, comprehensive approach," and as a matter of course, they factor issues such as transit, daycare services, and job training into their anti-poverty planning. Brooks attributes the spread of this approach, in part, to the work of the Waterloo, Ontario-based Tamarack Institute, which serves as a "community learning hub" that seeks to influence urban decision makers and planners.[17]

Change that starts on the street

Brooks describes an institution-led process: a think tank promotes a particular methodology so that civil servants and non-governmental players can bring it to specific communities and, if all goes well, put it into practice. But that's not the only way that change happens. In Hamilton, it's also common for plans to be hatched at street level and work their way upwards. The Hamilton Community Land Trust (HCLT), for example, is a relatively new organization that's trying to establish a novel model of social housing in the city. HCLT began as a project of the Beasley Neighbourhood Association (BNA), a volunteer community group serving a large chunk of downtown that's struggled with the double whammy of abandonment and decay, followed by rampant land speculation, inflated housing prices, and displacement.

Beasley is a kind of artificial amalgam (like a Yugoslavia or Iraq: a purely political creation that crammed different ethnic groups into one jurisdictional unit). It envelops residential enclaves but also warehouses, garages, and civic institutions—a hospital, a jail, the police headquarters—along with, of course, empty lots. Traditionally, most of the people who lived here were Italian immigrants struggling to realize the Canadian dream. For many, before achieving that, there was poverty and the feeling of being an outsider, recalls Charlie Mattina, who has assembled a small group of BNA members to discuss the neighbourhood's prospects.

Mattina remembers that, when he was a kid, the Salvation Army brought canned turkeys to his home at Christmastime and once gifted him with "a globe with a big dent in it, so for the longest time I thought there was a huge crater in the middle of China." Life was tough and the streets were sometimes dangerous, but the residents had dreams and a mighty sense of pride. As fortunes changed, the local Catholic churches started bringing Christmas baskets to poor families, with the canned turkeys replaced by pasta and panettone—familiar foods that didn't seem to come with a side order of condescension.

The exodus came later. "The goal," says Mattina, who now lives in Ancaster and works primarily in Toronto, "was to get out and move to *la montagna*" where the air was clean and the backyards were big enough to grow vegetables to last the whole year. As suburban flight accelerated, stores on these modest streets closed down and blocks of houses were demolished to make way for a sea of ground-level parking lots. When I met Charlie Mattina in Beasley, long after an influx of Torontonians had begun to reanimate the area, you could still stand on Cannon Street and look diagonally southwestward toward the downtown core and have a clear sightline—with no buildings rising above ground level—for what seemed like two or three kilometres.

This levelled landscape was especially bleak in the early 2000s, Mattina recalls, when the city accepted federal funds to move people (many of them with addictions) off the streets and into rooming houses in Beasley, mostly without supports or services. "By that time," says Mattina, "the neighbourhood had disintegrated." When the newcomers from across Lake Ontario started moving in a few years later, however, some of them became aware of a unique community spirit that had somehow survived.

"I'm from Toronto but I spent some time living on the East Coast, where people have identities that are beyond their careers and getting stuff," says artist Sylvia Nickerson,[18] one of the BNAers gathered at Mattina's pizza (whose owners are not related to Charlie) on Cannon Street. "That's the condition that can define big cities, but your identity can also be about taking care of people and having a sense of community. Here that's really strong. You can sense that in this neighbourhood and it's had an impact on me."

Mattina thinks Beasley's unique neighbourhood vibe is a gift passed down, in part, by the Sicilians who were once plentiful here and whose influence has not entirely faded. The biggest event in this neighbourhood used to be an annual festival with an origin story that dates back to the 1500s: it celebrates the appearance of a statue of the Virgin Mary, which was on its way to Rome but washed up on the Sicilian coast after a shipwreck. The locals took the statue's appearance to be a sign from God, built a church to commemorate the event, and vigorously resisted any attempts to retrieve the statue and ship it back to Rome. The festival that took place in Beasley each year to mark this miracle, with greased pole climbing, fireworks, battle recreations, and sizable crowds, is a fitting emblem for a community that distrusted authority and venerated self-reliance. Mattina says people here have always taken the initiative when they want something done: "If you want to show a movie in the park, nobody's going to get a permit from the city. You just get a car battery, plug in a generator, and show the movie."

Allison Maxted, director of the Hamilton Community Land Trust, first encountered the BNA in the midst of the association's initial efforts to make the community livable again. There had been a lot of drug use in neighbourhood parks and "absentee landlords and toxic waste on vacant properties right in the middle of the neighbourhood," she recalls. "The BNA had been working really hard to improve the neighbourhood, improve the safety of the neighbourhood. They started organizing community movie nights in the park, cleaning up the park, and getting rid of all the needles. They were doing a lot to transform the neighbourhood in a positive way." Concurrently, the influx of residents from outside also meant that a broader range of people started to come back in to public spaces and "there were people around at all hours."

Around this time, Maxted—who is originally from the Hamilton area—was working on a graduate degree in planning at the University of British Columbia. Having been interested in community land trusts for some time, she undertook a project to determine whether this model might help Beasley assert some control over future development by enabling the community to acquire land.

One of the earliest and most successful expressions of the land trust idea was the Dudley Street Neighborhood Initiative in Boston. It was created in 1984 as a response to deteriorating conditions in a fading working-class community where landlords would burn down their buildings for the insurance money and people would dump garbage in public places. The Dudley Street group won the right to expropriate vacant properties—a major advantage that does not exist for land trusts elsewhere. Community land trusts have since sprouted across Canada, including in Toronto's Parkdale neighbourhood, where the land trust recently bought a rooming house (which would otherwise have been sold for luxury accommodation) as well as a piece of land for a community garden.[19]

When Maxted presented the land trust idea to the BNA, her expectation was that—if they accepted the concept—the group would thank her for her time and begin work on the project on their own. "But that's not how it happened," she recalls. "They sort of asked me to help with getting it started." Since then, the land trust has formed partnerships with various organizations. The social planning council helped it secure a Trillium grant to fund putting all the organizational pieces in place and to scope out possibilities for future work. The Evergreen Foundation gave the trust use of its storefront community meeting place on James Street North. The Hamilton Community Land Trust (the choice of "Hamilton" in the name recognizes that rising Beasley land prices might force it to look beyond that neighbourhood for properties) was officially incorporated in December 2015.

The rapid inflation of Hamilton's real estate market—"We had no idea it would escalate the way it did," says Maxted—has complicated the trust's plans to buy idle properties. Land trusts, to be sure, face better odds in times when prices are low. Still, this fledgling institution has found a way forward. The city sold a small piece of surplus property to the HCLT for a symbolic two dollars, and the trust is partnering with Habitat for Humanity to build two town-houses on that parcel. The land trust will lease the land to Habitat but retain ownership, while the occupants will become owners of the actual homes. It's a kind of hybrid halfway between social and private housing.

"We're working on trying to find the right balance," Maxted explains. "One of the objectives of Habitat for Humanity is to build equity for the owner. So we're trying to make sure the owner can build some equity and maybe move on to owning a house somewhere else someday." At the same time, HCLT's control of the land ensures the property remains an ongoing resource for low-income Hamiltonians. "This is a way of giving families a way out of the cycle of poverty they are stuck in."

Maxted says this project is a likely model for future developments, with the land trust hoping to partner with Habitat over the long term. She also foresees HCLT carving out a niche in acquiring problematic properties "that are a weird shape or somehow are a challenge to develop. A traditional developer doesn't have the patience to do the creative things you need to do to develop them a lot of times," and consequently, they can often be bought more cheaply. The land trust has also had local people bequeath properties to it in their wills.

Two townhouses, in the face of the massive displacement of low-income people that continues in Hamilton, seems like a modest beginning. Matthew Green (who as councillor helped facilitate the transfer of the city property to the land trust) tells me that what the new organization is doing shouldn't be mistaken for an adequate solution to the city's immediate housing crisis. Only large-scale government action to build or fund more affordable housing could significantly affect the big picture, he says. On the other hand, the land trust offers opportunities for the future that haven't been fully defined yet.

"You need all those green shoots to start to sprout," says Rob Fiedler, an HCLT board member and community activist who holds a Ph.D. in urban geography. "In the case of the land trust, it's a hundred per cent true that it's had very small impact. But it's also very young, right? Before you take on something of any size, you have to prove that you can do something. We have to look to other cities to see how you go from a few units to something more substantive. In Vancouver, where the co-op movement is stronger, land trusts and co-ops are moving to do thousands of units, not just a few."

Hamilton's fruitful history of grassroots action

You needn't cast your sights all the way to the Pacific Coast to find historical precedents of projects with small beginnings that pay major dividends. This very area produced one of those "green shoots" that has since grown tall and mighty. A kilometre or two away, at the shores of Lake Ontario, Hamilton's Bayfront Park stands as a testament to the way that one inspired, committed person can ignite the power of a broader community, leading to transformative social and material change.

Bayfront Park is one of the nicest things about Hamilton today: a twenty-five-acre waterfront park with a 3.5-kilometre shoreline walking trail, a spectacular view of the lake, a thousand young trees (planted within the last four decades), and water that's clean enough to sustain myriad species of fish and birds. This is a far cry from the forsaken landscape that once blighted this stretch of waterfront.

"This was literally an industrial waste dump right up to the mid-eighties," says Chris McLaughlin, executive director of the Bay Area Restoration Council (BARC), an organization founded in 1991 to involve the broader public in multi-partner efforts to restore Hamilton's bay. "Trucks were backing up into the harbour here and dumping stuff right into the water. There are stories from the 1950s of kids coming out of the water all covered in oil and having to clean up from that. What are the health impacts of generations of kids doing that—we'll never know, right?" In addition to the clandestine dumping from trucks, a series of pipes pumped industrial effluent into the murky bay from the factories a few kilometres down the shoreline. All this coagulated not just as a major health hazard but also as a rising sense of public shame, to the point where Hamilton Harbour was described in the House of Commons in 1969 as "a stinking, rotten quagmire of filth and poisonous waste."

But the shame soon turned into outrage and then into action, the process ignited by a woman named Gil Simmons, who had originally emigrated with her husband from England to Burlington. The couple later took the unlikely step of decamping from that affluent suburb and relocating, with their three sons, to the downtrodden North End of Hamilton. That is where Gil took up the cause that would post-humously make her the first inductee into the Wall of Distinction created by BARC and the City of Hamilton at Bayfront Park.

In 1971, "Gil lived in one of those houses, you can see it through all the boat masts in Macassa Bay," says McLaughlin, pointing towards a stand of solid Victorian homes from a lush green patch along the waterfront. "Her kitchen looked out onto the bay where the dumping was taking place. She found what was happening here to be completely unacceptable, and so she started to gather people around her kitchen table, at first neighbours and people with a tangible connection to the area, and she also started to put on the pressure at city hall." Those informal kitchen-table confabs, soon formalized as the Save Our Bay group, became "really the turning point where people from the general public said, 'We're dumping on something that's marvellous. Most people would love to have a natural asset like we have here, and we're destroying it.'"

Fortuitously, this gathering storm of citizen activism meshed with a growing environmental consciousness, across North America and the world, that had begun to impact political priorities at higher levels. A decade after Rachel Carson's book *Silent Spring* had raised the alarm over unchecked pollution, and a few months after the first Earth Day, Simmons's protestations about the poisoning of Hamilton Bay began to resonate more widely. Growing governmental attention to water pollution would soon help propel action at the local level.

In 1972, recounts McLaughlin, Canada and the U.S. inked the first Great Lakes Water Quality Agreement, in response to a growing regional awareness of "the issue of contaminated water, contaminated sediment, the appearance of fish tumours, degraded environments, the disappearance of critters big and small, and public inaccessibility to bays and rivers." That landmark agreement led to huge investments in finding ways to end the dumping of raw sewage, which soon translated as a vast improvement in water quality.

"As the seventies progressed," McLaughlin continues, "scientists refined their methods and developed new technologies, which led to the discovery of problems we didn't know existed, particularly how chemicals in the environment could change us in unhealthy ways." This evolving understanding of the obviously pernicious effects of water pollution sustained public concern and convinced governments to negotiate new generations of water-quality agreements. Politicians were also keen to support partnerships with citizen organizations committed to the once unthinkable goal of returning badly despoiled waterways and shorelines—such as the nightmare scenario known as Hamilton Bay—to some semblance of their pristine, pre-industrial condition.

In Hamilton's case, it required considerable ingenuity to return life to the shoreline. Decades of dumping often-toxic fill had created an artificial shoreline, explains engineer and Hamilton Waterfront Trust executive director Werner Plessl, who had been responsible (while in the employ of the City of Hamilton) for the construction of new parkland along the waterfront. While the original bay had once sloped gently from shallow to deep water, says Plessl, that human-made ridge of hardened sludge had crept further into Hamilton's bay, forming a high wall that dropped off immediately into deep water. Such an environment does not encourage fish to spawn.

"Smaller fish generally grow up in a shallow area where the bigger fish can't eat them," says Plessl (another Hamiltonian who grew up close to my childhood habitat on the Mountain). "So, we used different techniques to make an environment that was friendly to the fish. In Bayfront Park in particular, we used forty-five different types of shoreline configurations using different types of stone and material to make it desirable for certain types of fish to spawn there."

One example is the restorers' use of large concrete pipes, which were dropped into the water and filled with logs and trees "so that there are areas for the little fish to hide and grow bigger and hopefully mature and survive in the harbour," Plessl says.

The restoration also involved creating artificial islands further into the bay. Explains Plessl: "By building an offshore island, you've got a huge perimeter around it and varying depths, so you've got a lot more shoreline than if you just use the shoreline without an island. We built about twelve islands that are connected by shallow shoals. In fact, there's a string of islands that are offshore about a hundred feet. Between the shoreline and this string of islands you've got a large shallow area with a lot of habitat."

Efforts to reclaim the area now known as Bayfront Park relied heavily on the expertise and imagination of engineers, in addition to a significant commitment of public cash. Further westward and past a bend in the shoreline trail, meanwhile, lies the Cootes Paradise marsh, the restoration of which has relied on the relentless slogging of legions of volunteers who aren't afraid of manual labour or mud. "We get grandfathers and students and all kinds of people out into the marsh in hip waders jamming little baby cattails down into the muck," says Chris McLaughlin. The replanting, which has gone on for years, is an essential part of efforts to clean up the water and create an environment suitable for fish to spawn, as they did in the pre-industrial days, when a massive commercial fishery operated in the waters nearby.

"It's getting to the point where fish are returning," declares Tys Theysmeyer, head of natural lands at the Royal Botanical Gardens. "The most fascinating part is actually getting the environment back to a place where you have clear, clean water, and where it actually supports things that you would never imagine seeing again. We've started to cross that line, although it's a big marsh so there are parts that still have a way to go." Besides fish, birds are also returning. "There are some grand concentrations of birds starting to occur again. It's quite something," says Theysmeyer. "There are trumpeter swans, waterfowl, red-winged blackbirds," as well as some A-level, celebrity residents: the bald eagles.

Some might describe that last example as close to a miracle. When experts considered where in Ontario's lower Great Lakes area the then-endangered bald eagle might be reintroduced, in advance of the first transplanting of eaglets in 1983, they "didn't even look at the Hamilton area because there's a mental barrier: there's not enough [suitable habitat] here. In the meantime, the bald eagles showed up [in 2013], set up their own territory, and for three years in a row we had two bald eagle chicks raised here, which is amazing for a spot that didn't even make the radar. [Hamilton] became the first spot where bald eagle chicks established themselves on Lake Ontario." Theysmeyer marvels at how unlikely this outcome was: "You know, when you're growing up you hear of bald eagles, but you'd never conceive of seeing one, let alone having one nest in your backyard."[20]

This natural revival at Bayfront Park has also fed a social renaissance. No one in the 1970s could have foreseen that the scarred and poisonous wasteland at the foot of Bay and James Streets would become a major tourist attraction, drawing locals and visitors alike with its abundance of natural beauty. But the scene on many summer nights down on Bayfront Park speaks of the almost-impossible becoming real. On warm evenings, the green space alongside that 3.5 kilometres of trail beckons a range of people: picnicking families with small children; James Street North hipsters walking their bandana-clad dogs; seniors and teenagers; people of all ethnic, religious, and economic backgrounds—all of them out to enjoy the sunshine and the warm lake breeze. Perhaps this is not precisely what Gil Simmons and her band of waterfront restoration advocates had envisioned. Maybe they dared not dream of something so successful; maybe they had no inkling of the rich social mosaic that would grow down here. But they put in place the conditions that allowed the waterfront to evolve in its own particular way. They committed to the idea that better is possible. Then this piece of waterfront took on a life of its own, the direction of its growth influenced by the efforts of new generations of contributors and shaped by shifting circumstances.

Will lessons from the past shape Hamilton's future?

The restoration work that coalesced over decades along the waterfront came as a response to what was likely the number one problem of Hamilton's industrial age: its pollution. In post-industrial Hamilton, the problems are different. If you had to rank the most pressing concerns of today's post-steel city, the intersecting evils of social inequality, poverty, and the lack of affordable housing would jockey for top spot. But there's been progress in these areas too. Huge as today's affordable housing crisis is, a cluster of organizations have been making a difference, developing infrastructure and expertise, providing models today for what could become commonplace tomorrow. Like the early environmental agitators who demanded that our waterfront no longer be treated like a cesspool, Hamilton's leaders in the social housing sector know not only what needs to be done but also which approaches work and which don't. Where they differ from the waterfront advocates, it seems, is that they don't yet have behind them the critical mass of support from governments and society at large that can make a pressing current problem something for the history books.

A handful of organizations in Hamilton have decades of experience developing housing solutions for people who have been failed by the private market. While these groups share a broad underlying goal—addressing the housing shortage that causes immense personal suffering and diminishes communities as a whole—they are differentiated from one another by their particular focuses. Individual people in different circumstances have different housing needs. The organizations that serve them have therefore developed their own specialized niches.

Alan Whittle from Good Shepherd says his organization differs from others, like Victoria Park homes and Kiwanis (which provides affordable housing for families) and CityHousing Hamilton (which administers social housing buildings and large complexes for the city), in that they "really want to focus on people who are not well served by others, like people with mental health or addiction issues, women who have experienced violence, and other people who have been victimized because of their gender or sexuality. Youth is another group. And seniors are becoming a big one" for them because of the large cohort of people now encountering the challenges of growing older.

The result of having multiple constituencies is that they've "developed quite literally a cradle-to-grave collection of services," says Whittle. On one end of the continuum, he continues, "we acquired a three-storey walk-up in the East End that we renovated and targeted it for teenage moms and their infants. The purpose of that program is to break two cycles of poverty. It gets the infants off to a healthy start. It's also intended to get the mother through school with the right skills to continue work and to improve parenting skills, if that's what's needed. We're now seeing success with the program: every mother that enters that program finishes high school." Other Good Shepherd programs address the needs of people at a range of critical junctures, including the provision of hospice care for people at the end of their lives.

Decades of experience has taught the agency's staff how to improvise to better meet the needs of distinct groups of tenants. For example, the acquisition of a new building for its emergency family shelter (one of five emergency shelters that Good Shepherd operates in Hamilton) allowed for a break from the typical communal living model. The new building "lent itself well to the building of apartments," says Whittle. In turn, placing families at risk of homelessness in their own apartments allowed those families "to live their lives, continue their lives normally so they could just focus on getting housing." They weren't distracted by issues that arose with many families living together, like having to agree what to watch on TV, adapting to different expectations for children's behaviour, or accommodating various dietary needs or restrictions (an increasingly prominent issue when people from different cultures inhabit the same space). The families can "just go and eat what they want to, when they want to, because they were expected to cook their own meals."

Adaptations are also necessary for people with special needs. Whittle recalls that in a building where tenants with mental health issues live, "we actually built a false floor, because [one of the residents would] constantly pound on the floor because she would hear noises in her head and would pound to try to make the noises stop. Other people would pound back or bang on the ceiling—a 'What are you bothering me for?' kind of thing. So we built this false floor that insulated it so people couldn't hear each other, and over time, it wasn't an issue anymore."

Beyond learning situational lessons and cultivating a talent for adaptability, Whittle says that Good Shepherd's work has also brought the organization face to face with some big truths. "What we've learned," says Whittle, "is that if a person has a safe, secure, affordable place to live, that really facilitates their ability to address many of the other issues they may have." In other words, institutions can be most effective in helping people improve their lives if they start with an understanding that finding housing shouldn't depend on first solving the tangled web of challenging circumstances they may face. Success almost inevitably comes from focusing first on the housing.

Whittle recalls a woman with a school-aged daughter who moved into a Good Shepherd subsidized apartment. That change became a turning point. "She had changed places to live seven or eight times and schools for her daughter four or five times," he recalls. "After she moved here her daughter said, 'Mommy, let's live here forever.' Because there weren't the constant changes in schools. There wasn't the daily ritual of looking for For Rent signs to get a better place that didn't have vermin. They didn't worry about paying the rent because they were in housing they could afford to live in. [The mother] started developing her own business, which is different than spending your time thinking, 'Do I have to go to the food bank to get something to put in my daughter's lunch? Do I have to go somewhere to get a hot meal because I don't have any food in the fridge for me?'"

Across town, a few steps down from Kenilworth and Main, in a ground-floor office in one of the Indwell organization's ten Hamilton housing projects, executive director Jeff Neven says he's also witnessed the transformative effect when people find decent housing. "When somebody gets housed," he says, "we see on day one that their addictions decrease, their mental health stabilizes. I'm not talking about a full recovery, immediately or even after years, but you can see the difference. Nobody's drinking gets better when they're underneath a bridge. Nobody develops more connections with employers and friends and family living under a bridge or in one of those houses carved up into boxes and rented out. That makes it nearly impossible to put your life back together."

Neven continues, "When people have housing that's safe, affordable, something they can be proud of, that reinforces people's sense of self-worth and dignity and you see people's lives start to change. People develop natural support networks, where a friend helps a friend, and you don't need a professional social worker to come in and ask how you are. The normal ways that communities for centuries have supported and helped each other start to come back into play."

This "housing first" approach dates back at least to the 1980s, when a New York City psychologist named Sam Tsemberis discovered that two-thirds of the homeless people he sent to the Bellevue psychiatric hospital for treatment would wind back on the streets. Eventually, Tsemberis was able to secure funding for a program to provide homeless people with housing that wasn't dependent on them having to conquer their addictions or mental health issues first. This allowed Tsemberis's team to test the notion that housing could be an effective stepping stone to wellness.[21]

The view of housing as a conduit for positive social interaction, explains Neven, is what motivated Indwell to name one of its buildings—across the street from where our conversation took place—in tribute to John Perkins. Perkins was a civil rights leader in the American South and a contemporary of Martin Luther King. His 1993 book *Beyond Charity* argued that empowerment, not simply spending, is key to helping disadvantaged people escape from poverty. "He said that if you want to break the cycle of poverty, that can only be done when people with networks extend those to people without them. And I think that's the core of our organization: we are deeply relational."

Indwell has also, like Good Shepherd, developed specialized technical expertise on how to bring housing for people with very low incomes to market. Almost all of its tenants survive on the disability or social assistance payments that have stagnated for decades as rents have skyrocketed. Since tenants have very little income to pay rent, almost all of the costs of planning, building, and operating Indwell housing must be covered by subsidies, and very little of those costs will be recovered after the fact through rents. Governments, which remain in austerity mode, are generally only prepared to provide a fraction of those subsidies. An essential skill for non-profits, therefore, is to find the missing resources.

Neven points to a new forty-five-unit Indwell project on James North (then in progress, since completed) that comes with a price tag in the vicinity of $17 million. The agency was able to access $6.3 million in public funds, says Neven, while Indwell's church partner (a presence in the neighbourhood for 130 years and in need of a new building) made a massive in-kind contribution by providing land on its new site and underwriting construction of the housing project's foundation and the roof. But that still left a $2 million shortfall, which had to be fundraised.

In this case and in the past, Indwell's ability to add to the supply of affordable housing has been dependent upon its special talent for securing private contributions. Neven says the organization had received support from some 180 private donors who had cumulatively contributed $22 million for its housing projects. The problem, however, is that it's not nearly enough. As gentrification accelerates and rents in the private marketplace rise, affordable housing is disappearing faster than it can be replaced.

"As a sector," says Neven, social housing agencies have "been building about fifty units every two years in Hamilton, although lately, with some federal initiatives, we've upped that to about fifty units per year." By contrast, Indwell calculates that, to serve people living on disability allowances who need supportive housing, "we need to build a fifty-unit building every two to three weeks. Every time we open a new unit, we get ten calls for it." And remember: those numbers only reflect the needs of "people who have been diagnosed with a permanent disability, which is just a subset of the population looking for housing."

Over at the Good Shepherd, Alan Whittle says responding to a sudden surge of housing insecurity is made more difficult not only by cost, but also by the amount of time it takes to turn an idea into reality. Although planning for Good Shepherd's King Street West housing complex for women began in 1999, for example, the building didn't open until 2012. That's why it's good to have a toolbox that's well stocked with a variety of solutions, such as rent subsidies (a significant element of the National Housing Strategy), that can "usually solve a problem in really short order." The availability of a rent subsidy allows a family that's been forced into a shelter because they can't afford their prior rent "to have a roof over their heads again in less than six weeks." But short-term solutions must be implemented alongside longer-term plans, says Whittle, since "we are a growing nation, with an increasing population, and there needs to be more places for people to live."

The magic ingredient is political will

So many good ideas. So many committed problem solvers. So many daunting obstacles that remain.

There's a sense of frustration among most of the people I spoke with over how frequently promising, well-designed plans get short-circuited in this city. Some point to petty bureaucratic obstacles, others to partisan posturing at city hall, others to large political and economic shifts that overwhelm any progress made on the ground. For every shining promise that leaps from the imaginations of Hamilton's cadres of visionary problem solvers, there seems to be a corresponding example of people in power moving in precisely the wrong direction.

Sometimes inaction has been the result of bureaucratic impediments that make innovations too costly or prohibit them altogether. Matt Thompson, co-chair of the Beasley Neighbourhood Association, points to potential of constructing "laneway houses" behind existing homes as a means of easing the housing crisis. Planning changes in Edmonton led to about 130 of these micro-projects going forward there. Landlords typically "were able to charge about seven hundred dollars in rent, and at this point that would be pretty affordable in Hamilton—actually, it would be great," he says. "I wish I had a house with a laneway so I could try it out." Beasley has abundant laneways, but city staff have been less than enthusiastic about populating them with small, inexpensive homes, although advocates continue to lobby to have them accepted. Thompson believes if laneway homes started sprouting in his neighbourhood, it might make up for the city having "missed the boat" on inclusionary zoning.

Whittle adds that citizens have made compelling arguments to try to erode city bureaucrats' reticence to green-light laneway houses. "You've got one part of the city wanting to do this," he explains, "and another part saying, 'This isn't appropriate—how are we going to fight a fire?' We've been saying, 'We're not going to have to fight a fire because we're going to put sprinklers in and do non-combustible construction and that kind of stuff.' But they still want to be able to put big fire trucks back there. There's some talk of smaller fire trucks, and that might be where this goes."

Proposing infill housing downtown is another case where potential solutions to the disappearance of affordable housing have met with resistance. John Neary, the other co-chair of the BNA and a physician at St. Joseph's hospital, reports that "in a lot of other neighbourhoods, people will fight a four- or six-storey infill building to the death." The primary motivation, he believes, is a self-interested concern with property values (although this is often couched in the language of wanting to preserve "the character" of their neighbourhoods). Resisting the construction of more units "keeps the supply down and the price [of existing homes] up," which obviously serves the economic interest of homeowners, notes Neary.

Urban geographer and community activist Rob Fiedler comments, similarly, "I don't see a lot of cases where you have considerable infill where there isn't contestation" from local residents. "In some cases, it's necessary because it produces a better outcome, but it also increases the time it takes and the cost," raising the chances that infill proposals will die.

Fiedler believes that a fundamental problem with plans to build more affordable housing in Hamilton is that they have too often been linked to the expansion of the private real estate market. Encouraging affordable housing growth through inclusionary zoning, for example, rests on the assumption that condo prices are high enough to convince developers to accept having to designate, let's say, 20 per cent of their units as affordable, simply as a cost of doing business.

But Fiedler questions whether the relevant segments of Hamilton's real estate market are robust enough to support this approach. "People who come from elsewhere to Hamilton seem to come because Hamilton offers them something Toronto doesn't: an urban existence but with a house. They like the transit and the walkability, but they also want the house with the backyard." Living in a high-rise in Hamilton, by contrast, is not yet many people's ideal of the good life. So, while a modest number of new condo and apartment towers have appeared on the skyline of downtown Hamilton, they aren't as mega-rise or pricey as their counterparts in Toronto or Vancouver and they don't generate the volume of cash needed to fund governments' plans for affordable housing through inclusionary zoning. On the other hand, says Fiedler, Hamilton's real estate market is buoyant enough that it can make it more expensive, and thus more difficult, to construct subsidized, non-market housing.

Furthermore, Whittle says, years after upper levels of government have withdrawn from the provision of social housing, the ministries that oversee their work have lost crucial capacities. Non-profits like Good Shepherd must sometimes "deal with government people who don't understand the development process. They've lost the people who know how to do this stuff. Governments haven't done any major developments since the early nineties in this province, and they don't have the people with the experience to understand what's involved."

Beyond the questions about governments' capacities to bring about change is the crucial matter of whether they have the will.

A shift in the political climate can erase years of hard-won progress and turn optimism back into despair. This was certainly the case after the election of Doug Ford's reconstituted, slash-and-burn Progressive Conservative party in the 2018 provincial election.

At first, it appeared that the new regime would honour the previous government's commitment to address the housing crisis and to support municipal programs. Shortly after presenting an April 2019 budget that appeared to make only modest cuts,[22] the Ford Conservatives made a separate announcement committing to one billion dollars in social housing spending ($29 million of that earmarked for Hamilton) to fund repairs to aging facilities, address long wait lists and overcrowding, and cover expiring federal subsidies.[23] The new government also defied expectations and reaffirmed the provincial commitment to fund Hamilton's LRT (although the province reneged on that pledge, later to reverse itself and recommit to the LRT).[24]

Within two weeks of the April 2019 budget announcement, however, it was becoming clear that a range of cuts that had been kept out of view amounted to something more like a bloodbath, and it was Ontario's most vulnerable citizens who would suffer most. The province made significant cuts to funding for public health (including killing a mobile cancer screening program in Hamilton aimed at people who have trouble accessing health services),[25] leaving municipalities to cover the shortfall. It withdrew millions of dollars in support from child-care programs and ended an addictions treatment program for people attempting to re-enter the workforce. It cut Ontario's legal aid program by 30 per cent, a move that would be especially injurious to refugee claimants.[26] Hamilton mayor Fred Eisenberger, who had previously said the provincial budget "isn't the slash-and-hack people were expecting,"[27] now complained that the province's "haphazard approach" and "in-year cuts inflicted . . . with no prior consultation" was making it impossible for the city to create a reliable budget or to meet its obligations.[28]

Although the government's hatchet hacked away at environmental programs, education, libraries, and other services,[29] it was the poor who seemed disproportionately targeted. The Hamilton

Roundtable's Tom Cooper called Ford's elimination of the Transition Child Benefit, which had provided a maximum of $230 per month to low-income families unable to access federal or provincial child benefits, "nonsensical," "beyond the pale," and "absolutely cruel because they are punishing the most vulnerable children in society." There were concerns that the health of the 1,800 children in Hamilton who received the benefit would suffer, and reports of many families being unsure of how they could pay their rent.[30]

The change in government also swiftly eliminated plans that had been years in the making. One example is the previous Liberal government's complicated deal to sell some surplus provincial land on the Mountain to Mohawk College, which would expand its campus and assume responsibility for restoring the historic Century Manor on the property. The province was to apply the proceeds from the sale to affordable housing in a new mixed-income development proposed for York Boulevard downtown. Despite all the contracts having been signed, the new government summarily scrapped the plan. Likewise, Ford's decision to end Ontario's participation in a cap-and-trade environmental program with California and Quebec (an income-generating initiative) foreclosed on $17 million in funding to retrofit and renovate social housing units in Hamilton.[31]

As 2019 drew to a close, it became clear that the past year had been one of the worst in recent memory, and the city's confidence had taken a beating. A few of the bad omens were only tangentially related to provincial budget slashing. For example, *Spectator* reporter Steve Buist, who had broken lots of bad news about Hamilton years earlier in the Code Red series, speculated that a spate of recent high-profile violent crimes and racist and homophobic confrontations was indicative of a deeper malaise rooted in growing inequality locally and the receptiveness of many Hamiltonians to a global wave of hate and reactionary politics.[32]

And then, less than three months after the close of a dismal year, the COVID-19 pandemic struck. Across the world, COVID's effects were especially devastating to people who were already vulnerable. Those who worked in low-wage and precarious jobs, unlike more privileged professionals who were often able to work remotely from home, were more likely to spend their work hours in crowded workplaces with fewer safeguards, putting them at greater risk of contracting the disease. For people in lower-income communities whose homes are generally smaller and more crowded, isolating an infected family member became nearly impossible. As a result, COVID had a much easier time of spreading quickly through families and across low-income communities. Meanwhile, the financial impacts of COVID-related shutdowns were particularly brutal for people without savings, people for whom survival was a struggle even in normal times, and especially for those who didn't qualify for the government's temporary relief programs.

In Hamilton, where, despite the ravages of the pandemic, prices for single-family homes shot up by a record 29 per cent in 2020,[33] the subsidiary impacts of COVID on people struggling to keep their footing in this unforgiving housing market quickly became visible on the streets. As *Spectator* columnist Margaret Shkimba wrote: "If you've been even half aware of what's happening in Hamilton, you will have noticed that our homeless situation has been escalating. It was bad before, but COVID-19 brought it out of the bushes and displayed it under our noses with no filter."[34] By the fall, some twenty encampments had appeared on public land, the largest of which was a sixty-tent settlement in front of the Wesley Day Centre on Ferguson Avenue. In spite of a human-rights-based legal challenge by a group of doctors, lawyers, and outreach workers seeking to prevent the city from removing the camps, in mid-October city workers moved in and tore them down. Although the city spent an extra one million dollars to create new shelter spaces during the crisis, shelter workers were unsure of whether they could meet the additional demand after the displacement of so many people who had been living outdoors.[35]

The one note of redemption emerging from this tragedy is that, by bringing existing social failures into the light of day, the COVID crisis may have forced a moment of reckoning. COVID-19 has compelled many Canadians to acknowledge, for example, the crucial importance of people who work for low wages (and in times like this, often at great personal risk) to keep grocery stores open, to clean and provide care in nursing homes, to deliver packages and take-out food to locked-down populations. Aren't these people—commonly described as "heroes" in the first phase of the pandemic—as much entitled to economic security and decent accommodation as the better-off?

Measures introduced to help Canadians ride out the pandemic also raised the question of whether we've been doing things wrong in the past, and whether Canada could easily take aim at the inequality that's been tolerated for too long. The federal government's Canada Emergency Response Benefit (CERB), designed to keep pandemic-displaced workers afloat and to avert a more general economic collapse by keeping money circulating, has been held up by some as the working model for a future Universal Basic Income program. That kind of permanent program could provide an ongoing stimulus to the economy while helping individuals move out of the conditions of poverty that trap too many Canadians.

Could the pandemic have also provided the jolt capable of pushing Hamilton out of the age of promising, small-scale experiments and towards actions ambitious enough to match the scale and urgency of its problems? A series of events in 2020—some pandemic-linked, others perhaps coincidental—provide some grounds for optimism. For one, the city has committed to using a pandemic-related $10.8 million infusion of federal funds to build forty-five subsidized units (housing fifty-three people) within a year. Housing on three sites will be constructed by transforming what is currently office and commercial space into accommodation, while prefabricated, modular housing units (cheaper to construct than conventional residences, and now a popular option for addressing the housing crisis in cities like Vancouver) will occupy a fourth site.[36] If this Rapid Housing Initiative hits its target, it will hopefully send a message that the red tape and planning hurdles that typically burden social housing creation can be overcome, making it possible to envision housing solutions that come online relatively quickly.

Meanwhile, Hamilton's major non-profit housing agencies—including Indwell, Good Shepherd, the YMCA, Kiwanis, Victoria Park Community Homes, and Sacajawea (which serves First Nations people)—have formed a consortium, dubbed Hamilton is Home, that aims to address both the need for speed and the imperative to build a far greater number of social housing units.[37] The consortium, which has won the backing of Hamilton city council,[38] is applying jointly to the federal government's National Housing Strategy program for funding to build some three thousand social housing units over three years. The price tag is estimated at $1.2 billion, and over fifty sites have been identified across the city. After years of playing catch-up—typical construction targets are two hundred new units a year, for example, which is far from sufficient to keep up with the growth in demand—Hamilton's social housing providers are now looking at a project that would make a serious dent in the city's 2021 subsidized housing waiting list of 5,100 applicants.[39]

The consortium's quest to build three thousand new social housing units is in addition to the 2020 announcement of a $400-million planned community in the East End. A partnership between private developers and the municipal agency CityHousing Hamilton, it will replace the old Roxborough School and a crumbling public housing development of 107 units with a mixed-income development in the vein of Toronto's redeveloped Regent Park. Roughly 800 units will include about "300 affordable market units" as well as subsidized homes in the form of apartments and stacked and back-to-back townhouses.[40]

After so much bad news—with waves of downtown displacement encouraged by gentrification; with an epidemic of "renovictions" of low-income renters across the city, courtesy of the desire of deep-pocketed real estate investment trusts to move their properties upmarket; with social spending cuts by the province; with the crushing impacts of the COVID-19 pandemic—could Hamilton be turning a corner? Could the city's fortunes be on the verge of changing? Whether there's still time to change the outcome of Hamilton's story is "the million-dollar question that no one has an answer for," says Rob Fiedler, who was interviewed before the COVID-19 crisis. "It's like we're in a baseball game where we're not in the first inning anymore, but nobody knows how deep into the game we are. Maybe we're in the fifth inning, but maybe we're in the sixth. It's not clear."

There are certainly factors that favour Hamilton being able to construct a more inclusive future, with room for people at all economic levels. One of those factors, says Fiedler, is the availability of ample property downtown, much of it owned by the city, for future development. In the past, when the city has turned over municipally owned property to private developers, it has been able to extract only a very low percentage of affordable units through inclusionary zoning. But, under different economic or political conditions, it might do better in the future. The abundance of city-owned property can also be a source of sites for future projects by social housing organizations.

Fiedler also finds cause for modest optimism in the potential for unintended consequences and quirks of fate—unforeseen occurrences that can impact cities in ways that no one would have anticipated. From the outdoor terrace of a café in the downtown district known as Durand, the urban geographer points to the neighbouring high-rise apartment towers, which provide an example of how the process can work. Although those buildings were originally constructed in the sixties and seventies with affluent young adults in mind, over time "they became an impressive stock of affordable housing in the city," he recalls. The same thing happened in Toronto with the development of the soaring St. James Town development north of Toronto's historic Cabbagetown neighbourhood. "They were intended as luxury housing," says Fiedler. Instead, apartments in St. James Town became low-cost rental accommodation while, ironically, the Victorian-era single-family dwellings that urban crusaders fought to preserve have become hugely expensive—well beyond the means of the working-class families and rooming-house tenants who once lived in them.

Another intangible that may have a positive impact on the way Hamilton develops is the city's unique social climate. Although his assessment differs from that of many other people interviewed for this book, Indwell's Jeff Neven believes that social housing providers are less inclined to face the headwinds of public resistance in Hamilton than in other places. "When we propose anything, particularly in the East End, we get nothing but support," Neven says.

"Neighbours come to the meetings not in opposition to affordable housing being built in the neighbourhood, but in celebration of it. You don't get that in other cities. In Hamilton, where we've had a history of people living here because it was affordable, and we've had our share of poverty, for us this isn't about somebody else. This is about us. This is about our brother, our mother, our sister, our child who needs affordable housing."

Neven adds that many newcomers to the city have embraced this idea of Hamilton as a diverse, multi-income community. Among the independent coffee shops that have proliferated in neighbourhoods across the city, "some of those are places that are not welcoming to marginalized people" while others "have been very intentional about welcoming marginalized people." In the latter camp is a coffee shop close by to Indwell's Main Street East premises.

"A couple from Toronto buys a building that was vacant and derelict," he recalls. "They have two children and they live upstairs and run their business on the main floor. They've invested into the building and invested into our neighbourhood. They treat our tenants with respect and dignity. They are building a type of community that I am really excited to be a part of. They know people personally and they welcome marginalized people. They even named a sandwich after one of our tenants."

The other advantage that favours Hamilton at this historical juncture is the accumulated experience—from here and from elsewhere—that points toward workable solutions. There's a formidable body of hard-won knowledge on how to create cohesive communities—on how to reduce poverty, homelessness, and inequality in cities—that planners and community builders can draw from. But will that happen? Will that magical ingredient—political will—be added to the mix, or will those great ideas stay confined to briefing booklets, of little use to anyone in the real world?

"Sure, there are all these opportunities," exclaims Deirdre Pike, from the social planning council. "The question is whether they'll come true." She effortlessly retrieves several examples of frustrated promises from Hamilton's recent past. "There was an opportunity when the new stadium was built to have good jobs [through community benefits provisions], but they weren't jobs for people in this community." And although this is a town where people frequently talk about the importance of living wages, when city hall was renovated a few years back, the café franchise was awarded to "a large, non-living-wage employer . . . so that everybody could see when you walked by there that we have a ten-year contract with an employer that pays poverty wages, when there's all sorts of other living-wage coffee shops in this community."

Big ideas with transformative potential have been the stuff of Paul Johnson's work days. But he, too, recognizes that if the political will to action somehow evaporates, those impressive ideas won't count for much. "Will we translate what we know into what we do?" he asks. "What is the gap between those two things? If, twenty years from now, we are still sitting around talking about what we know, what the research says, what the experience has been elsewhere, but not doing anything, then shame on us. We could still be having this conversation twenty years from now, but by then the situation will be much poorer than it is today."

Notes

Chapter One: Tectonic Shift

1   Bill Freeman, *Hamilton: A People's History* (Toronto: James Lorimer and Company, 2001), 83–86.

2   Greg Keenan, "US Steel Ends an Era in Hamilton," *Globe and Mail*, October 29, 2013.

3   "US Steel Closes Hamilton Blast Furnace and Steel-Making," CBC News, October 29, 2013, www.cbc.ca.

4   Steve Buist, "Code Red: Of Polls and Poverty," *Hamilton Spectator*, October 5, 2010.

5   The west Mountain neighbourhood runs between Upper Paradise Road, the Mountain Brow, Rice Avenue, and Mohawk Road West. The downtown neighbourhood is circumscribed by Wellington Street North, the harbourfront, Sherman Avenue North, and the railway tracks close to Barton Street.

6   "Worlds Apart," *Hamilton Spectator*, August 25, 2010.

7   "Great Divide of Extremes and Disparity," *Hamilton Spectator*, August 25, 2010.

8   The neighbourhood is bounded by Queen Street North, Cannon Street West, James Street North, and the railway track north of Barton.

9   "Code Red: Mental Illness: Poverty's Dark Side," *Hamilton Spectator*, April 16, 2010.

10 "Code Red: Starting Life on the Right Trajectory," *Hamilton Spectator*, April 13, 2010.

11 "Catch Ya Later, Toronto," Jason McBride, *Grid*, November 14, 2012.

12 Guy Dixon, "Hamilton Ready for Its Close Up," *Globe and Mail*, June 20, 2017; Nathalie Atkinson, "Steeltown's New Sheen," *Globe and Mail*, May 27, 2017.

13 Emily Glazer, "Lessons on Rekindling a Regional Romance: A Visit

to Hamilton Reveals a Percolating Urban Revival Canada Needs to Watch," *Spacing*, May 8, 2015.

14 Stuart Berman, "The New Hamiltonians," *Toronto Life*, July 2017.

15 Emily Badger, "The Deeper Problems We Miss When We Attack 'Gentrification,'" *Washington Post*, June 16, 2015.

16 Steve Buist, "Code Red: Barton Street's Lost Promise," *Hamilton Spectator*, May 18, 2013.

17 Badger, "The Deeper Problems We Miss."

18 Keisha St. Louis and Lena Sanz Tovar, "Infrastructure Is Not Enough: Coming Clean on Regent Park's Social Development Plan," *Spacing* 55 (2020).

19 Michael Kaminer, "Surfacing: Five Places to Go in Hamilton, Ontario," *New York Times*, August 24, 2017.

20 "Hamilton Housing Prices See Biggest Jump in Canada," *Hamilton Spectator*, September 16, 2015.

21 "Prices in Central Hamilton More Than Double in Ten Years," CBC, February 6, 2017, www.cbc.ca.

22 Tess Kalinowski, "Hamilton Is Having Its Moment. But the Days of a Cheap, Two-Story Victorian May Be Gone," *Toronto Star*, September 3, 2016.

23 Don Mitchell, "Hamilton Now Third Least Affordable Housing Market in North America, According to Study," Global News, May 21, 2021, globalnews.ca.

24 Joey Coleman, "Big REITs Buying Up Hamilton Apts, Leaving Vacant to Inflate Rents: Time for Speculation Tax?," *Public Record*, April 30, 2017, www.thepublicrecord.ca.

25 Natalie Paddon, "Report Shows Rental Market 'Out of Control,'" *Hamilton Spectator*, June 4, 2018, www.thespec.com.

26 Teviah Moro, "Homeless Campers Product of 'Out of Control' Hamilton Housing Market," *Hamilton Spectator*, August 1, 2018, www.thespec.com.

Chapter Two: Boom, Bust, and a Double-Sided Bohemian Renaissance

1 *Globe and Mail*, December 12, 1962, cited in Marsha Hewitt and Bill

Freeman, eds., *Their Town: The Mafia, the Media and the Party Machine* (Toronto: James Lorimer, 1979), 24.

2   Hewitt and Freeman, *Their Town*, 121–22.

3   Hewitt and Freeman, *Their Town*, 126–27.

4   Hewitt and Freeman, *Their Town*, 135.

5   The event launched editor and writer Sarah Hipworth's collection *Let Them Stay*, about American war resisters in Canada, and my own volume *Noble Illusions* (about kids' culture around the time of World War I). A Hamiltonian who returned to the city after living abroad for a while, Sarah played a vital role in the creation of this book by introducing me to many of the people who are interviewed in this chapter. She also participated in several of those interviews.

6   Rosemary Donegan, "What Ever Happened to Queen Street West?," *Fuse* 42 (1986), 10–24, available at http://openresearch.ocadu.ca/id/eprint/1862.

7   Toronto Arts Council, "No Vacancy: A Cultural Facilities Policy for the City of Toronto," 1986, www.artscape.ca.

8   Artscape, "Our Evolution," www.artscape.ca.

9   "The Tower Moving Statement," Facebook post, May 25, 2018.

10   The Tower: Hamilton's Anarchist Social Space, the-tower.ca.

11   "Now That It's Undeniable: Gentrification in Hamilton 2015," pamphlet, available at thehamiltoninstitute.noblogs.org.

12   "This Is How We Welcome You: 'Try Hamilton' Tries Fucking Itself," Hamilton Institute, June 26, 2016, thehamiltoninstitute.noblogs.org.

13   Nicole O'Reilly, "Police Arrest Suspect in Vandalism Spree," *Toronto Star*, April 6, 2018.

14   The Tower issued a statement on Facebook stating: "First, no, the actions on Locke and Aberdeen on Saturday night were not organized by the Tower, but yes, we support what happened and are in solidarity with those who carried them out." Facebook post, March 7, 2018.

15   This made me wonder why the authors of Tower-associated written materials don't try communicating more like our interviewees did in person. It's possible that they base their public communications style on a stereotypical conception of how working-class people think and talk. But that's just speculation on my part.

16 "Average Price of a Detached Home in Toronto Hits $1.15 Million," Susan Pigg, *Toronto Star*, June 3, 2015.

Chapter Three:
The "Creative Class" Creates a Global Urban Clash

1 Freeman, *Hamilton*, 62.

2 One of those economic forces, University of Toronto geographer Alan Walks told me, is the "financialization" of the Canadian economy. Walks sees the inflation of housing values by financial interests, as well as the presence of extremely well paid financial sector jobs in the Toronto area, as a primary cause of homes being priced beyond most people's reach in the GTHA. He foresees that "at some point the house price inflation we've seen is going to wane . . . so at some point in the future the price of housing will come back into balance with incomes." Walks believes relying on the financial sector as an economic driver is an unsustainable proposition in the long term. He recommends that cities like Hamilton consider reindustrializing, in anticipation of a return of Canadian manufacturing geared towards domestic consumption.

3 John Lorinc, "How Toronto Lost Its Groove," *Walrus*, November 2011.

4 Tanvi Misra, "This Chart Tool Shows How City Centers Are Doing Better Than Inner Suburbs," CityLab, March 2, 2015, www.citylab.com.

5 Lorinc, "How Toronto Lost Its Groove." When the article appeared in 2011, an average single family dwelling cost more than $450,000. Prices have continued to rise since then, with the average house hitting $1.56 million in early 2017 (Daniel Tencer, "What Toronto's Average House Price Will Buy You around the World," *Huffington Post*, March 9, 2017, www.huffingtonpost.ca) and continuing to rise since then.

6 Ben Spurr, "Waiting for a Bus That Takes Forever: Welcome to Toronto's 'Transit Desert,'" *Toronto Star*, April 25, 2015.

7 Edward Keenan, "Section 37—What It Is, and Why Everybody's Fighting about It," *Toronto Star*, January 16, 2015.

8 Alan Walks, "Stopping the 'War on the Car': Neoliberalism, Fordism, and the Politics of Automobility in Toronto," *Mobilities* (2014), doi: 10.1080/17450101.2014.880563.

9 Lorinc, "How Toronto Lost Its Groove."

10 Richard Florida, *The Rise of the Creative Class, Revisited* (Basic Books, 2012), vi.

11 Richard Florida, *Who's Your City?: How the Creative Economy Is Making Where to Live the Most Important Decision of Your Life* (Toronto: Random House Canada, 2008), 19.

12 Florida, *Who's Your City?*, 19, 27.

13 Florida, *Who's Your City?*, 27.

14 Florida, *Who's Your City?*, 30.

15 Chris Lehmann, *Rich People Things: Real Life Secrets of the Predator Class* (Chicago: Haymarket Books, 2011), 77.

16 Lehmann, *Rich People Things*, 81.

17 Lehmann, *Rich People Things*, 80.

18 "Cities in the Digital Age (an Interview with Joel Kotkin)," *Metropolis*, January 1, 2004, www.metropolismag.

19 Oliver Wainwright, "'Everything Is Gentrification Now': But Richard Florida Isn't Sorry," *Guardian*, October 26, 2017, www.theguardian.com.

20 Frank Bures, "Richard Florida Can't Let Go of His Creative Class Theory. His Reputation Depends on It," *Belt Magazine*, December 13, 2017.

21 Florida, *The Rise of the Creative Class, Revisited*, xi

22 Florida, *The Rise of the Creative Class, Revisited*, 385.

23 Richard Florida, "Canada's New Urban Crisis," brief, Martin Prosperity Institute at the University of Toronto's Rotman School of Business, April 2017.

24 Lawrence Ferlinghetti, *San Francisco Poems* (San Francisco: City Lights Foundation, 2001) 9.

25 Ferlinghetti, 9–10.

26 Ferlinghetti, 24–26.

27 Nathan Heller. "California Screaming: The Tech Industry Made the Bay Area Rich. Why Do So Many Residents Hate It?," *New Yorker*, July 7 & 14, 2014, 46–53.

28 Sarah Schulman, *The Gentrification of the Mind: Witness to a Lost Imagination* (Oakland, CA: University of California Press, 2012), 14.

29 Interview with Richard Moskowitz in "Art Districts," an episode of

the podcast *Benjamen Walker's Theory of Everything*, April 11, 2017, theoryofeverythingpodcast.com.

30 Schulman, *Gentrification of the Mind*, 29–30.

31 Schulman, *Gentrification of the Mind*, 33.

32 Schulman, *Gentrification of the Mind*, 27–28.

33 Patrick Butler, "Chattering Classes 'to Be Priced Out of Islington Housing Market,'" *Guardian*, London, October 3, 2013.

34 Carole Cadwalladr, "From Blair to Corbyn: The Changing Face of Islington, Labour's London Heartland," *Observer* (London), August 9, 2015.

35 Thomas Rogers, "The Life and Death of a 'Cool' City," *New Republic*, September 12, 2014.

36 Matt Shea, "Berliners Are Waging a War Against Gentrification," *Vice*, April 6, 2013, www.vice.com.

37 Philip Oltermann, "Unaffordable Cities: Berlin the Renters' Haven Hit by Green Fog of Eco-scams," *Guardian*, February 11, 2014.

38 Keanin Loomis, "Arts and Culture Now Drive Hamilton," *Hamilton Spectator*, March 23, 2015, www.thespec.com.

39 Meredith Macleod, "Hamilton Poised for Global Greatness," *Hamilton Spectator*, May 2, 2008.

40 Moskowitz interview, "Art Districts," *Benjamen Walker's Theory of Everything*.

41 Dave Beatty, "Masked Anti-gentrification Activists Disrupt Try Hamilton Real Estate Tour," CBC, June 27, 2016, www.cbc.ca; "Police Search for Masked 'Try Hamilton' Protester Wanted for Assault," *Hamilton Spectator*, June 27, 2016, www.thespec.com.

42 Molly Hayes, "Weekend Vandalism in Hamilton was Anti-gentrification Act, Blogger Writes," *Globe and Mail*, March 6, 2018, www.theglobeandmail.com.

43 "Hamilton Police Charge Leading Local Anarchist in Locke Street Vandalism," CBC, April 6, 2018, www.cbc.ca; "Police Arrest Suspect in Hamilton Vandalism Spree," *Toronto Star*, April 6, 2018, www.thestar.com.

44 "Hamilton G20 Activist Gets Bail," *Hamilton Spectator*, July 14, 2014, www.thespec.com.

45 Simon Orpana, "Much a-Dough about Nothing?: Donuts,

Gentrification and the Loss of the Commons in Hamilton," Raise the Hammer, May 1, 2018, raisethehammer.org; "Another Day, Another Broken Door: The Tower's Statement on Recent Events," Facebook post, April 8, 2018.

46 Adam Carter, "Hamilton Orders Removal of Anarchy Symbol, Calling It 'Hate Material,'" CBC, May 15, 2018, www.cbc.ca; Molly Hayes, "City of Hamilton Admits Classifying Anarchist Sign as a 'Hate Symbol' Was an Overstep," *Globe and Mail*, May 17, 2018, www.theglobeandmail.com.

47 Orpana, "Much a-Dough about Nothing?"

48 Carmela Fragomeni, "Panhandler Hounded by Fines Joining Constitutional Challenge," *Hamilton Spectator*, August 11, 2017, www.thespec.com.

49 Sarah Mann, "Creative Class Struggle: Gentrification and Sex Work in Hamilton's Downtown Core," *Briarpatch*, July 1, 2010.

50 "Street Level Sex Work in Hamilton: Community Engagement in the Sherman Neighbourhood," Social Planning and Research Council of Hamilton, January 2015.

51 Anna Francis, "'Artwashing' Gentrification Is a Problem—but Vilifying the Artists Involved Is Not the Answer," *Conversation*, October 5, 2017, theconversation.com.

52 Alexander Nazaryan, "The 'Artwashing' of America: The Battle for the Soul of Los Angeles Against Gentrification," *Newsweek*, May 21, 2017, www.newsweek.com.

53 "Art Districts," *Benjamen Walker's Theory of Everything*, April 11, 2017.

54 Nazaryan, "The 'Artwashing' of America."

55 "Defend Boyle Heights Statement about the Self Help Graphics Accountability Session and Beyond: Bombard the Artists Nonprofits!," Defend Boyle Heights, July 6, 2016, defendboyleheights.blogspot.com.

56 Joel Shapiro, "Goodbye to All That: Boyle Heights, Hotbed of Gentrification Protests, Sees Galleries Depart," *Art News*, June 8, 2018, www.artnews.com.

57 "Defend Boyle Heights Statement."

58 Rudy Espinoza, "On Defending Boyle Heights," July 11, 2016, www.inclusiveaction.org.

59 Bryce Kanbara was interviewed by Sarah Hipworth.

60 Paul Wilson, "New King at Cotton Castle on Sherman North,"

Hamilton Spectator, September 9, 2014, www.thespec.com; Jeff Mahoney, "The Cotton Factory Has Caught On," *Hamilton Spectator*, July 26, 2017, www.thespec.com; The Cotton Factory, "Building," www.cottonfactory.ca.

61   Solutions are something that the many street-level opponents of gentrification are mostly unconcerned with. At the Tower, "Peter" expressed a sense of resignation that nothing can be done, at a policy level, to stop gentrification from hurting the vulnerable: "I can't necessarily stop you [gentrifiers] from profiting off people's suffering," he said, "but I can stop you from being loved while you do it. The people who displace our neighbours and fuck us over in every way, at least we can hate them . . . We've just got to lay it bare. We can't necessarily stop this, but at least we can be real." Similarly, the goal of Defend Boyle Heights was to force the incoming gallery to "get the fuck out of Boyle Heights." Its literature expressed no objectives beyond that.

62   Orpana, "Much a-Dough about Nothing?"

Chapter Four:
A Blue-Collar Legacy—for Better and for Worse

1   Samantha Craggs, "Bill Scandlan Kept Up Morale during the Great Stelco Strike of 1946," CBC, October 30, 2019, www.cbc.ca.

2   Rob Kristofferson and Simon Orpana, *Showdown: Making Modern Unions* (Toronto: Between the Lines, 2016).

3   Kristofferson and Orpana, *Showdown*.

4   AGH, "History," www.artgalleryofhamilton.com.

5   McMaster Museum of Art, "The Herman H. Levy Collection," museum.mcmaster.ca.

6   Museum profile on Building Cultural Legacies Hamilton, buildingculturallegacies.ca.

7   Ian Young, "Gay in the Seventies," *Ottawa Journal*, December 17, 1977, walnet.org; Dakota Lanktree, "Hamilton's Pride Flag Is a False Promise of Safety," *Raise the Hammer*, June 24, 2019, raisethehammer.org.

8   Samantha Craggs, "'I Can't Breathe': Witness, Muslim Leader Question How Hamilton Paramedics Treated Dying Teen," CBC News, December 4, 2017, www.cbc.ca; Natalie Paddon and Carmela

Fragomeni, "Investigation Launched into Paramedics' Response to Good Samaritan's Shooting near Hamilton Mosque," *Toronto Star*, December 4, 2017, www.thestar.com.

9   Kayla Goodfield, "Hamilton Paramedics Charged in Death of Yosif Al-Hasnawi Fired," CP24, August 8, 2018, www.cp24.com; Natalie Paddon, "Al-Hasnawi's Family Launches $10 Million Lawsuit," *Hamilton Spectator*, January 26, 2018, www.thespec.com.

10   Nicole O'Reilly, "'Subconscious Biases' Influenced Hamilton Paramedics Behaviour Night Yosif Al-Hasnawi Died: Expert," *Hamilton Spectator*, January 26, 2021, www.thespec.com; Nicole O'Reilly, "Evidence in at Trial of Former Hamilton Paramedics Charged with Failing Dying Teen," *Hamilton Spectator*, January 26, 2012, www.thespec.com; Nicole O'Reilly, "Guilty Verdict Against Former Hamilton Paramedics a 'Light' for Yosif Al-Hasnawi's Family," *Hamilton Spectator*, June 8, 2021, www.thespec.com.

11   Kelly Bennett, "Hearing into Matthew Green Carding Complaint Gets Off to a Tense Start," CBC News, September 11, 2017, www.cbc.ca.

12   Molly Hayes, "Hamilton Police Officer Found Not Guilty in Carding Case Involving Black Politician," *Globe and Mail*, April 26, 2018, www.theglobeandmail.com; Ken Mann, "Hamilton Constable Not Guilty of Discreditable Conduct Regarding 'Carding' Complaint," Global News Radio, April 26, 2018, globalnews.ca.

13   Dan Taekema, "Defund Police Demonstrators Arrested after Refusing to Leave Hamilton City Hall," CBC News, December 2, 2020, www.cbc.ca; Sebastian Bron, "Defund Encampment Over—What Happened and What's Next?," *Hamilton Spectator*, December 9, 2020, www.thespec.com.

14   Claire Brownell, "Canada's Ten Worst Cities for Hate Crimes," *Maclean's*, December 12, 2018, www.macleans.ca.

15   "Man Sentenced in Hamilton Temple Arson Case Back in Court," *Hamilton Spectator*, December 20, 2014, www.thespec.com; Molly Hayes, "Third Man Pleads Guilty in Temple Arson Case," *Hamilton Spectator*, December 19, 2014, www.thespec.com.

16   Mark McNeil, "Mayor Fred Eisenberger Wants to Make Sure Violence at Hamilton Pride Festival Never Happens Again," *Hamilton Spectator*, June 16, 2019, www.thespec.com.

17   Samantha Craggs, "Cedar Hopperton Is on a Hunger Strike in Jail, Supporters Say," CBC News, June 24, 2019, www.cbc.ca.

18   Craggs, "Cedar Hopperton Is on a Hunger Strike."

19   Nicole O'Reilly, "Hamilton Police Charge Alleged Helmet-Wielding, Anti-Pride Protester from Kitchener," *Hamilton Spectator*, June 27, 2019, www.thespec.com.

20   "Editorial: Hard Lessons on Keeping the Peace from Pride Event," *Hamilton Spectator*, June 18, 2019, www.thespec.com.

21   Katrina Clarke, "Councillors Ask for Independent Review of Police Response to Pride Violence," *Hamilton Spectator*, July 12, 2019.

22   Meagan Deuling, "Hamilton Has the Highest Rate of Hate Crimes in Canada: Report," CBC News, July 23, 2019, www.cbc.ca.

23   McNeil, "Mayor Fred Eisenberger Wants to Make Sure."

24   Fifty-two per cent of workers in the Greater Toronto Area and Hamilton are in temporary, contract, or part-time positions, according to Lewchuk's 2015 report, entitled *The Precarity Penalty*, released by the United Way. A follow-up to Lewchuk's 2013 research for the same organization, it details numerous social consequences of this form of employment: precariously employed workers are twice as likely to report mental health problems, six times as likely to delay starting a relationship, and three times more likely to delay having children than workers in full-time, secure employment. Almost half of precariously employed workers say their employment structure (which often includes having no fixed work schedules) disrupts their family life. Sara Mojtehedzadeh and Laurie Monsebraaten, "Precarious Work Is Now the New Norm, United Way Report Says," *Toronto Star*, May 21, 2015.

25   Moro, "Homeless Campers."

Chapter Five: Slogging towards Tomorrow

1   Premier Wynn's Liberal government raised Ontario's minimum wage from $11.60 per hour to $14 per hour on January 1, 2018, and had planned to boost the rate to $15 per hour in 2019. The incoming Ford Conservative government froze the minimum wage at $14 per hour and abandoned the planned rise to $15, as it rolled back a series of Liberal

labour reforms. Mike Crawley and Andrea Janus, "Ford Government Freezing $14 Minimum Wage as Part of Labour Reform Rollbacks," CBC News, October 24, 2018, www.cbc.ca; Canadian Press, "Ontario Freezes Minimum Wage at $14 until 2020, Rolls Back Labour Reforms," CTV News, October 23, 2018, www.ctvnews.ca.

2   The $50 million is to be spent over ten years, divided between expenditures on social housing (particularly the repair of city-run public housing units that have become uninhabitable) and poverty reduction initiatives. The mayor stated that part of the intention of putting city money "on the table . . . here and now" is to leverage contributions from other levels of government. Matthew Van Dongen, "Mayor Lays Out $50M Plan to Curb Poverty in Hamilton," *Hamilton Spectator*, April 21, 2016, www.thespec.com.

3   Aaron Saltzman, "New Canada Child Benefit Program Payments Start Today," CBC News, July 20, 2016, www.cbc.ca.

4   Canadian Press, "Liberals' National Housing Strategy Calls for Billions in Spending, New Benefit for Low-Income Tenants. They're Also Pledging 100,000 More Units," *Huffington Post Canada*, November 22, 2017, www.huffingtonpost.ca; David Akin, "Analysis: National Housing Plan Will Help Thousands One Day but This Week It Helped Trudeau's Liberals," Global News, November 23, 2017, globalnews.ca; Bill Curry and Jeff Gray, "Ottawa Looks to Provinces for Billions to Support Housing Plan," *Globe and Mail*, November 23, 2018, www.theglobeandmail.com.

5   David Shum, "Ontario Basic Income Pilot Project to Be Tested in Hamilton, Lindsay, Thunder Bay," Global News, April 24, 2017, globalnews.ca.

6   The early cancellation of the pilot, writes Hamilton anti-poverty activist Laura Cattari, "is an unimaginable financial burden for those who contracted financially for a modest cable package, cell phone or internet." For others it "means not meeting financial obligations of a small business start-up opportunity or support in continuing education." Cattari says she knows one family for whom being denied the guaranteed income "means going back to not being able to pay for parking at hospitals when appointments or ER visits are necessary for

their very sick little girl." Laura Cattari, "Killing Basic Income Pilot Betrays Ontario's Most Vulnerable Residents," Raise the Hammer, August 9, 2018, raisethehammer.org.

7   "100 CEOs Urge Ford to Rescue Basic Income Project," *Starmetro Toronto*, October 18, 2018.

8   Ryan McGreal, "A Short History of LRT Planning in Hamilton," Raise the Hammer, September 14, 2011, raisethehammer.org.

9   "A 'Betrayal' of the City of Hamilton—Ontario Pulls Out of LRT," *Hamilton Spectator*, December 17, 2019, www.thespec.com.

10   Paul Shaker and David Premi, "All about the LRT Recovery for Hamilton," *Hamilton Spectator*, October 20, 2020, www.thespec.com; Christine Rankin, "LiUNA-Backed Review Puts Hamilton LRT Cost at $3.5B, Offers Funding Options," CBC News, August 27, 2020, www.cbc.ca; Matthew Van Dongen, "LIUNA Offers to Partner in Resurrected LRT Project Worth $3.5 Billion," *Hamilton Spectator*, August 26, 2020, www.thespec.com; Christine Rankin, "Premier Doug Ford Call Hamilton LRT a 'Good Project,'" CBC News, November 12, 2020, www.cbc.ca/

11   Ryan McGreal, "Train Drain: Inside the Seemingly Endless Campaign to Bring Light Rail Transit to Hamilton," in *Reclaiming Hamilton: Essays from the New Ambitious City*, edited by Paul Weinberg (Hamilton: Wolsak and Wynn Publishers, 2020), 291–94.

12   McGreal in *Reclaiming Hamilton*, ed. Weinberg, 297.

13   Laurie Monsebraaten, "Transit Connections in Weston-Mt. Dennis Offer New Possibilities to Solve Chronic Problems," *Toronto Star*, August 20, 2019, www.thestar.com.

14   Jonathan Mahler, "The Case for the Subway," *New York Times Magazine*, January 7, 2018, www.nytimes.com.

15   Matthew Van Dongen, "Convert 'Ghost Town' of Empty LRT Homes into Affordable Housing, Says Hamilton Tenant Group," *Hamilton Spectator*, January 13, 2020, www.thespec.com.

16   Stefanie Marotta, "Mississauga Could Build 174,000 Homes by Moving into the 'Missing Middle': Ryerson Report," *Toronto Star*, October 1, 2018, www.thestar.com.

17   David Brooks, "Winning the War on Poverty. The Canadians Are Doing It; We're Not," *New York Times*, April 4, 2019, www.nytimes.com.

18 Nickerson is an illustrator and artist who has published two books, *Creation* and *All We Have Left Is This*; www.sylvianickerson.ca.

19 Lisa Ferguson, "Community Fights Back Against Parkdale's Rooming House Crisis," *Now*, March 22, 2017, nowtoronto.com; Kate McGillivray, "Parkdale Neighbourhood Land Trust Purchases First Piece of Community Land," CBC, July 20, 2017, www.cbc.ca.

20 I originally interviewed Chris McLaughlin, Werner Plessl, and Tys Theysmeyer for a podcast on the Hamilton Waterfront commissioned by David Kattenburg for the Green Planet Monitor website: "Near Death Experience," February 16, 2016, www.greenplanetmonitor.net.

21 From "Housing First," chapter three of the *99 Percent Invisible* podcast series "According to Need," produced by Katie Mingle, www.99percentinvisible.org.

22 Carmela Fragomeni, "Provincial Budget Bodes Well for Hamilton: Mayor Fred Eisenberger," *Hamilton Spectator*, April 11, 2019, www.thespec.com.

23 Matthew Van Dongen, "Doug Ford Government Promises $29 Million for Housing, Homelessness in Hamilton," *Hamilton Spectator*, April 20, 2019, www.thespec.com.

24 Matthew Van Dongen, "Hamilton LRT Back on Track after Province Lifts Funding 'Freeze,'" *Hamilton Spectator*, March 29, 2019, www.thespec.com.

25 Joanna Frketich, "Doug Ford's Conservatives Cut Hamilton's Cancer Screening Bus," *Hamilton Spectator*, July 5, 2019, www.thespec.com.

26 Matthew Van Dongen, "Ontario Budget Surprise: The Cuts Keep Coming for Hamilton Services," *Hamilton Spectator*, May 1, 2019, www.thespec.com.

27 Fragomeni, "Provincial Budget Bodes Well for Hamilton."

28 Samantha Craggs, "Hamilton Mayor Tells Ford to 'Stop the Surprises' if He Wants Cities to Budget Better," CBC News, May 21, 2019, www.cbc.ca.

29 Kristin Rushowy and Robert Benzie, "Ford's Spending Cuts Extend from Trees to Libraries," *Toronto Star*, April 27, 2019, www.thestar.com. See also: Fatima Syed, "Here's Everything the Doug Ford Government Cut in Its First Year in Office," *National Observer*, June 7, 2019, www.nationalobserver.com.

30 Katrina Clarke, "Doug Ford's 'Absolutely Cruel' Decision to Axe Child Benefit Will Affect 1,800 Kids in Hamilton," *Hamilton Spectator*, September 16, 2019, www.thespec.com.

31 Matthew Van Dongen, "No Deal: Province Kills Brow Lands Deal Meant to Pay for Affordable Housing," *Hamilton Spectator*, October 5, 2018, www.thespec.com.

32 Steve Buist, "Steve Buist: Dark Clouds Are Gathering over Hamilton," *Hamilton Spectator*, October 12, 2019, www.thespec.com.

33 Jon Wells, "Hamilton Saw a Record Year for Home Prices in 2020," *Hamilton Spectator*, January 7, 2021, www.thespec.com.

34 Margaret Shkimba, "Mayor Fred, It Didn't Have to Be This Way," *Hamilton Spectator*, December 8, 2020, www.thespec.com.

35 Teviah Moro, "Hamilton Shelters Sees Spike after Encampments Cleared," *Hamilton Spectator*, October 17, 2020, www.thespec.com.

36 Dan Taekema, "$10.8 M from Federal Government Will House 53 People by End of the Year: Mayor," CBC News, December 15, 2020, www.cbc.ca; Ken Mann, "4 Rapid Housing Projects Get Funding in Hamilton through Federal Program," December 15, 2020, Global News, globalnews.ca; Lisa Polewski, "Hamilton Considering 'Modular Homes' to Increase Affordable Housing Stock," Global News, September 24, 2020, globalnews.ca; Christine Rankin, "Hamilton Gets $10.8M for Affordable Housing Units, but It Has to Build Them Fast," CBC News, October 30, 2020, www.cbc.ca.

37 Teviah Moro, "Hamilton Coalition Aims to Build 3,000 Affordable Units in Three Years," *Hamilton Spectator*, August 17, 2020, www.thespec.com.

38 Teviah Moro, "Council in Support of United Proposal for Massive Affordable Housing Boost," *Hamilton Spectator*, August 22, 2020, www.thespec.com.

39 Moro, "Hamilton Coalition."

40 Tracy Hanes, "Diverse, $400M Housing Plan Is a Focused Vision for Hamilton," *Toronto Star*, September 9, 2020, www.thestar.com.

Index

STEPHEN DALE is the author of four previous non-fiction books exploring issues ranging from the rise of the media-based environmental politics of Greenpeace; the impacts of suburban culture on politics in Canada and the United States; and the role of youth-focused propaganda in creating support for the bloodbath that was the First World War. He's been a freelance contributor to leading Canadian and international publications, was Canadian correspondent for InterPress Service news agency, and has created numerous radio documentaries for the CBC. He grew up in Hamilton and now lives in Ottawa, Ontario.